WILLS
of
WESTMORELAND COUNTY, VIRGINIA

1654 – 1800

Augusta B. Fothergill

Notice

In many older books, foxing (or discoloration) occurs and, in some instances, print lightens with wear and age. Reprinted books, such as this, often duplicate these flaws, notwithstanding efforts to reduce or eliminate them. The pages of this reprint have been digitally enhanced and, where possible, the flaws eliminated in order to provide clarity of content and a pleasant reading experience.

Originally published
Richmond, Virginia
1925

Reprinted by:

Janaway Publishing
2412 Nicklaus Dr.
Santa Maria, California 93455
(805) 925-1038
www.JanawayGenealogy.com

2007

ISBN 10: 1-59641-129-5
ISBN 13: 978-1-59641-129-6

Made in the United States of America

PREFACE

Every book should have a reason for its existence; that for presenting to those who are interested in old Virginia records this volume of abstract wills of Westmoreland County is the hope that the information contained therein will be of great assistance in compiling family records and establishing many historical facts.

A volume of wills of this county was published some years ago, but so many wills were entirely omitted, so many legatees left out and practically no legacies mentioned, aside from many inaccuracies occurring that in attempting to correct a volume of them for my own use, having had a great many requests for corrected information, I found that the only correct way was to make new extracts from the wills of record in order to have accurate working material. I was urged by many contemporaries to publish a new volume in order that others might have the privilege of their use with an expenditure of less time and effort than was necessary in my own case.

The wills in one entire volume, 1665-1677, were entirely omitted, which was particularly unfortunate as those of both John and Lawrence Washington were omitted which left the very beginning of one of our great history-making families to one's imagination. There were a number of similar instances which make it impossible to get any family record as complete as would otherwise be the case. In many of the Virginia counties it was the custom in the very early days to record all records in one volume, so in this instance it was very little more work to make abstracts of deeds of gift while making those of wills; these I entered in a large note-book which is in my files of county records from all over the State, but lack of space does not admit of their publication, nor does it of my copies of all of the marriage bonds to the year 1800 which I have filed with those from many other counties.

This edition is necessarily limited, since it is printed from type which has been distributed.

A Scandal Refuted

In the Pennsylvania Magazine of History and Biography, volume XLV, number 180, page 320, there was published an inaccurate and scurrilous article on the Washington family of Westmoreland County, Virginia, which was entitled "The Washington Pedigree; Conigenda and Addenda," by Charles H. Browning, of Ardmore in that State. Realizing the wide circulation of the said magazine and fearing that some people might give credence to some of the rather wild statements made by the above named writer, it seemed that some Virginian owed it to their history as well as to one of their most beloved and prominent families to write a refutation which would be published in permanent form, and I am doing so somewhat briefly but touching upon the main points made and giving dates with some circumstances in order that my readers may judge for themselves as to the inaccuracy of the said article, which in its entirety savors of hatred and malice, and could only have been written by a person of deep-dyed prejudice, and it would be beneath the notice of any accurate historical writer, but that some future readers, not having actual facts and dates available, might actually believe that, as alleged by the above said writer, his article was based upon certain actual documents extant or of record in Virginia, which a most careful personal examination made by me proved were neither extant nor of record. The writer finally acknowledged, in a letter written to the gentleman from the East who made use of Tyler's Quarterly Genealogical and Historical Magazine for January, 1923, as a medium for a refutation of the said article for a client who is a descendant of the said Colonel John Washington, of Westmoreland County, that he "began to see things" after reading certain published records and decided to write that before-mentioned article for the said magazine, which was unethical and certainly fatal to any writer of history or genealogy as it places their work in the class with fiction. The writer alone knows whether he wrote this distorted alleged account of the Washington family, accusing them of polygamy and illegitimacy, deliberately or as the result of misreading some published accounts, but he most certainly would have saved his reputation as an historical writer from much just criticism had he made a trip into the Virginia counties, where he alleges the documents are extant and of record, and made a careful personal examination of them as I have done.

One of his first statements is: "The fact is that the ladies and gentlemen of Washington blood are not descended from Colonel Pope, because his daughter Ann, though a wife of Col. John Washington, was not the mother of Col. John Washington's son and heir, Lawrence, their ancestor nor of any of his three sons"; that "those who have accepted this theory relied upon many printed pedigrees," which the writer evidently did himself, else he could hardly have distorted their pedigree in the manner in which he did. General George Washington left a pedigree in which he stated that he descended from Colonel Nathaniel Pope, and he certainly knew who his great-grandmother was. There is no recorded paper extant in which Colonel Pope styled his daughter "Ann Pope Broadhurst" in Westmoreland or any other Virginia county, nor did he sign any document of record with a mark as alleged, nor could he have achieved the position which he did if he had done so, as Virginia was controlled by men of education who came over here truly adventuring their fates and their fortunes. Colonel Pope is alleged to have made a power of attorney on May 11, 1659, to his daughter concerning some land; as a matter of record it was a deed in which he conveyed to her 700 acres of land "for my natural affection to my daughter, Ann Pope, alias Washington."

This is the special clause upon which the writer tries to base his theory that John Washington was a bigamist. He is evidently not acquainted with our ancient custom of styling a daughter thus in order to identify a married woman with her father's family, and was never done in Virginia as alleged "to prove her as not married by using her name with that of the man with whom she was living as a common law wife."

The famous letter of Col. John Washington written to Gov. Fendall of Maryland establishes the approximate date of the birth of his son, Lawrence, as a baptism was ordinarily within the month after the birth of a child; it was dated September 30, 1659, and stated that he could not appear at a certain session of court in that province, as his son was to be baptized at that time. Ann Pope-Washington died in the year 1668, and in the year 1669 Col. Washington married the twice widowed Mrs. Ann Broadhurst-Brett, notwithstanding the statement to the effect that "the exact date of the marriage of John Washington and Mrs. Broadhurst is unknown, and so is that of the date of the death of Mr. Broadhurst. Mr. Broadhurst's will was dated 26 January, 1658-9, and was not filed until in November, 1659." As a matter of record the will of Walter Broadhurst was entered for probate on 12 February, 1658, as will be seen on page three of this volume, this date proving that he died between the date 26 January, 1658, and that of 12 February, 1658, the making and probate of his will. The theory that a marriage between the last mentioned persons had been consummated before John Washington married Ann Pope was without proof, as she (Ann Broadhurst) as Ann Brett patented land in the county of Westmoreland in the year 1667 (land patents, volume 6, page 107), which was eight years after he had married Ann Pope.

On page 333 of the said magazine the writer states that Col. John Washington married as first and second wives two widows Mrs. Ann B., and that he married thirdly, while his second wife was still living, another widow, who survived him as joint widow and co-relict with his alleged second wife, Ann Pope. Had he not juggled dates by making the year 1698 the year 1678 he could easily have seen that the Mrs. Ann Washington who gave power of attorney to Caleb Butler was the widow of the son John of Col. John Washington and not of the latter.

At some time about May 10, 1676, Colonel John Washington married another widow, Dame Frances Appleton, the widow of Capt. John Appleton, their marriage agreement being of record in volume 1665-77, page 275, Westmoreland county.

As to the legitimacy of Col. John Washington, that has been dealt with most ably by Mr. T. Pape, B. A., who did exhaustive research work in England on the subject of the Washington family and, with the approbation of Dr. Lyon G. Tyler, I quote from his magazine that "when John Washington on 8 February, 1655-6, received letters of administration on his mother's estate he is described as 'the nrall (natural) and lawful sone of Amphillis Washington late of Tring in the county of Hertford.'" The word lawful was never used if there was any question of legitimacy either in England or Virginia.

The writer of the above mentioned article seemed to have gladly assembled all erroneous statements possible for him to obtain in order to try to bring into disrepute one of our most notable old families. Was it sectional prejudice? Washington belonged to our entire country, so why try to put a stain upon the fair name which he bore when he did so much for all of us? The original records of Westmoreland county contain nothing whatever disparaging to the character of any of the name, nor do those of any other county, but prove the various members of the family constantly rendering invaluable services to the colony and state.

AUGUSTA B. FOTHERGILL.

August 25, 1925.

WILLS OF WESTMORELAND COUNTY

VOLUME 1.

TASKER, JOHN, (Nuncupative) will. 12 January 1654.
John Draper said unto Tasker, master, I pray you you are very ill and sick do you make your will. He answered there is none here at present to do it, but I will give my whole estate to you. Proved by the oath of Gershon Cromwell. (First will on record.)

TEW, JOHN, 2 June 1655; 20 July 1655.
Legatees; wife Grace Tew; nephews John Hallowes Jnr. and Restitute Hallowes.

LOUDOUN, WILLIAM (Noncupative), 6 May 1654; 1 October 1655.
Legatees; George Day; sisters living in England; my estate in England; Mr. Thomas Speke, gent; Mrs. Anne Speke; Isaac Allerton Jr. a gun.

JONES, HUGH, (Nuncupative) 20 November 1655.
Robert Sharp aged 40, said as he was by Hugh Jones of Nominy when he made his will and gave all his estate to Walter Brodhurst, only paying 300 lbs. of tobacco to Mr. Curry, and 13 lbs. of tobacco to the deponet. John Wood aged 33 sweareth the same.

DRAPER, JOHN, 14 January 1653; 20 June 1656.
Legatees; friend William Spence my gun; Anne daughter of George Watts one heifer. John Bennett my house and plantation.

BOYCE, THOMAS, 1 August 1656; 15 October 1657.
Legatees; Elizabeth my now wife; Major John Hallowes; friend John Hillier; friend Thomas Wilsford; son Thomas Boyce aged about 32 years who was born in the Isle of Wight, and if he cannot be heard of his legacy to my sisters Eleanor and Dorothy and Jane Boyce. My executors shall write to the Mayor of Newport and inquire for my son Thomas and my sisters whom I left in Gotyam near Newport and if they are not heard of estate to friends Major John Hallowes, John Hillier and Thomas Wilsford, gents.

HILLER, JOHN, 12 October 1657; 20 February 1657.
Legatees; dau. Elizabeth Rozier and grandchild John Rozier, Jnr. to have all my estate save child of Mr. Webb my late wife's godchild one cow and calf; son in law John Rozier, clerk, to be executor.

BRENT, MARY, 23 July 1657; 21 June 1658.
All my goods to my sister Mrs. Margaret Brent, and after her death to my brother Mr. Giles Brent.

BRODHURST, WALTER, 26 January 1658; 12 February 1658.
Son Gerrard and if he die without issue my land to my son Walter and then to my daughter Elizabeth Brodhurst. Wife Ann exx, and if she marry, Mr. Thomas Gerrard, Mr. Nathaniel Pope and Mr. Robert Slye overseers of my children.

BALDRIDGE, WILLIAM, 20 March 1658; 20 July 1659.
Wife Elizabeth and son Charles; friends Daniel Hutt and Edmund Lindsey.

BRENT, EDMUND, 26 March 1658; 20 July 1659.
Wife Rebecca exx. and guardian; son Edmund my two plantations at Nominy; dau. Katherine plantation at Aquia River and land at Peace 300 acres; children under age; Witness; Giles Brent.

POPE, NATHANIEL, of Appomattox, 16 May 1659; 20 April 1660.
Son Thomas when 21; son Nathaniel; wife Lucy; son in law John Washington; son in law William Hardidge; Witnesses; John Washington, Law Washington, John Rosier.

DADE, FRANCIS, 29 December 1663.
William Storke aged 39 swears that 1 May 1663 that Mr. Francis Dade coming out of England in the last shipping in the "Maryland," merchant whereof Capt. Miles Cook is Master, and falling sick at sea did make his verbal will in these words, that he gave his whole estate to his wife and she to have the tuition of their children until of age. Assignment from Edward Griffith of Mulberry Island, James River, to Francis Dade son of Major Francis Dade, deceased, "mentions other brothers and sisters of said Francis the heir and in case of their mortality the said land to revert to Mrs. Bethland Dade late wife of Major Francis Dade.

SOLLEY, THOMAS, 12 October 1663.
Wife Elizabeth exx; son John Rosier and dau. Elizabeth Rosier.

ASTIN, ROBERT, 28 April 1663; 24 February 1663.
To Mr. Edward Nan * * *, all my estate.

MUNN, THOMAS, 24 April 1659; 20 July 1659.
Wife Elizabeth my plantation; Gervace Bell to look after estate of my daughter Elizabeth until she arrives at the age of 21 years.

PEYTON, HENRY, of Aquia, gent. 17 May 1658; 20 October 1659.
Wife Ellen exx.; sons Valentine and Henry when

they arrive past the age of 21 years; brother Valentine Peyton and my uncle Thomas Partington of London, draper, to be overseers of the estate.

SPEKE, THOMAS, 1 December 1659; 14 January 1659.
Son Thomas (under age) to be exr; wife Frances Speke; brother John Speke to have 2000 acres of land if he settle in this country; my godson Thomas Gerrard; my youngest sister; my father in law Thomas Gerrard and my mother in law Susanna Gerrard; my father in law and my brother in law Mr. Robert Slye to be overseers.

MADISON, JOHN, 10 Novmber 1659; 10 January 1659.
My brother Thomas Perkins to be exr; my aunt Grace Isham; to John Biddle; my brother Edward Madison.

BALDRIDGE, JAMES, 26 November 1658; 10 January 1659.
My wife Dorothy to be exx. and have my estate save one mare foal; Daniel Sisson.

ARMSLEY, JOHN, of Nominy, 4 September 1657; 10 January 1659.
Wife Anne; daughter Anne Armsley until she be 16 years old or marry to remain with my wife. Witness; Rice Maddox, Richard Flint.

POPE, NATHANIEL, 16 May 1659; 28 April 1660.
To son Thomas the plantation upon the cliffs, five cows at the age of 21 years. To son Nathaniel plantation whereon I live; wife Lucy land whereon I live for life or until marriage. To son in law John Washington money which he oweth unto me. My son ——; son Thomas to be exr. and if he die son Na-

thaniel; son in law William Hardidge. Witnesses: Joseph Rosier, Laurence Washington, John Washington, William Hardish.

ROZIER, JOHN, 25 February 1659; 15 December 1660.
Wife Elizabeth until my son John come of age; wife exx.

JONES, HUMPHREY, 13 December 1660; 15 November 1660.
All my estate to friend John Vaughan.

BELL, MARY, 12 September 1660; 13 February 1660.
To Elizabeth the wife of Robert Maphe; to my goddau. Mary Maphe dau. of the aforesaid; my son Richard Bell; all estate to be divided among my children.

LUND, THOMAS, merchant; 29 January 1660; 10 February 1660.
To my kinsmen the eldest sons of my brothers William and Robert Lund; Nathaniel Jones of Machodick and James Walker of Maryland to be overseers; to Henry Paite; to my kinsman Christopher Lund.

DOYLE, CHRISTOPHER, 24 November 1660; 10 June 1662.
My servants Teague Conners and Alexander Sumett to be given to Mr. Welch; brother John Heabedred; friends Edmond Kelly and Thomas Daniel.

BLAGG, THOMAS, 3 August 1661; 9 October 1661.
Wife Joane; land at Machodeck to two children Ralph and Thomas Blagg.

JONES, NATHANIEL, Upper Machodick, Northumberland County, planter, 3 June 1662; 20 Aug. 1662.

To my children; Mary Mathe daughter of Robert Mathe goddau. to my wife; Judith Eastaff dau. of Thomas Eastaff; George Haines son of Sibley Haines now my servant. My wife Judith Jones.

INMAN, ABRAHAM, 18 April 1662; 20 August 1662.
Legatees; Sarah and Margaret daus. of Nathaniel Jones; Daniel White, Michael Phillips and Nathaniel Jones.

BROOKS, HENRY, shipwright, 21 June 1662; 3 February 1662.
My wife Joane to be exx.; dau. Dorothy Brooks; grandchild Lidia dau. of Lawrence Abbington; Henry Saxton my godson and his father Nicholas Saxton; dau. Jane Higden; dau. Lidia Abbington; Richard Cole to be overseer.

BALDRIDGE, DOROTHY, Appomattox, Westmoreland Co., 2 Nov. 1662; 11 March 1662.
Grandson Charles Baldridge; William son of my nephew James Baldridge; Joshua son of Thomas Butler; John Stands; grandchildren Elizabeth, Anne and Mary Bayanham, son in law Thomas Butler to be exr.

MAPHE, ROBERT, 5 September 1662; 11 March 1662.
Dau. Mary; servant Ralph Eversly; wife Elizabeth to be exx.

PRESCOTT, EDWARD, bound to sea from New England; New London 12 Sept. 1661; 11 March 1662.
My kinsman Henry Alldy; friends Nathaniel Jones and Thomas Dutton to be exrs. of my estate in Maryland and Virginia. 1000 acres rice manor to Mary daughter of Capt. Josias Fendall of Charles Co. Md.

FOWKE, THOMAS, gent., 11 May 1660; 24 June 1663.
Wife Susanna; brother Gerard Fowke to be exr.

SMITH, HERBERT, gent., 4 December 1663; 24 February 1663.
To Herbert Burwell if he lives to be of age; to Rebecca Burwell if she lives to be of age; my now wife Rebecca Smith to be exx.

CAREY, EDWARD, 9 December 1663; 24 February 1663.
To John Axton; bro. Christopher Carey.

SHORE, ARTHUR, 16 December 1663; 27 April 1664.
To Penelope Webb; wife Susanna; daus. Patience and Susan; my wife and George Weeden and Henry Cossum exrs.

COLE, RICHARD, Parish of Appomattox; 4 November 1663; 27 April 1664.
Widow Brooks; Nicholas Saxton; my goddau. Jane the wife of Richard Higden; Joice Arbell; Thomas Webb; the widow Brooks to be exx. Witnesses; John Brook and John Bell.

VAUGHAN, JOHN, 9 January 1663; 27 April 1664 (of Nominy Parish).
Wife Ellen exx. and guardian of two sons, Samuel & William; son in law John Watts and his wife Elizabeth 1000 acres of land on Mattox Creek.

REYNES, JOHN, clerk, of the county of Westmoreland. No date; probated 31 Aug. 1664.
My servant Magdalen Jones; all of my estate to John Whistens.

BALDRIDGE, JAMES, 20 April 1664; 31 August 1664.
My son William to be under his mother's care during his minority; wife Elizabeth.

WALKER, RICHARD, planter; 28 October 1664; 30 November 1664.
My wife Mary to be exx; to my nephew Richard son of my bro. Thomas Walker.

QUOANES, ELIZABETH, 4 November 1664; 30 November 1664.
My son John whose father's name is John Beard; friend Mr. Anthony Bridges to be guardian of my son.

PEYTON, VALENTINE, gent., 27 November 1662; 29 June 1665.
My wife Frances to be exx; son in law Thomas Speke when he comes to the age of 21 years; father in law Thomas ——— Esq., and Mr. Robert Sligh both of Maryland to be overseers of will.

LANDSDOWNE, NICHOLAS, 11 December 1664; 29 June 1665.
Wife and dau. Mary; Colonel Valentine Peyton and John Whitstone to be overseers of will.

COLEMAN, WILLIAM, 12 April 1665; 6 September 1665.
All my goods etc. to my bro. Richard Coleman; my friend John Ward.

DUCKWORTH, WILLIAM, 13 July 1665; 17 November 1665.
Legatees: Daniel Hutt to be exr; William son of John Baseley.

VINCENT, HENRY, 19 February 1666; 8 March 1666.
Son John Lord; wife Elizabeth; son John Vincent; cousin William Salter; my wife's dau. Elizabeth Ireland.

ANGIER, JOHN, 4 January 1666; 8 March 1666.
All my estate to Mr. Anthony Bridges.

WALKER, JOHN, no date; probated 8 March 1665.
John Lampkin; George Lampkin; eldest dau. Connegan Lampkin all her mother's clothes; my son in law Thomas Lampkin.

JOHNSTON, THOMAS, 14 February 1665; 10 April 1666.
Wife Joanna and Peter Lett's eldest dau.

MAUNDER, WILKES, gent., 20 August 1665; 6 September 1666.
Wife Sarah and unborn child.

MORGAN, JOHN, joiner, no date; probated 12 February 1666.
All my estate to William Newberry of Westmoreland, carpenter.

GREY, FRANCIS, 7 June 1667; 31 July 1667.
Wife Alice; son Francis; dau. Ann the wife of William Rush; Anne Launcelott the wife of John Launcelott.

CLAY, FRANCIS, 20 March 1665-6; 31 July 1667.
Wife Anne all my estate.

TRUSSELL, JOHN, 22 May 1667; 31 July 1667.
Son Daniel Trussell; dau. Elizabeth Trussell; wife to be exx.

ABBINGTON, LAWRENCE, No date; probated 25 May 1670.
Wife, Lydia; son Lawrence; daus. Mary, Lydia, Abigail and Jane.

SAXTON, NICHOLAS, 7 February 1669; 25 May 1670.
Sons William, Henry, Nicholas; daus. Elizabeth, Ann; wife Alice; executor Mr. Richard Chapman.

WILSFORD, THOMAS, 1 September 1666; 11 September 1667.
To son Andrew Wilsford my plantation lately bought of John Watts; son James and son Thomas; Witnesses; James Ward, Robt. Nurse.

JOURNEW, SISLEY, 13 January 1667; probate obliterated.
My husband Journews debts to be paid; my sons Robert Jadwin and John Jadwin and Jeremiah and Cisely; to Bartholomew Jadwin the son of John Jadwin when he arrives at the age of 21 years.

STURMAN, RICHARD, 5 March 1668-9; 7 April 1669.
My estate in Maryland, Virginia and England to my wife Rebecca and my three children, Richard, Valentine and Margaret Sturman; if my wife be now with child, my brother Thomas Hall and his son Thomas Hall of London, merchants, to be overseers of my will; my friends Colonel Nicholas Spencer and Lieut. Colonel John Washington to aid my wife; wife and children to return to England.

DODSON, THOMAS, 17 October 1668; date of probate obliterated.
My wife Frances; my son Thomas who is under 21 years of age.

PAYNE, JOHN, of COPLE, 9 December 1668; probate obliterated.
Son John Payne to work for his mother until he is 21 years of age; my dau. Elizabeth; wife Milicent, son James.

OLATHMAN, TEAGUE, 20 December 1668; 24 February 1668.
To Walter English's children; to Thomas Collins children otherwise Thomas Attwell's children.

WEBB, WILLIAM, 4 January, 1669; 25 May 1670.
To son William Webb; to George Campians eldest son William; to my wife Joane.

ALDAY, HENRY, 27 April 1670; 27 July 1670.
My daughter Mary Alday; wife Grace.

BELL, JOHN, No date; 27 July 1670.
My wife Mary Bell; friend Thomas Webb.

WHISTON, JOHN. No date, 27 July 1670.
To son John; to Restitute Whiston; my wife Ann.

MARTIN, THOMAS, 18 February 1669; 25 May 1670.
To Mr. Thomas Pope; to Lawrence Abington; my wife and dau. Mary.

BROWN, PHILIP, No date. 25 May 1670.
To wife Joane Brown all my estate.

WILSON, JOHN, 6 April 1671; 31 May 1671.
To Henry Dunkin and Ann Hull; to Penelope and Mary Hayden; Henry Owen.

RECORDS 1665-1677.

HARPIN, HENRY, 24 June 1671; 29 November 1671.
My son young Walter English all estate; one cow to Mary dau. of Thomas Atwell. Witnesses; John Ward; Thomas Blundell.

HARPER, DANIEL, 7 March 1670; 25 February 1671.
Estate to my master William Court and Adam Wophendall.

SMITH, WILLIAM, 13 December 1671; 28 February 1671.
Wife Mary; daughter Elizabeth Smith.

LEWIS, FRANCES, 31 January 1671; 28 February 1671.
Legatees; John Moon; dau. Christiana and Margery land purchased from Mr. Robert Harrison; daughter Margery to care of Mr. Richard Chapman and dau. Christiana to care of Mrs. Brereton; John Moon to care of William Webb.

FOSTER, THOMAS, 24 January 1671; 28 February 1671.
Cozen William Hardichs.

HARFORD, THOMAS, (Nuncupative) No Date. probated 28 February 1671.
Sworn to by William Batts aged 26 years. Said Harford left Henry Kirke 100 acres of land; 2 chests to said Batts and residue of estate to Col. Nicholas Spencer.

LAUNCELOT, JOHN, of Washington Parish, planter; No date. Probated 29 February 1671.
Wife Joane; issue: John, William, Ann. Land on Potomack.

READMAN, JOHN, 2 March 1672; 25 June 1673.
My loving wife Mary and my children all estate. Witnesses; John How, Edward Franklyn, Robert Bletso.

HULL, ANNE, 3 March 1670; 31 July 1671.
To daus. Anne, Winifrett and Penelope Hull a bed and what goes with it, wearing clothes each. To son Thomas Ewell my biggest brass kettle; to son Richard Ewell one great iron pott; grand daus. Anne, Winifrett and Penelope Ewell tobacco to buy one cow and calf each. Witnesses; Joseph E. Smith, John How.

NORRIE, DAVID, 22 December 1671; 31 July 1671.
Son John Norrie land called Fair Fountain; wife Bridget and child unborn rest of land and estate.

WALKER, RICHARD, 30 November 1664; 26 February 1672.
Wife Mary one half of all my land. Nephew Richard son of my bro. Thomas Walker the other half.

MOULTON, JOHN, 1 March 1672; 30 April 1673.
Son John to live with Malachi Peale; my horse to Mr. William Hardwicke when he comes to this country.

GARRARD, THOMAS, 1 February 1672; 19 9br. 1673.
To be buried by deceased wife Susanna; son John and loving and deare wife Rose estate in Va., Md., and England. Dau. Mary land in Mrs. Whites Neck; to son in law Blaxtones, 300 acres adaj: Mr. Cole, Mr. Salles. Son Justinian. Grandson Gerrard Peyton. One mare to Gerrard Tucker; my sons in law and daughters in law; my 3 sons and 2 daughters; my eldest son Justinian my land in England. Witnesses: John Waugh; Isaac Allerton; J. Lee, John Cooper.

JENKINS, NICHO, 27 July 1673; 20, 9br. 1673.
Wife Anny and my three children. Overseers of will: William Clements and Robert Edwards.

PIPER, JOHN, 25 January 1669; 19 9br. 1673.
Son John land and cattle etc. Dau. in law Mary Evans one pigg; wife Rebecca personal property. Witnesses; Robert Foster; William Smith.

WITHRINGTON, EDWARD, 29 January 1676; 21 November 1677.
Wife Constance exx. To William Stoddard 18 head cattle. Witnesses: Jeremiah Nash and Thomas Blundell.

WHITE, DENNIS of NOMINI, 26 August 1677; 21 November 1677.
Wife Ann; no children mentioned; a servant man and maide to have cows etc. when free. Solomon Ratte one cow.

SHARP, THOMAS, 1 March 1676; January 1677.
Two sons John and Thomas (?) to have my land.

WASHINGTON, JOHN, 21, 7br. 1765; 10 January 1677.
To be buried on plantation where I live by ye side of my wife yt is already dead and two children of mine. To my eldest sonne ──── by my father Pope made over to me. To son Lawrence 5000 acres (my share of land) in Stafford Co. taken up by me and Col. Nicho Spencer, other land on Rosiers Cr. etc. To son John W. land where I live purchased of David Anderson, land at head of Rappanock Cr. etc. Wife her thirds for life; Ann Washington dau. a diamond ring. Bro. Thomas Pope; sister ──── ten pounds I have in England. Bro. Lawrence Washington and wife Mrs. Anne Washington.

TUCKER, JOHN, 5 May 1671; 31 May 1671.
To my two daus. Sarah and Rose Tucker when they are 17 years old; to the child my wife now goes with; my eldest son; my wife Rose to be exx.

PHELPS, THOMAS, 16 April 1669; 31 May 1671.
To wife Ann all my estate.

VOLUME II.

COLLINSWORTH, THOMAS, planter, 14 March 1690; 29 September 1691.
100 acres of land to my two sons Thomas and John under 18 years of age; son in law John Davis land already given him, under 18 years of age; Thomas Greentree; wife Jane to be exx.

STOPPER, CHRISTOPHER, No date. Probated 29 September 1691.
Robert Readman to be exr; John and Mary Lancelott clothes; to Bridges Rosier westcoat, breeches and hatt.

STURMAN, RICHARD, 2 June 1691; 29 September 1691. (Cople Parish.)
Friend John Sturman 100 acres of land; servant Penelope Higgins one servant; friend Patrick Spence; friend Alexander Spence trooping saddler and furniture; friend Elizabeth Hardidge rest of land in Va., utensils etc. William Hardidge exr.

PIECROFT, NATHANIEL, 26 January 1694-5; 27 March 1695.
My son in law Edward Whetstone land which doth of right belong to him; daus. Margaret, Deborah, Philadelphia; friends John Crumpton and John Tanner.

YOUELL, THOMAS, Cople Parish, 7 December 1694; 29 May 1695.
  95 acres of land to my wife and she to be exx; my grandsons Youell English, Youell Watts and Thomas Spence; daughter Ann Watts; John Atwell; daughter Spence; dau. Winifred English.

MARMADUKE, MILES, 16 May 1695; 28 August 1695.
  My wife Jane home plantation for life; son Christopher residue of estate when 16 years of age; Jacob Remy and Morgan Williams to be trustees of my estate.

BAILEY, BASIL, 20 April 1694; 28 August 1695.
  Son in law Caleb Smith; second son in law John Smith 2 cows each; daus. Ann and Mary Bailey. wife Ann; brother in law Thomas Robins.

SHOARES, WILLIAM, 7 October 1693; 28 August 1695.
  To Elizabeth and Ruth Parker daus. of William Parker land adjoining John Middleton who is to use tan flatt; to William son of John Landman; Edward Minty and William Short; my father in law Mr. John Hicks at home.

JONES, JOHN, 4 January 1695; 25 March 1695.
  Son Ashton Jones when 18 years of age; dau. Elizabeth Jones; sons Manwaring and John Jones to live with their mother in law Mary Jones and she have all personal estate and plate until they are 20 years of age; wife to be exx.

VEALE, MORRIS, 3 October 1695; 29 July 1696.
  My three sons Morris, John and William when they are 21 years of age my land; personal property to three daus. Amey, Elenor and Mary; wife Dorothy; Darby Sullivant, Richard Hancock and Tobias Butler to be overseers of will.

SPENCER, ANNE, 29 August 1695; 27 May 1696.
Son Richard 1,100 lbs. of tobacco left to him by my former husband Richard Chapman; to Richard Chapman; dau. Elizabeth Haley; Ann Lucas; two sons William and Richard Anckram; Joshua Hudson. Witnesses; Samuel Lucas and Richard Wall.

EVANS, PETER, 23 November 1696; 27 January 1696.
Son Richard 2 mares and one shilling; Mathew Wonsbear 1 cow; wife Elizabeth and daus. land, stock, household goods etc; daus. Hester, Mary, Sarah and Rebecca Evans; friends Thomas Marson and Joseph Hudson to be exrs. Witnesses; Ruth Hudson and Frances Franklyn.

JORDAN, JOHN, 6 February 1693; 27 January 1696.
To son Alexander Spence's dau. Dorcas one negro boy; to son Patrick Spence's son Patrick one negro boy; to dau. Elenor Munroe's dau. Elizbaeth one negro girl; to godson Jordan Weedon one negro girl; son John Spence 25 acres of land; son Thomas Spence 2 negroes etc; god-dau. Dorcas Sturman 5000 pounds tobacco; sons John Sturman, Andrew Monroe and George Weedon; to Elizabeth Sturman; gold rings; Jane Hubard £9; my wife Dorcas to be exx.

RICE, JOHN, of Nomini, 26 January 1696; 24 February 1696.
50 acres land to son John; grandson John Rice 50 acres; son Zorabable one cow; dau. Ann Rice 2 cows etc; William Rice one chest; son Ralph and dau. Elenor part of residue.

BLAGG, ABRAHAM, 4 June 1694; 31 March 1697.
Estate to wife Margaret.

MIDDLETON, ROBERT, 1 February 1696-7; 26 May 1697.
Son John 50 acres of land, and rest of my lands to sons John and Benedict jointly and that the eldest

heir male enjoy my plantation Taniherne with 364 acres of land. My sons or their heirs shall not at any time sell or mortgage any of my land save to each other. To John and Nathaniel sons of Nathaniel Garland one crown to buy gloves. To Daniel and Jeremiah sons of Nathaniel Garland 500 pounds tobacco each. To John, Robert, Thomas and Elizabeth Middleton, children of John Middleton 500 pounds tobacco each when of age. Sons John and Benedict residue of estate and the negroes upon my plantation and Alimbeck be not divided.

NEWTON, JOHN, 19 August 1695; 28 July 1697.

To eldest son John my lands at Carlton and Camilsforth, in Yorkshire in England, and the house in Hull, which was my father's, also the land bought of Joseph Laycock, to said son John and his four children I leave 1,000 lbs. of tobacco each; to son Joseph and his three sons 1,000 lbs. of tobacco each; to son Benjamin and his daughter 1,000 lbs. of tobacco each; son Gerrard and wife Rebecca live at ye Little Falls and have 1,000 acres in the freshes of Rappahannock with a mill and four negroes; to daughter Elizabeth Newton one-half of a tract of 2,150 acres and one negro; to my wife all my plate for life and then to my dau.; to son Thomas 350 acres and a mill at Totoskey; to wife Rose Newton 5,000 lbs. of tobacco each year for life and various other bequests; to son Thomas four Negroes; to grandson John the son of Joseph Newton, 200 acres of land. John son of son Joseph Newton. My three English sons one negro if they are living at my death.

RUST, WILLIAM, 18 March 1696-7; 28 July 1697.

One half of land to son William; das. Anne and Margaret Rust one-half of land; George Eskridge use of lands 20 years; wife Margaret and children personal property. Ann Smith 2 cows and 1 mare.

HINES, ZACHARIAH, being bound for England, 13 March 1697; 28 July 1697.
One third estate to wife Jane; Mary Evans dau. of Rebecca Hurst; Simon son of Simon Come; Caleb Smith son of Thomas Smith deceased; William Smith orphan of Humphrey Smith 100 acres of land; John son of John King; William Horton to be exr.

READ, ANDREW, Parish of Cople.
Sons Coleman and Andrew Read land and other bequests. (record mutilated from here on)

WASHINGTON, JOHN, 22 January 1697-8; 22 February 1697.
To be buried on home plantation by father, mother and brothers; wife Ann home plantation at Appamatox; son Lawrence land on upper Machodick, Stafford Co. purchased of Mr. Francis Dade; son John home plantation after death of wife Ann; sons Nathaniel and Henry personal property. My brother Lawrence have the care of son in law; son Nathaniel land at head Appamatox Creek; son Henry land in Stafford.

WASHINGTON, LAWRENCE, gent., 11 March 1697-8; 30 March 1698.
To be buried by father, mother, sisters, brothers and my children. Friends William Thompson, clerk and Mr. Samuel Thompson one mourning ring each; godson Lawrence Butler 1 mare and 2 sows; sister Anne Wright's children slaves etc.; sister Lewis; cousin John Washington, Snr., of Stafford; cousin John Washington's eldest son Lawrence my godson one servant; godsons Law, Butler and Lewis Nicholas 275 acres of land; wife Mildred one-fourth of estate; sons John and Augustine one-fourth of estate each; dau. Mildred Washington one-fourth of estate and 2500 acres on Hunting Creek, Stafford Co.; brother

Francis Wright; wife exx; and cousin John Washington of Stafford and Mr. Samuel Thompson.

PAINE, WILLIAM, of Cople, gent., 31 January 1697-8; 23 February 1697.
Eldest son William when 16 years to be exr; son Edward 700 acres in Stafford; my eldest dau. Anne by a former venture 6 cows, 6 ewes, furniture and etc; my daughter Betty one negro; daughter Mary 10,000 lbs. of tobacco at age of 16 years; daughter Anne and son William exrs; my said daughter Anne to go after my decease to Colonel Lee's house; Richard Lee one horse; my loving wife;

CARRIER, JOHN, Cople, 10 January 1697; 23 February 1697.
Wife Elizabeth whole estate; father in law Joseph Hardwick.

JADWIN, JEREMIAH, 2 December 1697; 23 February 1697.
To cousin Jeremiah son of Bartholomew Jadwin the son of John Jadwin all my lands at the age of 21 years; exr. John Tanner; Deborah Foxcraft 10,000 lbs. tobacco; god-daughter Dorcas Spence daughter of Alex Spence one heifer; god-dau. Anne Payne dau. of William Payne negro girl Moll for 22 years then to be free; friend Richard Bond £20; negro man, his wife and children free.

BENNETT, WILLIAM, 17 January 1697—; 23 February 1697.
To Robert Moore chest; to John Butler clothes; to Sarah Tabutt my wife's clothes; to my master Henry Rosse residue of my estate.

PAYNE, JOHN, 4 October 1697; 23 February 1697.
Wife Elizabeth one-third of estate; sons John and William residue of estate.

BAILEY, STEPHEN, 8 December 1697; 23 February 1697.
To son John 50 acres; son William home plantation; dau. Anne Smith one iron pot, one mare and one shilling; Anne Bailey dau. of Stephen Bailey deceased one heifer; Mary dau. of William Walker deceased one heifer; dau. Mary Smith.

CLARKE, WILLIAM, 26 December 1697; 23 February 1697.
100 acres of land to wife Mary; son James 100 acres and the 100 acres of his mothers at her death; son William 300 acres on Pohick Creek; daus. Anne, Elizabeth, Mary, Jane and Francis 340 acres of land.

WICKLEFF, ROBERT, 26 January 1697; 30 March 1698.
Son David; wife Margaret; brother David Wickleff; my father in law Col. Wm. Pierce.

HARDWICK, JAMES, 7 February 1697-8; 30 March 1698.
Son William land I live on; son Joseph land adjoining; dau. Lydia Hardwick a caudle cup, ring and land; son Joseph silver hilted sword and belt given me by Capt. William Hardwick; my wife's dau. Ann one shilling; dau. Lydia to remain with my son William until age of 14; personal estate to wife Ann and children Joseph, Lydia, Thomas and James; my brother Joseph Hardwick.

FLEWELLING, JOHN, 15 March 1697-8; 30 March 1698.
One heifer to god-dau. Margaret; Law. Abbington exr; Estate to be sold for tobacco and the amount of same goes to sons William and Thomas Flewelling at the age of 16 years.

FOXHALL, JOHN, 10 February 1697; 30 March 1698.
To Robert Vaulx and Sarah Elliott all my estate in Great Britain lying in Birmingham, Warwickshire;

to James Vaulx and John Elliott; to Susannah Comocke plantation on Popes Creek; to Mary and Martha Elliott colt and mare; my loving brother Caleb Butler exr.

CHURNELL, JOSEPH, 4 April 1698; 27 April 1698.
To be buried by the side of my boy William; George Sammons debt due me; Robert Sparrow tobacco and 3000 nails; Widor Rust debt due me; John Blyton; William Clift; William Edge rest of his time and tobacco; to Ann Wilkeson dau. of John deceased; to Henry Pickell father of William Pickell; to Mary, Henry, John Richard and Jane children of Henry Pickell 200 acres in Talbot Co. Md.

THORNE, GEORGE, 3 August 1693; 27 April 1698.
To wife Frances all estate; 151 acres whereon I live.

BROWN, ORIGINAL, 5 February 1697-8; 27 April 1698.
Chest of drawers to dau. Jane Pope; dau. Judith Roe 10 shillings; dau. Mary Brown at age of 16 years one negro girl, feather bed and furniture; son William horses, pistols and bayonets; Law. Abbington one-half stock, books, etc.; wife Jane exx. and residue of estate.

TUNBRIDGE, GEORGE, 30 March 1698; 27 April 1698.
To Mary Brown dau. of Original Brown and Jane his wife all my estate; latter to be exx; said Mary under age.

NICHOLAS, LEWIS, 19 March 1697; 27 April 1698.
All estate to wife Vasula; lands, stock etc.

PEARS, JOHN, 20 February 1697-8; 27 April 1698.
Wife Mary and son George one-half of estate each.

PENNELL, THOMAS, 27 March 1698; 27 April 1698.
To Henry Hornbuckle and my godson Thomas Hornbuckle use of plantation four years; godson Thomas Wheeler one heifer; to the first of my brothers' sons who shall come here for it all my lands, cattle, tobacco, household furniture, etc.

WEST, RICHARD, 7 April 1687-8; 27 April 1698.
To Charles son of Peter Dunkan one horse; to John Baker a mare; to Mary Baker one cow; to Eliza Baker one calf; Peter Dunkan exr; Peter son of Peter Dunkan my gunn.

OMOHUNDRE, RICHARD, 21 March 1697; 27 April 1698.
Sons Richard and Thomas land when they become 16 years of age; son John when of age 3,000 lbs. of tobacco; dau. Ann after my wife's death one feather bed; my six children; son William my gun; dau. Elizabeth one flock bed; wife Ann exx., rest of estate.

BARTON, JOHN, 28 February 1697; 27 April 1698.
To James son of James Tayler land I live on; wife Mary exx. and rest of land and estate.

HARRIS, ARTHUR, 14 January 1697; 27 April 1698.
50 acres of land and houses to wife Ellenor for life; son Arthur; son William all my coopers' tools and 50 acres of land; daughter Ann Harris one heifer; wife exx.

GORDON, ALEXANDER, 5 October 1697; 27 April 1698.
Son in law Valentine Harris 300 acres of land; wife Elizabeth; to George son of Thomas Hord when 8 years old a cow yearling; son in law Valentine of age when 18 years old, one gun which was his fathers; to William Smoot one horse colt.

KIMBALL, LYDIA, 28 March 1698; 27 April 1698.
Son William 100 acres; son Lawrence Abbington; son in law Mark Cullum 100 acres of land; grandson Joseph Abington 1 mare and feather bed; grandson Brooks Abington; my dau. Elizabeth Cullum and her daughter Mary Cullum one calf, cow, feather bed and household goods; dau. Mary Rodgers mare and bed; Exr. Law Abington or (Elizabeth Kellum).

MILLER, JOHN, 3 April 1698; 27 April 1698.
To Richard Cradunck one horse; to Philip Camose one horse; to Elizabeth Booth one horse; to John and Wantsford Arenton gun and powder horn; to Thomas Spillman carsey coat! to Elizabeth Colston a trunk; to John Bell shoes etc; to Frances Spillman 6 eels of linen.

DEBRIA, LEWIS, 27 April 1698.
Inventory of estate of Lewis Debria by Elizabeth Debria.

WEBB, WILLIAM, 20 March 1698; 25 May 1698.
Home plantation to eldest dau. Hannah Webb; dau. Elizabeth; cousin Ann Maiders Jnr; cousin Robert Mascey; cousin Ann Maider's children; Thomas Redman; exrs. friends Robert Redman and Robert Lovell.

BEARD, THOMAS, 16 March 1697; 25 May 1698.
Home plantation to eldest son John; youngest son Thomas; dau. Mary Beard; bro. in law Robert Redman and sister in law Mary Redman exrs. and to look after my children; cousin Francis Readman.

HEARN, PHILIP, 18 December 1697; 25 May 1698.
To Thomas Hallwell one ewe lamb; to William House one ewe lamb; daughter Alice Hearn and wife Alice one-half estate each.

SIMMONS, LAWRENCE, 30 March 1698; 25 May 1698.
Sons William and Jacob lands; daughter Margaret Allison one bed, furniture etc; son Thomas feather bed, furniture, table ware etc.

HEWES, THOMAS, 25 May 1698. Inventory Returned.

PENNELL, THOMAS, 25 May 1698. Inventory Returned.

THOMAS, JOHN, 26 May 1698.
Inventory of John Thomas by Margaret Thomas.

JOHNSTON, JAMES, 22 January 1695; Codicil 29 May 1698; 29 June 1698.
Son James land in Maryland at 16 years; my four daughters Elizabeth, Barbara, Frances and Ann 100 acres of land; to John Gerrard my black mare; to Mary Gilbert one cow; 350 acres among daughters; wife Elizabeth money in house etc.

ETHELL, JOHN, 28 March 1698; 29 June 1698.
One feather bed to son in law Thomas Shadreck; my children of age at age of 16 years; daughter Katherine one bed and furniture and her mothers clothing; son Abraham one bed, furniture and linen; exrs. Charles Tyler and John Chelton.

LISSON, FRANCES BUTLER, 11 February 1697-8; 23 February 1697-8.
Buried near my father and mother in Appomatox; cousin Nathaniel Pope; godson Lewis Pope son of Nathaniel 2 cows; cousin Lewis Nicholas servant and tobacco; children of my friend Law. Washington Snr. residue of estate and he to be exr.

WINDZOR, ANTHONY, 7 February 1697; 29 June 1698.
Wife Margaret lands for life, then to daughter Mary; daughters Elizabeth, Anne and Sarah residue of estate.

WEBB, MICHAEL, carpenter, 12 December 1697; 29 June 1698.
Elizabeth Hid daughter of Thomas one cow; Anne Hid one cow; wife Rebecca lands and if she dies without issue to Evan son of Evan Price.

TALBOT, JAMES, 29 June 1698. Inventory Returned.

PAYNE, JOHN, 29 June 1698.
Inventory of John Payne by Elizabeth Payne.

CLARK, WILLIAM, 29 June 1698.
Inventory returned by Mary Clark, relict.

BROWN, ORIGINAL, 29 June 1698.
Inventory returned by Mrs. Jane Brown, relict.

TUNBRIDGE, GEORGE, 29 July 1698.
Inventory returned by Mrs. Jane Brown exx.

NOTTS, JOHN, 29 June 1698.
Inventory returned by Jane the relict.

WILLIAMS, MORGAN, 29 June 1698.
Inventory returned by Katherine, the relict.

WICKLIFFE, ROBERT, 29 June 1698.
Inventory returned.

PEARCE, JOHN, 29 June 1698.
Inventory returned by Mary the relict.

WHITE, PHILIP, 29 June 1698.
Inventory returned by Alice White alias Dunn of her deceased husband Philip.

PEPER, JOHN, 29 June 1698.
Inventory returned by Margaret the relict.

HOGG, WILLIAM, (Nuncupative) 29 June 1698, recorded.
Joshua Hudson deposes that he desired Hannah Butler should have what was in his chest. Rest of estate to bro. Roger Hogg and Hannah Butler.

HARDWICK, JOSEPH, 22 June 1698; 31 August 1698.
To Sarah Clark my housekeeper 20,000 lbs. tobacco; Mr. William Sanford Snr. his debt to me; to Henrietta Buckley her mothers trunk; to Richard Sutton 200 acres of land and 10,000 lbs. tobacco; Richard Middleton; to kinsman James Hardwick 5,000 lbs. tobacco; to friend Temperance Blanchflower my Bible; cousins Janes and Thomas Hardwick land; friend Col. William Peirce one horse; friend Captain William Bridges ring; the children of William Earle to remain with my exr. during their time; friend Benjamin Blanchflower exr.

KNIGHT, TERRELL, 5 April 1698; 31 August 1698.
150 acres of land to son Richard; wife Ellenor and the child unborn, stock, tobacco, household goods; wife exx; and friend James Taylor to assist.

BUTLER, TOBIAS, 17 February 1687; 31 August 1698.
My wife and two children one not as yet in being; son James to friends John Quinsberry and his wife, estate at 20 years of age; wife and John Quinsberry exrs.

JONES, THOMAS, 9 May 1698; 31 August 1698.
To Frances Thorne widow a man servant named Richard Coggin having 5 years to serve; to John Mourning, cooper one hatt; to William Horton 3 yards serge; to Thomas Longford 2 buck skins; exx. Frances Thorne.

SMITH, ISAAC, * * *; 31 August 1698.
Godson Williamson Rosier, and to Bridges Rosier all

movable estate and to have land in his charge until Williamson Rosier comes of age. Bridges Rosier to pay his mother 700 a year for life.

BOOTH, GEORGE, 31 August 1698.
Inventory returned by Elizabeth the relict.

GULLOCK, THOMAS, 31 August 1698.
Inventory returned.

COX, VINCENT, 5 July 1698; 26 October 1698.
300 acres of land to son Carnock, my 3 daus. Martha, Ann and Elizabeth; son Vincent home plantation and 346 acres of land; son Thomas 370 acres of land; sons Carnock and Vincent silver etc.

DAVIS, JOHN, 2 January 1697-8; 26 October 1698.
Son John all my carpenters tools and mare; son Elias mare and colt; wife Ann exx. and residue of estate.

REED, SAMUEL, 7 October 1698; 26 October 1698.
Land to son John; my two grandsons David and John Peper at age of 10 2 heifers; land to son William, sword, gun etc; daughters Margaret, Elizabeth and Mary stock, household goods.

HARRIS, JAMES, 2 April 1698; 26 October 1698.
My lanlord James Coleman; friend Edward Berry to have estate.

NEWELL, JOHN, 26 April 1698; 26 October 1698.
Son William to friend William Horton, gent., until 18 years cf age; Mr. Richard Cradunck; my son being 10 next September; exr. W. Horton.

MINOR, JOHN, 22 Feb. 1698; 30 Mar. 1698.
400 acres of land to eldest son Nicholas; second son William 300 acres; youngest son John 300 acres; eldest daughter Frances Minor 200 acres of land;

youngest daughter Elizabeth Minor 200 acres of land; wife Ellenor her clothing, one-third of estate and residue land; to William Read 100 acres; to Morgan Williams 20 shillings to buy ring; wife and son Nicholas exrs.

SULLIVANT, DARBY, 2 December 1698; 29 March 1699.
Wife Elizabeth all my estate.

LENHAM, JOHN, 4 October 1692; 29 March 1699.
Wife Joshan all my estate, 50 acres of land and to be exx.

WICKLIFF, HENRY, 23 February 1698-9; 26 April 1699.
Mentions Mrs. Ann Washington; Mr. William Thompson Snr; leaves his estate to a negro woman and her 8 mulatto children and appoints Mrs. Ann Washington exx. She to purchase 2 negroes in place of 2 mulatto children to be set free.

WATTS, JAMES, 31 June 1699; 30 August 1699.
My two sons John and Spencer Watts 300 acres on the Eastern shore; wife Elizabeth exx. and personal estate. She was daughter of Thomas Youell (will 1695).

RUST, WILLIAM, Page is lost.

GEORGEHAM, JOHN, Page is lost.

VOLUME III.

ALLISON, THOMAS, 24 September 1701.
Inventory returned by Margaret the relict.

PURKINS, JOHN, 29 October 1701.
Inventory.

CHUBB, HENRY, 1 November 1701.
Inventory.

READ, ROBERT, (Nuncupative) 10 September last; probated 29 October 1701.
His landlord to take all he leaves and see him buried.

BLANCHFLOWER, BENJAMIN, 1 October 1694; 1 November 1701.
Wife Temperance all estate in Va., lands, negroes, etc. and she to be exx.

VINCENT, JOSEPH, 6 June 1701; 1 Dec. 1701.
Estate to friends Erasmus Green and Richard Evans and they to be exrs.

BUCKLEY, ABRAHAM, 23 Octboer 1701; 26 Nov. 1701.
Wife Elizabeth; son John to Thomas Thompson until 21; wife and Thomas Thompson exrs.

WESTMORELAND COUNTY WILLS

GOOD, FRANCIS, (Nuncupative) 26 November 1701; 1 December 1701.
Estate to friends in Ireland if anything left after burial by William Cohern.

SCOTT, JOHN, of Mattox, 28 May 1700; 2 December 1701.
My two sisters and their children that I believe are In Ireland and whose maiden names are Jane and Rebecca Scott £100; my brother James' son Gustavus; my brother Gustavus; to son John land I now dwell on; my dau. Jane; my wife Sarah; son John when 8 or 9 to go to England to my bro. Gustavus of Bristol to be educated; exrs. William Graham and Anderw Munroe; wife's former husband Mr. George Cross and their child George Cross.

WHITE, THOMAS, 1 December 1701.
Inventory returned.

ENGLISH, WALTER, late of Parish of Cople; 1 December 1701.
Inventory returned.

CLEMENTS, JOHN, 28 January 1701.
Inventory returned by Jane Clements the admx.

BUCKLEY, ABRAHAM, (Nuncupative) 28 January 1701; 2 February 1701.
Elizabeth the relict guardian to son John.

ROBERTS, MAURICE, (Nuncupative) 17 December 1701; 2 February 1701.
All estate to John Igdon at whose house he died.

PIERCE, COLONEL WILLIAM, of Cople, gent.; 20 February 1701; 7 April 1702.
To Pierce and Stanley Gower 300 acres of land;

grandson Samuel Bayley son of John land; grandson William Pierce at 20 years of age; daus. Elizabeth Bridges, Margaret Graham and Mary Rowsey; Thomas Marson and Rachel his wife 1,000 lbs. tobacco; exrs. Thomas Marson and grandson William Pierce; my son John Pierce the deceased father of grandson William; my wife Sarah one negro and her thirds.

TILSON, ROGER, 24 October 1701; 29 April 1702.
60 acres to dau. Rebecca when 18 years of age; 70 acres to son Robert when 17 years of age; wife Hannah one feather bed, stock etc; exr. William Carr and George Eskridge.

LAMBEE, WILLIAM, 9 April 1702.
Inventory returned.

DEMENET, LUKE, 29 April 1702.
Inventory returned by Mary Cockerill the relict.

PAINE, EDWARD, 8 June 1702.
Appraisement of estate returned.

SCOTT, JOHN, CAPT., 1 September 1702.
Supplement of inventory returned.

WILLIAMS, JOHN, planter, 27 May 1702; 26 August 1702.
Land to son John; dau. Susan Jones one shilling; dau. Ann Tillary one shilling; dau. Jane Walker feather bed and furniture; dau. Elizabeth pewter tankard; dau. Mary Laham pewter dish; grandau. Elizabeth Walker brass kettle; wife Jane home plantation, stock and household goods.

HAWKINS, JOHN, merchant, 25 August 1702.
Inventory returned by Caleb Butler.

SMITH, ROBERT, 1 September 1702.
Inventory returned by Robert Johnson and Mary his wife.

DUDLEY, RICHARD, 27 October 1702; 25 October 1702.
To John Cockerill 100 acres of land by Westd. Court House; to John Follins one cow, horse etc; to James Taylor's son William one heifer; wife Mary Dudley residue of estate and exx.; James Tayler and Ann Tayler witnesses.

BOOTH, WILLIAM, 2 October 1702; 25 November 1702.
Wife Elizabeth 200 acres of land and at her death to Mary daughter of Law. Abingdon; to Alexander Webster one gold ring and Ann his wife 15 shillings; to Sarah wife of Capt. Benj. Berryman 3 half crowns; to Thomas Shaw one gun; sister in law Sarah dau. of John Blagdon late of this county deceased to be exx.; Alexander Webster trustee.

HAWLEY, EDWARD, 5 November 1702; 2 December 1702.
Household goods, stock etc. to wife Sarah and two children; son John a year old 19 December 1702 and dau. Elizabeth 4 years old 11 of August 1703.

ROZIER, JOHN, 25 November 1702.
Inventory returned by John Rosier, Jr.

CAMPBELL, JAMES, 20 November 1702; 30 December 1702.
To John Higdon's sons, Original, Daniel and John one heifer each; to Nathaniel Pope's two children Mary and William late of Richmond county when 21 years of age two cows and calves; to Elizabeth Higgins' two sons 5 shillings each; to Mary Triplett 10 shillings; to Original Roe 2 years schooling; wife Jane exx. and estate not willed.

ALLERTON, ISAAC, 25 October 1702; 30 December 1702.
1050 acres and 600 acres to dau. Sarah Lee; grandson Allerton Newton land in Stafford; £10 to church of Cople Parish; dau. Elizabeth Starr who lives in New England 600 acres on southside Rappahannock River; my dau. Travers had her dowry at marriage; her three daus. Elizabeth, Rebecca and Winifred Travers 1,000 lbs. tobacco each; son Willoughby Allerton exr. and residue of estate.

CANADA, JOHN, 30 December 1702.
Inventory returned.

CARR, WILLIAM, 13 January 1702-3; 24 February 1703.
Home plantation to son Joseph; daus. Sarah and Elizabeth plantation; daus. Hannah 100 acres, Martha 100 acres, Mary 150 acres, Ann 70 acres; land to Jane Carr; wife Sarah; friends Daniel McCarty and George Eskridge trustees and guardians.

FOSTER, ROBERT, 8 October 1702; 24 February 1702.
Godson Robert Marcy; goddaus. Sarah Beard and Mary Walker; godson William Graham; wife Ann exx.; colts to God children.

BENNETT, WILLIAM, 2 February 1702-3; 24 February 1703.
Son Corscomb; dau. Margaret plantation in Stafford; dau. Mary plantation adjoining home plantation; my wife and her son Christopher; my two sons in law John and Thomas Christopher; friend Daniel Field Trustee.

JONES, STEPHEN, gent.; Cople, 30 January 1702-3; 31 March 1703.
Silver fruit dish, silver tumbler and spoon to Lettice wife of Honl. Richard Lee; Robert Osborne for making my will; to Paul Howell for caring for me in sickness one hogshead tobacco.

WESTMORELAND COUNTY WILLS 35

GARLAND, NATHANIEL, 16 January 1702; 31 March 1703.
Whereas Robert Middleton and Mary his wife did in their lifetime give to my sons John and Nathaniel each a mare and whereas both sons are dead, etc., 6000 lbs. tobacco, still tubb and worm, servant who was sent out of England for use and rescue of son John; my son Jeremiah Garland exr; my brother Thomas Garland to be guardian until son is 21 years of age.

SHEPPARD, GEORGE, 31 March 1703.
Inventory returned by Elizabeth Sheppard alias Thornbury.

BONAM, SAMUEL, 14 February 1702; 5 May 1703.
My three sons Samuel, Philpot and Daniel 280 acres of land; wife Katherine exx. and rest of estate.

PICKERILL, HENRY, 5 May 1703.
Inventory returned by Elizabeth Pickerill.

LUCAS, JACOB, 5 May 1703.
Inventory returned by Charles Lucas.

ATWELL, CAPT. THOMAS, gent., 13 March 1702-3; 26 May 1703.
Brother Francis feather bed; brother John Atwell one horse; son Francis 5 years of age to Thomas son of my brother John Atwell; Ann Pye daughter of John Pye, deceased; Frances and Hannah Tanner daughters of Thomas and Mary Tanner; brother Francis exr.

WEBSTER, ALEXANDER, 2 May 1688; 26 May 1703.
Wife Ann exx. and whole estate.

GARNER, JOHN, 22 January 1702; 1 January 1703.
Sons John and Henry 800 acres of land to be divided between them where they are now seated; Henry my chest and wearing apparel; son Vincent plantation whereon I live and land in Horn Point, my long gun and hanger and a yoke of oxen. Also one-half of money of sloop the Outcry; Vincent to pay sons Thomas and Parish 2000 lbs. tobacco and to son Benjamin 2000 lbs. tobacco at age of 21 years; son James 2000 lbs. tobacco; to daughters Mary, Susan, and Martha each a thomb ring; wife Susan residue of estate; Witnesses; William Gardner, John Williams, William More.

HORRELL, PAUL, 6 July 1703.
Inventory returned by Elizabeth Horrell.

HENMAN, BENJAMIN, 6 July 1703.
Inventory returned.

ROBINS, SIMON, 28 June 1703; 25 August 1703.
Silver caudle cup, dram cup and ring to Ellis Brown; my servant Owen Brannan razor and hone; to Sarah Newstubbs cattle; to Simon Lynn land etc; to James Brown and Robert Phillips 500 lbs. tobacco, my morning gown and sash.

WOODLOCK, THOMAS, 10 February 1702-3; 25 August 1703.
Estate to Ruth Coneland, widow, after debts are paid.

ORCHARD, JAMES, 24 April 1694; 29 September 1703
Estate to wife Rebecca; land on Totusky between Westmoreland and Richmond counties.

SCOTT, JANE, September 1703.
Inventory of estate most being that of her deceased father Mr. John Scott.

LEGG, ROBERT, 12 February 1702-3; 1 December 1703.
Wife Mary to have care of son James until 18 and daughter Elizabeth until 16 years of age, wife exx.

DAVENPORT, RANDLE, 1 December 1703.
Inventory returned by Mary Davenport.

WILSFORD, THOMAS, gent., 17 September 1700; 23 February 1703.
Friend Richard Watts all my land, cattle and rest of estate.

KNOBLE, ROBERT, medicus, 25 February 1703-4; 23 Feb. 1704.
To friend Lewis Markham all goods in Va. for the use of my wife Mary of Wormouth, Co., Dorset and my three youngest children and he to be exr.

WARE, JOHN, 24 July 1703; 29 March 1704.
All lands to son John and if he dies without issue to daughter Elizabeth Ware; sons in law Anthony Morgan and Robert Morgan; wife Elizabeth exx. and residue of estate.

REDMAN, ROBERT, 18 January 1703; 29 March 1704.
Thomas Beard; to Mary Lovel 160 acres of land; my son Francis exr. and all rest of estate.

ROZIER, BRIDGES, 29 January 1703; 29 March 1704.
Son John; my wife Elizabeth exx. and home plantation; son John lands and other estate.

WEEDON, GEORGE, 5 September 1703; 29 March 1704.
Lands in Westmoreland county to son Jordan;

daughter Mary Weedon; to George son of Thomas
Weedon and George son of Benjamin Weedon; wife
Susannah; brother John Weedon, son Jordan and
wife exrs; overseers of will Andrew Munroe, John
Washington and Thomas Weedon. Personal estate
to wife and two children.

MARSHALL, THOMAS, carpenter; 31 May 1704.
Wife Martha exx. and if she should marry then
David Brown, Snr. and John Brown Jno. to be
guardian to my children; to Elizabeth Rozier one
heifer; son William my plantation when of age and
if he should die without issue to next heirs.

HULL, EDWARD, 31 May 1704.
Inventory returned.

RANDOLPH, FRANCIS, 31 May 1704.
Inventory returned by Henrietta Randolph.

HUDSON, JOSHUA, 6 June 1704; 26 July 1704.
Son John plantation he now lives on; son Joshua 100
acres of land I live upon adjoining William Bush;
sons Caleb and Rush Hudson land; wife Elizabeth
exx. and residue of estate.

WICKERS, THOMAS, 4 April 1704; 26 July 1704.
Son Benjamin in Parish of Southley £40 sterling;
Jacob Martyn exr. and George Cross his son in law;
to Thomas Chancellor Jr. my gun; to Charles Tankersley clothes.

NOBELL, ROBERT, 26 July 1704.
Inventory returned.

SPENCE, ALEXANDER, gent., of Yocomico, 2 May 1704;
30 August 1704.
9 negroes and one-ninth of estate to son Patrick;

daughter Mary Spence 6 negroes and one-fifth of estate; daughters Dorcas and Elizabeth Spence one-third estate each; to my wife I bequeath nothing but her wearing apparel; friends William Allerton and George Eskridge exrs. and one horse each.

WARE, JOHN, 27 September 1704.
Inventory returned.

THORNE, GEORGE, Jr., 28 February 1704.
Inventory returned by Frances Thorne.

HARDWICK, GEORGE, planter, 27 May 1704; 28 February 1704.
To son Robert and his son George land when latter is 18 years of age; my wife Mary; Mary, Katherine and Susannah Stewart daughters of William Stewart; Blanche Hopkins daughter of Rice Hopkins if grandson dies without issue; exr. James Westcomb. Witnesses; Thomas Sorrell and Lettice Sorrell.

ROZIER, JOHN, 28 September 1705; 31 October 1705.
To Nathaniel Pope clerk of Stafford and practitioner at law all land which I formerly gave to my daughter Elizabeth Leftwich, 130 acres for which he to pay exx. 3500 lbs. of tobacco; rest to wife Mary Rozier, exx.

GREEN, ERASMUS, 27 February 1705.
Inventory returned.

FLINT, MARTHA, MRS., 5 March 1705.
Inventory returned.

JARVIS, RICHARD, 4 April 1706.
Inventory returned.

WELLINGTON, MICHAEL, 9 October 1701; 27 March 1706.
One gold ring to daughter Ann Robinson; grandson William Robinson one gold ring; grandson Michael Robinson one gold ring; granddaughter Elizabeth Blundell one gold ring; my wife and son John my house and good will in Coadrill (?) Co. of Hereford, Gt. Britain and in Virginia.

LANCELOTT, WILLIAM, 26 June 1706.
Inventory returned by Jane the relict.

WHARTON, HENRY, 26 June 1706.
Inventory returned by Elizabeth Wharton.

CARTER, FRANCES, wife of Thomas Carter, deceased of Westd., 22 July 1706; 28 Aug. 1706.
To be buried by husband George Thorne; Joseph Hennings and Thomas Butler exrs.; Daniel Mills and Thomas Langford cattle; to Gerard Ford one gun; estate to my exrs; my boy James Nevitt one damask vest, breeches etc.

MIDDLETON, JOHN, 14 March 1705-6; 25 Sept. 1706.
Son John two negroes; son Robert one negro; son Thomas one negro; son Benjamin one negro; personal estate to be divided among children Elizabeth, Mary and Alice; wife Elizabeth one-eighth or a child's part; if wife remarry land to sons as they reach age of 17; brother Benedict and Wm. Hammock exrs.

VOLUME IV.

RICE, JOHN, 22 February 1706.
  Inventory returned by Elizabeth Rice.

HORNBUCKLE, HENRY, 11 October 1704; 26 March 1707.
  Wife Ellenor estate for life; sons Thomas and Richard estate at death of wife.

BEARD, ANTHONY, 23 October * * *; 26 March 1707.
  Most of estate to sons John and Andrew who are 11 years of age now; dau. Sarah 2500 lbs. tobacco; wife Elizabeth plantation for life and at her death to son Andrew.

ASBURY, HENRY, 3 February 1706; 30 April 1707.
  Son Henry 400 acres of land; son Thomas 400 acres of land and if he dies without issue to son Benjamin; to son Benjamin 100 acres and personal property; dau. Catherine one cow; wife Mary Exx.

BROWN, THOMAS, 14 March 1706; 30 April 1707.
  Wife Elizabeth; dau. Frances Brown; sons George and Thomas; my bros. George and William Brown exrs. My estate between my wife and children.

SMOOT, WILLIAM, 12 April 1706; 30 April 1707.
  Daus. Sarah and Mary Smoot tobacco and personal

property; wife Ellenor; sons William and Thomas; dau. Winnyfrut; sons are under age.

PIPER, JOHN, 25 June 1707.
Inventory mentions that Thomas Harper had married the relic of John Piper.

HOGG, ROGER, 24 September 1707.
Inventory returned.

SMITH, WILLIAM, 10 October 1707; 26 November 1707.
Land and best bed and furniture to my wife; granddaus. Jane and Sarah Ashton bed, furniture etc; dau. Temperance Lucas 1 feather bed and furniture; dau. Mary King feather bed and furniture; son in law William Danks one horse; grandson Smith King 150 acres of land; wife, daus. Temperance and Mary exx.

COLE, ROBERT, 7 February 1707; 25 February 1707.
Horse and land to son Maryday Cole; wife Mary exx. and 12 head of cattle.

UNDERWOOD, MARY, 9 January 1707-8; 25 February 1707.
All estate to Morris Hurley.

COHOREN, WILLIAM, 25 February 1707.
Inventory returned.

MOSS, ROGER, 25 February 1707.
Inventory returned by Elizabeth Moss.

ELLIOTT, JOHN, 9 January 1707; 31 March 1708.
Land to my sons John and William; wife Sarah exx.

MANNER, JOHN, 4 April 1708.
Inventory returned.

SAXTON, WILLIAM, 31 March 1708.
Inventory returned.

POWELL, WILLIAM, 31 March 1708.
Inventory returned.

HANCOCK, RICHARD, 31 March 1708.
Inventory returned.

CHILTON, JOHN, Sr., 15 November 1706; 29 April 1708.
1 negro and 1 horse to dau. Sarah Chilton; dau. Mary wife of John Sharp of Lancaster; 1 negro man to dau. Elizabeth wife of Bryan Groves; son Thomas £10 Sterling; grandson John son of William Chilton £5 Sterling; grandson John son of John Chilton £5 Sterling; wife Jane and all my children; daughter Sarah my side saddle; son John exr.

HUDSON, JOHN, 22 April 1708; 28 July 1708.
Daughter Margaret plantation I live on; daughter Mary plantation where Edward Maning lives; uncle William Rush and brother Joshua Hudson exrs; daughters of age at 16 years and all my estate equally divided.

SPENCER, JOHN, of Nominy, gent., 20 June 1708; 28 August 1708.
200 acres of land to Joseph Taylor, planter; son Nicholas Spencer 350 acres of land; daughter Frances Spencer land adjoining son Nicholas; wife Mary exx.

CASH, WILLIAM, 16 February 1707; 25 August 1708.
Home plantation to wife Elizabeth and she to be exx; sons William and Thomas 100 acres of land each; sons John, 124 acres of land and if they die without issue to Howard, Joseph and Peter; William 19 years old 5 March 1708; Thomas 11 years old 2 August 1708; daughter Anish Cash 15 years old 31 July 1708; personal property to wife.

WESTMORELAND COUNTY WILLS

TANNER, THOMAS, 10 August 1708; 29 September 1708.
Sister Hannah Tanner of Honiton in Devon if living; daughters Frances and Hannah Tanner 150 acres of land.

JORDAN, DORCAS, of Cople, 25 October 1708; 24 November 1708.
2 negroes to grandson Patrick son of Alexander Spence, gent. deceased; Jordan Weedon and his sister Mary Weedon now wife to son of Bunch Roe; Dorcas Sanford dau. of my eldest dau. Elizabeth Sturman; dau. Jane Spence one negro; Ellenor Munroe; friends John Sturman, John Higgins and Lawrence Pope exrs; Ann Sturman Jr; grandson Patrick son of Patrick Spence; son in law John Sturman one pair silk stocking and Spanish leather shoes; my 13 grandchildren.

PRICE, MERIDAY, 14 April 1708; 24 November 1708.
Land to son Thomas; son in law John Butler chest and coat; dau. Mary Cole one stear; daughter Grace one bed and furniture; sons Meriday and John 200 acres of land each; daughter Katherine to keep daughter Grace.

RUCH, WILLIAM, 23 February 1708.
Inventory returned.

BOOTH, ELIZABETH, 27 October 1708; 26 January 1708.
One-half household goods, one flock bed and furniture to daughter Ann Grimstead and her husband Thomas 5 head of cattle and hogs; their sons William one mare and Thomas Grimestead one mare, 1 cow and calf; Joan Stephens; son in law Esward Mazingo 500 lbs. tobacco to buy nails; and 5 head of cattle; grandchildren Sarah, John and Mazingo bed, furniture, pewter, 1 mare and 1 heifer.

COCHREN, CHRISTIAN, 26 October 1708; 23 February
1708.
Daughter Elizabeth Cochren all estate, plantation,
tobacco, stock, household goods and she to be exx.

BUTLER, CALEB, 16 February 1708-9; 25 May 1709.
3 negroes to wife Mary; daughter Jane 6 negroes;
son in law Robert Vaulx and his deceased Uncle
John Foxhall 5000 lbs. tobacco, 1 negro, furniture
etc; Sarah Elliott daughter of Sarah Elliott and her
deceased uncle John Foxhall £30 Sterling; son in
law James Vaulx gun, sword, and 5000 lbs. of tobacco;
my sister Ann wife of Joseph Bayley £25
Sterling; to Thomas Robins clothing; to Mary daughter
of John Butler deceased 3000 lbs. tobacco; to
Thomas Clayton Sr. tobacco he owes me; to Thomas
Boyleston tobacco he owes me; sister Sarah Elliott,
widow, debt to me; to Jenny wife of Thomas Shaw
1000 lbs. tobacco; to Elizabeth wife of Captain Richard
Craddock £12 Sterling; friend James Taylor one
mourning ring.

HAM, MANUEL, 21 March 1708.
Inventory returned.

HARPER, WILLIAM, 14 July 1709; 28 September 1709.
Colonel Allerton; to cousins William and Thomas
Harper all land and personal estate, my iron bound
case and cabinet.

VOLUME V.

GERRARD, JOHN, 25 April 1711.
My brother in law William Newton and his wife Barbara; my brother in law William Davis and Elizabeth his wife; my wife Jane; my mother Elizabeth Johnson; my brother James Johnson; my sisters Frances and Anne Johnson.

HIGGINS, JOHN Mr. 1712.
Inventory returned by Augustine Higgins.

HORE, JOHN, Washington Parish, 16 February 1711; 26 March 1712.
Son Elias land in Stafford; son John land where I now live on Mattox Creek, silver hilted sword; son James land on south side of Mattox Creek which I bought of John Beard and Mary his wife; until my children come of age sons John and Elias are to be exrs.

RUSH, WILLIAM, 6 April 1712.
Inventory returned by Elizabeth Rush; son William.

VAULX, JAMES, 23 February 1711.
Inventory returned.

COLE, JOHN, 8 July 1712.
Inventory returned.

DUNKAN, CHARLES, 8 July 1712.
Inventory returned by Frances Dunkan.

EDWARDS, MERIDA, 17 June 1712; 27 August 1712.
One feather bed, furniture, sword, gun etc to son John and he to be exr; my wife Ann 5 cattle; son William 76 acres of land, 4 cattle and sheep, one feather bed and furniture; my granddaughter one heifer; godson John Maders one heifer; daughter Ellenor gown and petty coat; son Thomas 4 head of cattle and 76 acres of land.

OFFILE, WILLIAM, 23 August 1712.
Inventory returned.

ARRINGTON, JOHN, 20 April 1712; 24 September 1712.
Whole estate to wife Susanna and daughter Mildred Arrington; brother Thomas and my wife exrs.

WEEDON, BENJAMIN, 7 October 1712.
Inventory returned by Susanna Weedon.

BROWN, JOHN, 26 November 1712.
Inventory returned by Mary Brown.

LANCELOTT, JOHN, 21 August 1706; 28 January 1712.
To cousin John Lancelott my two plantations one formerly my brother William's and the other that which Gilbert Atwood now lives on, but his mother Jane Lancelott to live on it during her life; in case John Lancelott dies then to his sister my cousin Jane Simmons failing which to my cousin William Butler and * * *; to my wife Mary remainder of estate; brother William's children; my cousin to be kept in school until he can read Bible and cousin Jane same.

BUTLER, JOHN, ———; 28 Jan. 1712.
George Purvis; William Cutler; Richard Coggin; wife Catherine and my children; wife and brother William Butler exrs; eldest son Thomas; sons John and James; my brother James Butler.

NEWTON, ROSE, 1 December 1712; 4 February 1712.
To son Thomas Newton land in Va. and Md. my late husband Thomas Gerrard left me.

BLANCHFLOWER, TEMPERANCE, 12 December 1711; 4 February 1712.
One feather bed, furniture etc, to Ann Davis when 17 years of age; my grandchildren the children of my two sons Gerard Hutt and Osman Crabb residue of estate.

HORE, ROBERT, 28 January 1712.
Inventory returned by Sarah Hore.

HARDWICK, GEORGE, 25 March 1713.
Inventory returned.

WASHINGTON, LAWRENCE, 3 April 1698.
Account of estate of Captain Lawrence Washington returned 3 Apr. 1713; divided into 4 parts.

GARNER, JOHN, 3 Feb. 1712; 25 March 1713.
Land in Northumberland to son William and if dies without issue to my sons John, Abraham, Joseph and Jeremiah; to son Abraham land in Ragged Point and 100 acres in Horn Point; to son John lands where Thomas Merchant and John Kersey live with 300 acres of land adjoining my old mill upon Blices Run; son Joseph 200 acres adjoining Johns land; to son Jeremiah plantation I live on; to daughter Jane Joyce Self land where Richard Organ lived which land was purchased by me of Thomas Watson, also land adjoining Middletons and Mr. Samuel Rusts mill branch; also 66 acres where Susanna Moon liveth; to daughter Susanna Garner lands adjoining Colonel Richard Lee, Robert Smith, John Jenkins, Waddy Cox and Selfs; to son William 500 acres of land in Stafford; to son Abraham 180 acres in Forest of Nominy; legacy due from Jane Joyce or Steadam,

grandmother to Abraham Garner and Jane Joyce Self is £10 Sterling; wife one-tenth of estate; son William exr; my wife my negro woman Cate if she marry.

COX, VINCENT, 3 February 1712; 1 April 1713.
Negroes, stock, household goods to daughter Winifred Cox under 21, and to her a diamond ring that was her mother's, she to be under the care of my wife Jane and latter to be exx; daughter Ann residue of estate.

MOORE, JAMES, 5 June 1713.
Inventory returned by Ann Moore.

JONES, JOHN, 10 January 1707; 5 June 1713.
Son Nathaniel; daughter Elizabeth Jones; daughter Sarah Jones, son Charles; John son of William Overall and William Overall, Jr. one heifer each to Mary Overall one mare; daughter Ann Jones one crown; my wife; William Overall exr; lands to Nathaniel and Charles Jones; household goods to other children and wife.

HINDMER, JOHN, 2 December 1712; 5 January 1713.
Grandson Hindmer Shephard when 10 years of age 2000 pounds of tobacco; his mother my daughter Ann Shephard; my wife Sarah for life residue of estate and then to daughter Ann.

MOORE, THOMAS, 5 February 1709; 5 January 1713.
60 acres to son William; Thomas rest of land; to Margaret Moore when 18 years of age 1 cow and calf; wife Margaret exx.

MARSON, THOMAS, 5 June 1713.
Inventory returned.

FLETCHER, ROBERT, 5 June 1713.
Inventory returned by Ellnor Jennings.

CRADOCK, RICHARD, CAPT., 6 June 1713.
Inventory returned by Mrs. Elizabeth Porten.

GARLAND, WILLIAM, 6 June 1713.
Inventory returned by George Garland.

MARKHAM, LEWIS, 15 Mar. 1712; 13 June 1713.
To Joseph Bayley and his wife Ann; my eight children; son William, plantation at Mattoax at death of my wife Elizabeth.

ATWELL, JOHN, 6 Apr. 1713; 30 June 1713.
Sons Thomas, Youell and Samuel my land at 21 years; personal estate to daus. Hannah, Lydia and Frances and wife Elizabeth personal estate.

CLEMENS, DAVID, 10 December 1711; 30 June 1713.
Whole estate to wife Isabella; dau. Sarah Beard one-half crown; dau. Grace Downton one-half crown; dau. Susanna Arrington one-half crown.

JONES, JOHN, 24 June 1713.
Inventory sworn before Capt. Benjamin Berryman.

WOOD, EDWARD, 3 July 1713.
Inventory returned.

CHARLES, THOMAS, 24 June 1713.
Inventory sworn before Major Henry Ashton.

WATTS, WILLIAM, 3 July 1713.
Inventory returned.

HEMMONS, JOHN, 7 August 1713.
Inventory returned.

WESTMORELAND COUNTY WILLS 51

HASELRIGG, JAMES, 7 August 1713.
Inventory returned by Richard Haselrigg.

WRIGHT, FRANCIS, MAJOR, gent., 7 August 1713.
Inventory returned by Martha Wright.

BAGGE, MARY, wife of John Bagge, clerk, 2 February 1712; 5 September 1713.
Mentions marriage articles between her and her husband of date 19 Dec. 1711; one slave, household goods; my emerald ring with 10 diamond sparks to my dau. Jane Butler; my late husband Caleb Butler; to son Robert Vaulx and his dau. Mary £15 Sterling and one ring; son John Duddlestone £100 Sterling; dau. Elizabeth Porten 2 rings and 6 silver spoons; Mr. Daniel Porten one ring; husband John Bagge negro, one plate etc; to James son of Elizabeth and John Jarvis 1 slave and 2000 lbs. of tobacco; to William Moxley Sr. if living some clothing.

ATWELL, JOHN, 5 September 1713.
Inventory returned by Elizabeth Atwell.

WASHINGTON, JOHN, Mr. gent., 5 September 1713.
Inventory returned by Nathaniel Washington.

HARRISON, GEORGE, 2 October 1713; 10 December 1713.
Sons Thomas, George, John, William, James, Peter, and Willoughby Harrison all my lands and personal property.

MORRIS, JOHN, (Nuncupative) 13 November 1713; 24 February 1713.
William son of John Collin; Vincent son of William Wyatt; wife Elizabeth exx; sons Samuel, Edward, John, Charles and William Morriss; son Robert estate.

HEADLEY, ANN, 22 July 1713; 25 November 1713.
Sons Robert, William, Henry, daus. Barbary Webb, Elizabeth Headley and Ann Headley; son John personal property and stock.

NEALE, DANIEL, gent., 19 December 1713; 2 March 1713.
One negro to dau. Hannah Neale; sons Presley, Daniel, Christopher, and Rodham one negro each; wife Ursual one negro and she to be exx; dau. Frances Neale one negro; son Presley plantation where I live. Residue of estate to wife and children.

WILSON, HENRY, 10 Feb. 1713-4; 2 March 1713.
Dau. Ann Wilson; Richard Vanlendgen exr. and to have care of dau. Ann and use of estate.

CURTIS, JOHN, 3 March 1713.
Inventory returned.

SMITH, JAMES, 9 Dec. 1713; 9 April 1714.
Land to son James when 20 years of age; wife Ann; my three daus. Jane, Ann and Elizabeth Smith; residue of estate and personal property to wife and four children.

CAHOE, ALEXANDER, 31 March 1714.
Inventory returned.

WATTEY, GEORGE, 31 March 1714.
Inventory returned.

WILLIAMS, WILLIAM, 31 March 1714.
Inventory returned.

TANCELL, JOHN, 31 March 1714.
Inventory returned.

WILLIS, WILLIAM, 31 March 1714.
Inventory returned.

POWELL, THOMAS, 31 March 1714.
Inventory returned.

BROWN, WILLIAM, 26 May 1714.
Inventory returned by Hester Brown.

MUNROE, ANDREW, gent., 30 Dec. 1713; 9 June 1714.
Land to son Spence; brother William Munroe; son Andrew land and negro woman; dau. Susannah Munroe one negro boy, 2 cows, 2 steers, household furniture and 10,000 lbs. of tobacco; to Andrew son of my brother William 1 horse, 1 feather bed and furniture; dau. Elizabeth Arrington and her son John 1 cow, 1 feather bed and 5,000 lbs. tobacco; my wife Sarah; son in law William Elliott 1 mare; daus. in law Elizabeth & Sarah Elliott horse and cow; to Thomas Mustin one coat; friends Charles Tyler and Richard Watts and brother William Munroe, exrs; son Spence negro given him by his grandmother Jordan; to two sons 9 negroes.

SMITH, CHARLES, Parish of Sittenburn; 16 February 1709; 9 June 1714.
Lands to son William and daughter Mary Smith; Nathaniel Pope Sr. and Mr. Joseph Bayley trustees; son Francis feather bed and furniture; wife Ann and children residue of estate.

WRIGHT, JOHN, Cople Parish, 21 January 1713; 9 June 1714, (blacksmith).
Grandson Thomas son of my dau. Hester one heifer; granddau. Mary dau. of my dau. Susanna 1 heifer; my son John and the child my wife goes with land in Richmond county; four negroes and land where I live; best of my smith's tools and largest anvil to son John; to Anna dau. of Thomas and Elizabeth Sorrell 1 heifer; son Thomas Blundell and my bro. Thomas Walker, trustees; wife Anne.

GRAY, JOHN, 28 July 1714.
Inventory returned.

CARROLL, DANIEL, 28 July 1714.
Inventory returned by Mary Carroll.

BUTLER, THOMAS, 2 May 1714; 2 September 1714.
Sons William and James; grandson Thomas son of John Butler near where Katherine Butler lives; John and James sons of James Butler; Ann Baker dau. of Elizabeth Baker; to dau. Elizabeth Baker all her mother's clothes, exrs. sons James and John.

BUTLER, JAMES, 29 September 1714.
Inventory returned.

BUTLER, JOHN, 28 November 1714.
Inventory returned.

BUTLER, THOMAS, 29 September 1714.
Inventory returned by James Butler and John Baker.

PRATT, JOHN, 20 September 1714; 30 November 1714.
Granddau. Margarte Pratt; grandson John Lovell 400 acres of land, 2 negroes and 4 cows; dau. in law Mrs. Mary Pease 2000 lbs. of tobacco; son John Pratt £100, horse, 2 feather beds, furniture, lands in Virginia and Great Britain.

ALDERSON, GEORGE, 10 November 1714; 3 December 1714.
Daus. Jane, Mary and Margaret Alderson; my mother Mary Baxter care of children until 16 years of age; mother and Jane exrs.

LUKE, NICHOLAS, 26 January 1714.
Inventory returned.

GOWER, PIERCE, 26 January 1714.
Inventory returned.

MURPHY, BRYANT, 27 April 1715.
Inventory returned.

BUTLER, CALEB, 27 April 1715.
Inventory returned.

ATWOOD, GILBERT, 27 April 1715.
Inventory returned.

EATTLE, BENJAMIN, 27 April 1715.
Inventory returned.

BONAM, KATHERINE, 25 May 1715.
Inventory returned.

LEE, RICHARD, Cople Parish, 3 March 1714; 27 April 1715.
To eldest son Richard the land granted to my father in the year 1650 whereon I live; to son Henry land in Westmoreland; to son Philip land in Maryland, Dorchester Co.; son Francis land in Gloucester called Paradice; son Thomas land in Northumberland; dau. Ann Fitzhugh land in Stafford, 4000 acres of land patented by my father deceased; exrs. Richard, merchant of London, Thomas and Henry Lee in Virginia.

JOHNSON, JAMES, 9 February 1714; 10 January 1715.
To my mother during her life land left to me by my brother John Gerard and after her death to my godson Gerrard Davies; sister Ann Johnson 300 acres in St. Marys, Md.; godson John Newton 200 acres of land in Md.; cousin Elizabeth Wigginton; cousin William son of William Davies; friend John Footman; John Hines; John Hardy; exx. mother Elizabeth Johnson.

MARREAN, DANIEL, 7 August 1712; 10 January 1715.
Son John land; son William horse; arms etc; to dau. Hester pewter; wife Elizabeth exx.

ARRINGTON, THOMAS, 16 October 1715; 8 December 1715.
1 negro to wife Elizabeth; 3 negroes to son John; brother Wansford Arrington 1 negro and if he dies my son John land on Bull Run, Stafford Co; daus. Dorcas and Jane 2 negroes each; son Thomas £30.

THOMPSON, THOMAS, gent., 17 January 1715; 28 March 1716.
My two daus. Alice and Anna Thompson estate at 20 years of age; friends Thomas Lee and William Pierce 1 horse each; friend Edward Ransdell a gun; son in law Patrick Spence pistols, hostlers and breast plate; son in law Thomas Spence my violin; to Elizabeth Colson 1 feather fed and furniture; dau. Anna 1 bed and furniture and she to live with Mrs. Sibella wife of William Pierce; said William Pierce my rapier.

FINN, THOMAS, 30 Jan. 1715; 28 March 1716.
Dau. Elizabeth to friend Morris Hurley and to have her estate when 16 years of age; to Mary Couch one servant; to Daniel Conniers 2 cows; to Thomas Lankford 1 sow; Terrence Conniers exr.

CARDWELL, RICHARD, 4 December 1715; 30 May 1716.
Wife Mary stock, household goods etc; son Richard to have his estate at 21 years of age, 1 horse; dau. Margaret 1 heifer and dau. Winifred 1 mare.

WALKER, THOMAS, 6 Jan. 1715; 30 May 1716.
Sons Thomas 30 acres; George 100 acres, Edmund

100 acres and Samuel 120 acres; wife Mary 2 negroes and personal property; daus. Margery 2000 lbs. tobacco; Ann one shilling; to John 1 lamb; to Thomas Wright 1 lamb; daus. Mary 1 bed and furniture, and Rachel 1 heifer; son Benjamin home plantation; dau. Alice 1 mare.

WESTCOMB, JAMES, gent., 27 June 1714; 30 May 1716.
Servant Judith Lavcock to be free; friend Mary Collins alias Collier exx.

ERWIN, JOHN, 10 April 1716; 30 May 1716.
My godchildren John son of George and Anne South; Frances dau. of John Sorrell and Anne his late wife; Jemimah dau. of John and Hannah Awbrey; John son of John and Frances Awbrey; John son of Charles and Temperance Lucas and Elizabeth dau. of Thomas and Elizabeth Sorrell, all to have 2 year's schooling each; to William Clark my overseer; friend John Awbrey land purchased of John Hobson late deceased; friend Thomas Sorrell plantation and to be exrs.

SMITH, ANNE, 16 January 1715; 30 May 1716.
To Alice Beckwith 100 acres of land for life; dau. in law Mary Smith land and she to be exx; probated by Mary Gerrard the exx.

HOWARD, JOHN, 30 May 1716.
Inventory returned; at house of Susanna Howard.

GARNER, SUSANNA, 30 May 1716.
Inventory returned by Benjamin Garner; clothing among her daughters.

HOBSON, JOHN, 30 May 1716. Cople.
Inventory returned.

WALKER, CHARLES, 30 May 1716.
Inventory returned at house of Elizabeth Walker.

REDMAN, FRANCIS, 16 April 1716; 25 July 1716.
1 bed and furniture to Margaret Lambert; to James son of Robert Lovell my gunn; to Israel Chapman my clothes; exr. kinsman Robert Lovell lands and residue of estate.

BEARD, THOMAS, * * *; 25 July 1716.
All estate to cousin Lovell Massey and Mary Lovell and they exrs.

CROUTCHMAN, JOHN, * * *; 25 July 1716.
To wife Sarah all estate and she to be exx.

WATERS, JOHN, 25 July 1716.
Inventory returned.

ROE, SUTTON, 25 July 1716.
Inventory returned.

SMITH, ANNE, 25 July 1716.
Inventory returned at house of William Gerard; signed by Mary Gerrard.

WHEELER, THOMAS, planter, 30 Dec. 1716; 29 August 1716.
Linen and 2 trunks to sisters Mary Thornbury and Elizabeth Hicking; to Samuel son of William Wheeler my colt, saddle etc; to Anne Gough 1 yearling and her husband Robert his debt to me; my two brothers William Wheeler and Samuel Thornbury my clothes; exr. Joseph Bayley.

VOLUME VI.

BAXTER, MARY, widow; 5 October 1716; 31 October 1716.
The estate that is in my hands that belongs to the orphans of George Alderson to be set aside; son Thomas; dau. Anne; granddau. Jane Alderson; dau. Mary; granddau. Ann; sons Abraham, Thomas and William; all estate to be divided.

WORDEN, JOHN, physician, 17 Jan. 1714; 31 October 1716.
½ estate to Godson Worden Pope; friend Nathaniel Pope and Joseph Weeks other half of estate; Jane wife of Nathaniel Pope.

SPEED, RALPH, planter, 13 September 1716; 31 October 1716.
All estate to friend Abraham Griffen and he to be exr.

WATTS, RICHARD, 23 April 1715; 31 October 1716.
Plantation at mouth Mattox to son Richard; son John plantation where my mother lives on north side Mattox Creek; my five children and wife Mary personal estate; residue of estate to 2 sons.

BLAGG, ABRAHAM, 6 October 1716; 28 November 1716.
Mother Margaret Blagg exx; son Abraham; my bro. Richard Watt's children; personal estate to son and and wife; if mother dies William Reed exr.

MANLEY, WILLIAM, 30 May 1716; 28 November 1716.
Wife Penelope; daus. Penelope and Jemima; son John negroes and estate; wife Penelope, Lawrence Pope and John Elliott exrs.

SHEADRICK, THOMAS, 29 April 1716; 28 Nov. 1716.
My three children to be of age at 16 years; eldest son John my land; son Thomas; my wife and my brother Abraham Ethell exrs.

RAWLINGS, ANTHONY, 21 April 1713; 28 Nov. 1716.
My sons Richard and Samuel land and personal estate at death of wife Martha.

PORTEN, DANIEL, 31 Oct. 1714; 19 Nov. 1716.
To Mary Furlong daughter of my sister Anne Furlong lot in Norfolk town and in Norfolk Co.; son Cradock Porten land in Norfolk and Princess Anne counties; my father in law Major Samuel Boush exr; wife Elizabeth lands and personal estate.

DOWNING, RALPH, 10 Aug. 1716; 30 Jan. 1716.
To friend Mr. John Chilton 1 pair of silver spurs; my brother in law John Howell violin and clothes; residue of estate to sister Ruth Howell.

GRAHAM, WILLIAM, 28 Nov. 1716.
Inventory returned.

WEEKS, JOSEPH, 4 Jan. 1716; 30 Jan. 1716.
Wife Mary 2 negroes; my two eldest children Sarah

and William 1 cow and calf each and to William 1
negro man; wife residue of estate.

WELCH, GARRATT, 9 Sept. 1709; 30 Jan. 1716.
My debts to be paid and my friend John Pratt Jr. to
be my exr.

OCANNY, DANIEL, planter, 27 Feb. 1715; 30 Jan. 1716.
Grandson Daniel Crabb 130 acres of land; to John
Crabb 250 acres of land; grandson John Crabb and
my son in law Thomas Sorrell; friends William Allerton and Henry Lee to be exxs; grandson Daniel
Crabb to inherit my land if John Crabb dies without
issue.

HAVEN, STEPHEN, 13 Jan. 1716; 30 Jan. 1716.
My son Arthur all my estate in Ireland and Great
Britain; daughter Elizabeth Haven household goods,
her mother's rings and lockets. exx. Margaret Herra
with friend George Eskridge to assist her.

ABBINGTON, BROOKS, 6 Feb. 1716.
Inventory returned.

BRYANT, WILLIAM, 23 Jan. 1716; 27 Feb. 1716.
Daughter Sarah 1 feather bed and furniture; son
William 1 feather bed and furniture; my daughters;
Margaret Watts to have tuition of my dau. Sarah;
Richard Walls and his wife Mary exrs.

BATEMAN, WILLIAM, 18 Feb. 1716; 27 Feb. 1716.
Eldest dau. Mary 2000 lbs. of tobacco; second dau.
Elizabeth 2000 lbs. of tobacco; third dau. Sarah
2000 lbs. tobacco; son John 3000 lbs. of tobacco,
stock, and household furniture; wife Elizabeth residue of estate.

ROBERTSON, PRISCILLA, 8 Jan. 1716; 27 March 1717.
All estate to dau. Mary Robertson; William Humphreys to have care of her until she reaches the age of 16 years and he to be exr.

SELF, ROBERT, 18 June 1716; 27 March 1717.
One chest to son John; wife Jane exx. and residue of estate; land to son Stephen; 80 acres of land to grandson Walter Self.

HEADLEY, JOHN, 15 December 1716; 26 June 1717.
Wife Frances all my estate; witness Robert Headley.

SHAW, THOMAS, 5 March 1716; 26 June 1717.
Son Thomas 1 cow and horse; wife Jane land and estate for life; brother in law John Elliott guardian over two children; dau. Mary 1 cow.

MOON, JOHN, 10 June 1717; 26 June 1717.
Two cows to son John; to Elizabeth Hawley my wife's granddau. 1 pot and hooks; wife Elizabeth residue of estate.

CHILTON, CHARLES, 26 June 1717.
Inventory returned.

NETHERTON, HENRY MR., 26 June 1717.
Inventory returned.

ROBOTTOM, WILLIAM, 25 July 1717.
Inventory returned.

SUMMERVILLE, JOHN, 19 June 1717; 28 August 1717.
5 negroes to wife Mary and land in Stafford; son in law William Thompson land in Stafford devised him by his mother; Susanna Thompson one negro boy; son in law John Watts; to William Sturman a gold ring.

PARSONS, DOROTHY, 16 Feb. 1716; 28 August 1717.
1 mare to dau. Mary Finch; son John Finch; grandson John Finch; granddau. Ann 1 heifer; grandson Lawrence Abbington 1 heifer and 1 cow; son James Abbington horse, cows and household goods; son John Parsons 1 horse, feather bed; son Joseph Parsons; dau. Mary Nicholls; son Robert Finch a mare.

JONES, ROBERT, 12 September 1717.
Inventory returned.

HOWARD, SUSANNA, 13 September 1717.
Inventory returned.

JENKINS, JOHN, 13 September 1717.
Inventory returned.

WATTS, RICHARD, 13 September 1717.
Inventory returned.

SHAW, THOMAS, 15 October 1717.
Inventory returned by Jane Shaw.

NEWJENT, ELIAS, 14 Oct. 1717; 27 Nov. 1717.
All estate to my mother; Robert Vaulx exr.

PRICE, THOMAS, 3 Sept. 1717; 27 Nov. 1717, (Of Washington Parish.)
Home plantation to wife Margaret and 1 horse; eldest son William 100 acres in Stafford; son Thomas 88 acres of land; son Meridice 50 acres of land; son John, 30 acres on Wedoen's Dam; dau. Sussana Price 1 negro child; son William 1 horse etc; brother Meridice Price overseer of will; wife exx.

WATERS, DOROTHY, 6 Nov. 1717; 27 Nov. 1717.
My silk crape suit to dau. Sarah Williams; dau. Sarah Owen serge for suit; dau. Ann Dunkan bed and furniture; son Blanchflower Dunkan bed and

furniture; Henry and Jarrett sons of John Medford,
to Jarrett Medford if he pay estate 6000 lbs. tobacco;
son William Macclanacon exr; to each child 1 silver
shilling.

QUISENBERRY, JOHN, 23 Nov. 1714; 27 Nov. 1717.
Son William all land and if he die without issue to
my son Humphrey to whom I leave one gun and a
horse; wife Ann rest of personal property. Witnesses, Frances Quisenberry, William Griffin, Humphrey Pope.

GILBERT, MICHAEL, 2 Oct. 1717; 27 Nov. 1717.
Lands to sons William and John, and lands to son
Michael if his bros. die without issue; grandson William Shortridge; wife Jane 2 feather beds and furniture and 1 horse; wife Jane and son William exrs.

BAYLEY, JOSEPH, 5 Dec. 1717; 29 Jan. 1717.
My bro. Michael and his son Thomas Bayley money
in hands of Capt. John Waters; Goddau. Mary Butler 1 negro girl, a feather bed and furniture; residue
of estate to wife Ann whom I appoint my exx.

BONAM, THOMAS, gent., 18 Nov. 1717; 29 Jan. 1717.
My wife's clothes, 2 amber necklaces, 1 pearl necklace, a locket and other jewelry to Sarah Baker
daughter of John Baker to whom I leave a slave;
my deceased wife; bro. Capt. George Eskridge 1
horse; nephew Samuel Bonam 1 negro man and boy
and one-third of goods in store; nephew Daniel Bonam same bequest; to nephew Philpott Bonam the
same as his brothers and also my lands.

SPARROW, ROBERT, 17 Feb. 1717.
Inventory returned.

RUST, SAMUEL, 16 Aug. 1717; 26 March 1718.
The plantation where he lives to Mr. Patrick Spence

and his father in law Capt. George Eskridge; sons Jeremiah, Peter, John, Matthew, George William and Benjamin Rust my lands and personal property; daughters Ann Harrison and Hannah Rust; wife Martha and son Jeremiah exrs; the heirs of John Clements to have my land called Middleton's Neck.

ROLLINS, WILLIAM, 4 December 1717; 26 March 1718.
To Sarah Sebastian 1 calf; my three children Phillip aged 12 years, Mary aged 9 years, and Thomas aged 7 years to Phillip Dolin until they come of age.

GARNER, BENJAMIN, 31 March 1718; 28 May 1718.
My clothes to my brother Parish Garner; cousin Henry Garner; cousin Thomas son of Henry Garner my clothes; counsin Joseph son of John Garner; godson Benjamin Walker 1 heifer; cousin Vincent son of William Lewis 1 heifer; brother Thomas Garner my gun and hat; sister Mary Price my looking glass; sister Martha a trunk; cousin James Garner one calf and his father James Garner 200 acres of land on which I live and residue of estate; brother James Garner exr.

STONE, THOMAS, 31 March 1718; 28 May 1718.
Friend Robert Bernard exr. No bequests made.

MARLOE, JOHN, 28 May 1718.
Inventory returned.

KING, ARTHUR, 28 May 1718.
Inventory returned.

BENNETT, COSSOM, 25 June 1718; 18 July 1718.
Wife Katherine 1 feather bed and furniture; dau. Lucy 1 negro child; dau. Susan 1 negro child; sons William and Cossom residue of estate; Mr. Dade Massey to act as trustee.

ALLWORTHY, ROBERT, (Nuncupative) 25 June 1718; 10 July 1718.
Estate to wife Ruth and she to pay my debts.

SMITH, JOSEPH, 13 May 1718; 25 June 1718.
Son Nathaniel 1 shilling; dau. Mary cow etc; dau. Joyce Smith 1 cow and table ware; son Joseph my lands and rest of estate and he to live with his brother Nathaniel for 4 years.

PALMER, SARAH, 2 March 1717; 25 June 1718.
Dau. Sarah wife of Edward Turner 1 shilling; granddau. Sarah Turner 6000 lbs. of tobacco; granddau. Jane Turner tobacco and she to be my exx.

HEMMINGS, JOSEPH, (Nuncupative) 25 June 1718; 10 July 1718.
To godson John Jones a suit of clothes and a hat; Mrs. Jane Pope a reading glass; wife Elizabeth residue of estate.

WIGGINTON, ROGER, 3 March 1717; 14 August 1718.
To my son William my watch and 1 negro; son Roger my shoe buckles and 1 negro; daus. Elizabeth and Ann Wigginton 1 negro each; son Henry 1 negro, feather bed and furniture; brother William Wigginton and Willoughby Allerton exrs.

THOMAS, HUGH, 6 Nov. 1717; 14 Aug. 1718.
Two sons Daniel and Hugh all my lands equally; brother John Thomas; personal property to wife Ann and my children.

MUCKLEROY, ELIZABETH, 12 Feb. 1717; 14 Aug. 1718.
To Granddau. Elizabeth dau. of John and Elizabeth Pope 1 cow, 1 mare and 500 lbs. of tobacco; to granddau. Jemima the dau. of my son Lawrence Pope and his wife Jemima (Waddy) 1 Russia leather

trunk; grandson Thomas Youel son of Harman and Dinah Youel 2 calves, cows, mare, gun etc; granddau. Elizabeth dau. of same, 2 cows, 1 feather bed, a Bible and a ring; residue of estate and 15 shillings to Dinah Youel, she and her husband Harman exrs.

ALLEN, WILLIAM, 31 March 1718; 30 July 1718.
All my land to my son William who was born 21 Oct. 1704; exr. James Courtwell and he have care of my son.

MOTHERSHEAD, BROOKS, 15 Aug. 1718.
Inventory returned.

SPELLMAN, THOMAS, 15 Aug. 1718.
Inventory returned.

CLAYTOR, THOMAS, 23 July 1718; 18 Oct. 1718.
Grandson Thomas son of William Claytor 40 acres of land adjoining the 60 acres already given to William Claytor by Edward Cony; son Thomas the rest of my land; my wife Katherine personal estate. Son Thomas and wife exrs.

HIGDON, JOHN, 7 Sept. 1718; 21 Oct. 1718.
Sons Daniel and John land, 1 negro and personal property; son John exr.

POTTER, WILLIAM, * * *; 4 Nov. 1718.
To my wife Frances her mare and saddle; son John ¼ of estate, son James ¼ of estate and daughter Frances ¼ of estate.

WARD, JOHN, 30 Aug. 1718; 4 Nov. 1718.
To son Henry 1 horse, 1 cow and calf; son in law James Brisco 1 cow; dau. Jane Ward residue of estate and she to be exx.

OWEN, EDMUND, 23 Aug. 1718.
Inventory returned.

STONE, THOMAS, 28 July 1718.
Inventory returned.

McBOYD, PATRICK, 13 May 1718; 29 Dec. 1718.
Son Thomas 100 acres of land in Stafford, 1 horse and cattle; wife Mary residue of estate; David Conner and cousin Carran Barnham exrs.

HARDWICK, WILLIAM, 31 Oct. 1718; 10 March 1718.
To wife Elizabeth one-third of estate; son James my plantation and my still; dau. Frances 1 mare and a still; son George 1 mare and a still; my dau. Dorcas to stay with my wife until she comes to the age of 16 years.

VEAL, JOHN, 20 Nov. * * *; 10 March 1718.
Land in Stafford to sons John and Morris; dau. Susan 1 mare; wife Deliverance and my three sons exrs; brother Humphrey Pope and Caudry Vaughan trustees.

EATON, PETER, 7 March 1719.
Inventory returned.

DUNN, JOHN, 1 Feb. 1718; 25 Feb. 1718.
Wife Katherine and 2 daughters all estate and wife educate them if she is able.

KENNER, RICHARD, 17 Nov. 1718; 10 Jan. 1719.
To son Winder Kenner land where I live to the land where Mr. William Chandler now lives; son Richard land extended 1 mile into the woods; son Rodham land; wife Elizabeth land and personal property; my mother in law Elizabeth Winder a living out of my estate for life; daus. Elizabeth and Frances Kenner; children now under age; Major Henry Ashton and John Awbury exrs. in trust.

WILLSON, JOHN, 22 July 1718; 10 June 1719.
Estate real and personal to wife Mary and at her death to my children, the land going to my son Allen; children Allen, John, William, Sarah and the child my wife goes with.

BATCHELLOR, THOMAS, planter, 15 April 1719; 3 Aug. 1719.
¼ of personal estate and all of my land to my grandson John Morton; dau. Ann Morton; wife Mary ¼ of personal estate and she and my grandson John Morton exrs.

ANDERSON, ABRAHAM, 3 Aug. 1719.
Inventory returned.

LANE, JAMES, 3 Aug. 1719.
Inventory returned.

REDMAN, SOLOMON, 4 Aug. 1719.
Inventory returned.

MASON, WILLIAM, 23 Sept. 1719; 16 Dec. 1719.
Estate to William Jennings whom I appoint my exr.

LEWIS, WILLIAM, 30 Sept. 1719.
Inventory returned.

THOMAS, ANN, 16 Dec. 1719.
Inventory returned.

CARTER, DORCAS, 8 March 1719.
Inventory returned.

CRABB, OSMAN, 25 Jan. 1719; * * * March 1719.
Personal property to sons Osman, Gerrard, Daniel and John and dau. Lettice; land in Nominy to sons Osman and Gerrard; wife Sarah exx. and brother in law Thomas Sorrell trustee.

WOODIER, THOMAS, 9 March 1719.
Inventory returned.

POPE, NATHANIEL, gent., 9 March 1719.
Inventory returned.

BUSHROD, JOHN, 26 Jan. 1719; 30 March 1720.
Daus. Apphia Fauntleroy and Elizabeth Meriwether 20 shillings each; dau. Hannah Bushrod 1 negro, £100, 12,000 lbs. of tobacco when 17 years of age; dau. Sarah 1 negro, £100 and 12,000 lbs. of tobacco when 17 years of age; son Richard land; son John land and 13 slaves when 19 years of age; son Thomas 900 acres of land, 14 slaves, stock, silver etc; to wife Hannah the plantation whereon I live and she to be exx.

GILSON, BETHETHLAND, 20 Aug. 1716; 30 March 1720.
To grandson David Massey 1 silver tankard; grandson William Storke residue of estate and he to be exr.

KELLEY, WILLIAM, 17 Nov. 1719; 12 April 1720.
To the child my wife Ann now goes with 2 negroes; to Dorothy Anderson's dau. a feather bed and furniture; residue of estate to my wife and child; exrs. Lawrence Butler and Jarrat Ford.

VOLUME VII.

DRISKALL, DARBY, 11 May 1720; 8 July 1720.
To Mrs. Katherine McCarty and to Capt. Daniel McCarty 2 negroes; to Robert Bayley my clothes; to John Gore my stockings; to David Williamson and Edward Clark clothes; to godson Daniel McCarty 5 shillings Sterling.

FIELD, DANIEL, 17 April 1720; * * *; July 1720.
2 plantations and 1 negro to dau. Joyce Hudson; Emma Price; sons Abraham and Henry my still and worm; son Henry 50 acres of land and the land in the fork of Rappahannock River to Abraham and Henry; son John Wheeler exr; Evan Price land in Stafford county; son Daniel Field land on Popes Creek.

POWER, ROBERT, 26 March 1720; * * *; July 1720.
5 cows and feather bed to dau. in law Ursual Whiting at age of 16 years; wife Hannah and son in law William Whiting residue of estate; Lovell Massie and Robert Lovell; wife exx.

MARTIN, JOHN, * * *; 29 June 1720.
Brother William Martin and his son John horse saddle and clothes; sister Elizabeth Smith clothes; Elizabeth Collins 4 yards of linen; friends William, Vincent and Matthew Wyatt clothes; John Morris 1 deerskin; James Dunn 550 lbs. of tobacco and linen; bro. William exr.

HIGDON, JOHN, 28 April 1720; 29 June 1720.
Son John; bro. Daniel; wife Magdalene exx; son and wife equal parts of estate.

HIGGINS, AUGUSTINE, gent., 9 July 1721.
Inventory returned by Ann Higgins.

SPENCER, FRANCIS, of Cople, gent., 3 Dec. 1715; * * * July 1720.
100 pounds Sterling and 10,000 lbs. of tobacco to my bro. John's daughter Frances Spencer; to Rev. James Breechin 2 suits of clothes; friend Daniel McCarty residue of estate after 1 negro Sam to George Eskridge, Jr.

ROBINSON, THOMAS, 22 April 1717; 4 Aug. 1720.
Daus. Mary, Elizabeth and Susannah 1 shilling each; to son Thomas and his children my entire estate.

SOUTH, GEORGE, 29 Feb. 1719; 13 Sept. 1720.
Land to son George begot by me on the body of Ann my wife late wife of Issac Shepherd; son John begot by me on the body of Ann my wife ½ of my land; wife; sons George and John and dau. Hannah; my sons' godfather Thomas Lambert 1 bed and furniture; debt from Jane Dunn now wife of Benjamin Lampkin to my wife Ann; John and Francis Awbury exrs.

SUTHERLAND, JOHN, 1 April 1720; 13 Sept. 1720.
My wife's oldest and youngest son 1 cow and yearling each; wife Katherine and dau. Catherine rest of estate.

CLAYTER, KATHERINE, 22 June 1720; 6 Oct. 1720.
Son Thomas 1 shilling; dau. Jane Carter 1 shilling; dau. Ann Goff and grandson Thomas Clayter residue of estate equally.

BYARD, JAMES, 6 Sept. 1720; 6 Oct. 1720.
Son John exr; dau. Sarah Byard; wife Mary; son and daughter land; wife and children personal property.

BUTLER, JAMES, 7 Oct. 1720.
Inventory returned by William Butler.

HANDLEY, JONAS, 8 Dec. 1720.
Inventory returned.

LONGWORTH, JOHN, 8 Sept. 1722.
Inventory returned.

TUCKER, ELIZABETH, 3 May 1722; * * * Oct. 1723.
Dau. Mary Woodward 1 black gown; dau. Sarah Minor a black hood; dau. Rebecca Tucker clothes; son Benjamin residue of estate; Joseph, John and Henry my sons; dau. Martha Tucker 1 bed and furniture; son Joseph Woodward exr.

TAYLOR, JOSEPH, 24 Aug. 1722.
Inventory returned.

SPILLER, DOROTHY, 20 April 1722; * * * Nov. 1722.
Money, 2 cows, 1 bed and furniture, kettle to William son of Benjamin Berryman; granddaus. Verlinda and Jane and grandson John clothing and residue of estate; exr. Benjamin Berryman.

GAMON, JOHN, 9 Nov. 1722.
Inventory returned by Francis Gamon.

POPE, JOHN, 9 Feb. 1722.
Inventory returned.

BELL, RICHARD, 5 March 1722.
Inventory returned.

SANDERS, PHILLIP, 9 Dec. 1722; 6 April 1723.
Land to son William; dau. Urslee Taylor use of land; grandson John son of William Sanders plantation where I live; land to grandson Phillip Sanders; granddaughter Mary Sanders pewter; wife Elizabeth and daughter Urslee Taylor residue of estate.

MUSE, JOHN, 6 April 1723.
Inventory returned.

POPE, LAWRENCE, 23 March 1723; 10 May 1723, Washington Parish.
Land I live on to sons Humphrey, Thomas and John; Thomas land in Cople Parish; John land at Pope's Creek; dau. Elizabeth 1 negro and furniture; dau. Ann 1 negro and furniture; dau. Mary 1 negro and furniture; dau. Jemima Spence 1 negro woman; dau. Penelope 1 negro etc.; dau. Catherine 1 negro; James son of Benj. Waddey; godson John son of Nicholas Minor 1 mare; wife Jemima; bro. Humphrey Pope and bro. Nicholas Minor 33 shillings gold for rings; wife and son Humphrey exrs; to children horses, cattle, household goods.

COLEMAN, JAMES, 22 March 1722; 10 May 1723.
2 negroes and 70 acres of land to wife Jane; 2 elder sons James and John land in Yeocomoco Neck; son Richard land; son James land he is seated upon after decease of my son's mother in law; son in law Joseph Carr 1 negro man, 1,000 lbs. tobacco for schooling of James Carr; to Martha Sparrow 2 negroes at death of wife Jane; Elizabeth Carr.

KITCHING, WILLIAM, 5 May 1723.
Inventory returned at house of Elizabeth Kitching.

VAULX, JAMES, 16 Oct. 1710; 6 Sept. 1711.
To James son of Elizabeth Field negro and tobacco;

my bro. and sister Richard and Elizabeth Cradock 2 servants, money in England; bro. Capt. Richard Cradock; to sister Jane Butler the silver hilted sword of my father Butler; to Mary Baxter 500 lbs. tobacco; to Joseph Merkes 40 shilling; exr. bro. Robert Vaulx remainder of estate.

ROWLAND, DAVID, 28 June 1711; 6 Sept. 1711.
100 acres of land to Bryant Brannen; to Edward Hoburd 150 acres; to Rebecca Dab my iron pot; to Robert Barn's father pair of shoes.

GERRARD, SUSANNA, 29 Aug. 1711.
Inventory returned.

GERRARD, JOHN MR., 7 Sept. 1711.
Inventory returned at house of Mrs. Jane Gerrard.
(The 1711 records recorded in Vol. 7.)

VAULX, ROBERT, CAPT., 30 Nov. 1721; 5 Dec. 1721.
Land to sons Robert and James; my wife and three children (third child un-named) residue of estate; land at head of Popes Creek; wife Elizabeth, Augustine Washington and Richard Kenner exrs.

RAMEY, JACOB, Snr., July 1702; 5 Dec. 1721.
Furniture in her room to wife Mary; youngest son Jacob 200 acres of land; eldest son William 1 shilling upon demand.

BROWN, WILLIAM, Jr., 11 July 1723.
Inventory returned.

DAMOURVELL, SAMUEL, DR., 12 April 1723; 8 Aug. 1723.
To son Samuel 6 negroes and 200 acres of land in Stafford Co.; dau. Magdalene Rust 100 acres of land in Stafford; dau. Elizabeth Harrison 140 acres of land in Stafford; wife Hannah 2 negroes, 2 horses, 2 beds and furniture.

JENKINS, THOMAS, 9 Dec. 1722; 8 Aug. 1723.
Son Jeremiah to stay with his mother in law until 19 years of age, then to have 800 lbs. of tobacco, clothes and personal estate; wife Elizabeth exx. and use of estate.

LUTTRELL, SIMON, 1 Aug. 1723; 8 Oct. 1723.
Son Simon 1 negro; son John 3,500 lbs. of tobacco; dau. Margaret Luttrell 2,000 lbs. of tobacco, 1 feather bed and furniture; my daughters; wife Elizabeth exx. and residue of estate.

MUSE, JOHN, 5 April 1723; 8 Oct. 1723.
Son Thomas 1 shilling; dau. Jane Pritchett 1 shilling; dau. Ann Wilson 1 shilling; dau. Mary Quisenberry 1 shilling; residue of estate to dau. in law Ann Muse.

EALES, JOHN ALLERTON, 6 July 1721.
Inventory returned.

MURPHY, ELIZABETH, 6 July 1721.
Inventory returned.

FROUD, JOHN, 4 March 1717; 1 Aug. 1721.
Dau. Jane Lamkin 60 acres of land; granddau. Winifred Lamkin plantation where I live, stock, household goods etc at death of my wife.

WATSON, THOMAS, 1 Aug. 1721.
Inventory returned.

BAKER, SUSANNAH, 23 July 1721; 6 Sept. 1721.
Land I live on on Popés Creek to John Steel; to John Keesee 50 acres which I had by my husband John Baker now occupied by Robert Turner; to John Gannack 50 acres, 1 feather bed, furniture and personal estate.

GOLDING, HANLETT, 30 Aug. 1721.
Inventory returned.

BREECHIN, JAMES, 19 Oct. 1721; 6 April 1722.
My late wife Ann; sons William and James land at falls of Potomac; to Mr. John Rele 50 acres; to Dennis Lynsey 100 acres of land; to Thomas Poindexter 300 acres of land; dau. Anna and Jane land; to James and Anna Sorrell 1 hogshead tobacco each; kinsman Thomas Sorrell a mourning ring; wife and Capt. George Turberville exrs., the latter to have a mourning ring; wife Sarah personal estate.

WIGGINGTON, WILLIAM, 7 Nov. 1721; * * * March 1721.
2 negroes to son James Johnson Wiggington; dau. Elizabeth Wiggington 2 negroes stock and plantation in Md.; wife Frances; dau. Ann 2 negroes; bro. Henry Wiggington if he should come to Virginia.

ONEAL, GARRETT, 3 April 1722; 7 May 1722.
Horse and saddle to dau. in law Elizabeth Butler; sons Garrett and John my plantation and movable estate; dau. Ellenor Oneal; my four daus. when 18 years of age 40 shilling each; exr. friend Henry Washington.

DUDLEY, MARY, 20 April 1722; 7 May 1722.
Son John Collins; granddau. Mary Collins estate after debts are paid.

NEWTON, WILLIAM, 1 March 1721; 4 Jan. 1722.
Son John land in Westmoreland and in King George, also land and money in Great Britain; sons William and Benjamin land in Stafford; wife Elizabeth; daus. Frances, Sarah and Elizabeth Newton; personal estate to wife, 3 daus. and 3 sons.

VOLUME VIII.

STURMAN, JOHN, aged 73 years, * * *; 27 Nov. 1723.
Land in personal property to wife Anna; son John one-third land and grandson Dick; son Thomas one-third land in Md. or Va. of my father or grandfather; dau. Neale silver tumbler and 500 lbs. tobacco; dau. Dorcas Sanford land; son William one-third land; dau. Jemimah Stone land; personal property to wife and children.

BALL, ROBERT, 29 May 1723; 9 Dec. 1723.
Son Robert home plantation; son George 2,000 lbs. of tobacco; son Emanuel bed and furniture; son Gerrard Ball 1 heifer; dau. Sarah Ball 1 bed and furniture; my wife and children Daniel and Benoni; Ralph Elston coat and breeches; bro. Gerrard Ball of Maryland exr. and care of 3 sons; child unborn.

REED, JOHN, 3 Jan. 1723; 10 March 1723.
My four sons John, William, Claytor and Thomas lands; dau. Mary Reed 3 head of cattle; wife Jane and Giles Carter exrs. 1 mare, saddle and heifer to wife Jane.

BAKER, THOMAS, 31 Jan. 1723; 10 March 1723.
Estate to John Jewell, Sr., and appoint him exr.

DAVIS, ELIZABETH, widow, relict of William Davis, 6 Feb. 1723; 10 March 1723.

Son William land given me by my father and if he dies without issue to dau. Elizabeth; my four daus. Frances, Sarah, Barbara and Ann; sons Gerrard and William.

ALLERTON, WILLOUGHBY, gent., 17 Jan. 1723; 8 April 1724
Land, stock and 3 slaves to wife Hannah; son Isaac land whereon I live and 300 acres of land and two-thirds of estate; dau. Elizabeth Allerton 200 acres and one-third estate; son exr; my wife's daus. Hannah and Sarah Bushrod personal property of their father and mother. Land on Machotick; land formerly Capt. John Bushrod's and personal estate of his to my wife and her daus.; to wife the school master Joshua Nelson and 3 more white servants.

McCARTY, DANIEL, 29 March 1724; 9 June 1724.
25 negroes to son Dennis and all land in Stafford; son Daniel lands in Westmoreland; to son Billington lands in Farnham, Richmond co. that was my grandfather Billington's land; son Thaddeus land in Richmond that was Capt. John Rice's land purchased by me; land in Northumberland to Billington; daus. Winifred £500 for land and Sarah £500 for land. Mrs. Anna Barbara Fitzhugh 2 negroes; to each of my grandchildren 2 negroes; to wife's son Henry Fitzhugh a ring; my son Daniel who is now under care of Mr. John Gilpin of Whitehaven to be continued until his education comes to £100 to be paid on his arrival in Virginia and when he does arrive to have all my law and gospel books; son in law William Payne; pictures of son and dau. Fitzhugh to their son when 7 years old, but the pictures of myself and first wife to remain in my dwelling house; exrs. in trust Col. John Tayloe, Humphrey Pope, Nicholas Minor, John Fitzhugh and Samuel Peachey, gents., until son Thaddeus be 17 years of age; my first wife's

daus. Elizabeth Sherman and Mary Burns; my uncle Mr. Joseph Taylor late clerk of Lancaster; to my aunt Mrs. Barbara Tayloe and her son Joseph; my brothers Philip, Francis, Thomas and Henry Lee; friend Capt. Eskridge; my wife Anna and her brothers Col. and Capt. Lee a ring each; wife Anna 12 slaves, use of plantation and personal property for life and use of her children; 12 slaves and 1,000 acres of land to wife; soup ladle to Sary; porriger to Lettice; John Warner to serve rest of time; also his wife, then 100 acres at Aquia; he to continue to teach school and keep accounts and wife to help his mistress; home plantation to son Daniel at death of his mother.

RANSDELL, EDWARD, 1 May 1724; 24 June 1724.
Still, tools, gun, hogs, etc., to son Wharton; sons John and Edward bed and furniture each; my wife's plantation in Rappahannock; wife Amy the estate which formerly did belong to her first husband Capt. John Kelley, bed, tobacco, household furniture and bee hive; the orphan of Capt. John Kelley; Elizabeth Jeffreys; dau. in law Mary Kelley 1 heifer; Nicholas Stephens; to William Longworth suit and clothing; son Wharton exr; daus. Elizabeth Talbott and Milicent Longworth residue of estate.

ASHTON, CHARLES, 9 Sept. 1724; 30 Sept. 1724.
Land in Mattox to son John; youngest sons Charles and Burdett residue of my land; my dau. Jane 3 negroes and to be educated by her aunt Storke; my bro. Burdett Ashton to be exr; all of my children now under 18 years of age.

BROWN, GEORGE, 18 May 1724; 20 July 1724.
Nephew John son of my brother William Brown dec'd 100 acres of land; to Thomas son of my bro. Thomas Brown 100 acres of land; to George son of George During 100 acres of land; to John Fryer land; to

George the son of William and Elizabeth Hardage 280 acres of land, she being my sister; to Priscilla Fryer the dau. of William Fryer after the decease of my wife Rose my mill and 2 acres of land; to Daniel Jackson land whereon I live; to William and Katherine son and dau. of John Fryer bequest; Frances and Rose dau. of William Fryer; George and Elizabeth children of Daniel Jackson; Katherine dau. of John Fryer residue of estate.

MARCEY, EDWARD, 28 May 1724; 30 Sept. 1724.
Sons John, Edward and Thomas 150 acres of land; dau. Ann Marcey 1 feather bed and furniture; wife Martha residue of estate and she to be exx.

BERNARD, ROBERT, 4 Dec. 1724; 27 Jan. 1724.
To George Pierce a saddle and my clothes; to his son John Pierce 2 heifers; to George son of George Pierce 2 heifers; to Elizabeth Manning 2 heifers; to Stephen Latharam 2 hogs; to Edward Riley 1 mare; to Dr. Cooper my bay mare; my wife residue of estate; she and George Pierce exrs.

DOWLING, JAMES, 16 March 1724; 26 May 1725.
Dau. Mary Dowling 1 horse, pewter and household furniture; wife Joanna residue of estate.

FRANK, SARAH, widow of Robert * * * 20 June 1725.
(Nuncupative.)
Eldest son Thomas; children Robert, Samuel, Martha and Neremiah to John Piper and his wife Mary until they come of age. Attested to by John Plunkett.

SMITH, CALEB, 15 June 1725; 28 July 1725.
To eldest son John 162 acres of land; son Caleb an equal share with John; wife Elizabeth household goods, horse and cattle; my five children; brother John Smith.

MORRIS, ABRAHAM, 22 July 1725; 25 July 1725.
To Mary Harvey 1 heifer; wife Margaret, my son and dau. residue of estate; exr. my friend James Horde.

SMITH, JOHN, * * *; 25 Aug. 1725.
Sons Thomas and John; wife Mary.

HOPWOOD, RICHARD, 25 Jan. 1725; 23 Feb. 1725.
Wife Mary and son Moses my land and orchard; son in law John Borrer my weavers tools and loom; to Henry Borrer 1 gun; if my son Moses die without issue my land to James Hamilton, Jr.

PEACH, GEORGE, 6 Nov. 1717; 25 Feb. 1725.
Son Thomas my land in Richmond County; dau. Mary land in Richmond Co.

BROWN, JOHN, 26 Dec. 1725; 23 Feb. 1725.
Land to sons Richard & David when 18 years of age; rest of estate to 2 sons and dau. Sarah; son William Brown's widow to stay on the plantation during widowhood.

MASON, JOHN, 16 Jan. 1725; 23 Feb. 1725.
Land, stock and pewter to cousin John Higdon when 20 years of age; to Richard Wroe my tools; to William son of William Brown 3 years schooling; to Mary Brown 20 shillings; to Hannah Wroe 20 shillings; to Walter Brown a heifer; to Original son of John Wroe ½ of my personal estate; exrs. Capt. Augustine Washington and William Brown.

MARTIN, MATTHEW, 22 Nov. 1725; 23 Feb. 1725.
Son Stephen 1 shilling; wife Hester corn, fowls and hogs; son Elias 2 hogs and one-third of personal estate; granddau. Nanie Martin 2 years schooling and to remain in care of my wife.

ROBINSON, JOHN, 8 Nov. 1725; 23 Feb. 1725.
To wife Mary 1 bed and furniture; dau. Ann 1 feather bed and furniture; Elizabeth my dau. 1 feather bed and furniture; residue of estate to wife and 2 daus. Executor my brother Thomas Chancellor.

LOVELL, ROBERT, 15 Jan. 1725; 23 Feb. 1725.
To dau. Elizabeth Nicholson 1 feather bed and furniture; dau. Mary Harrison 1 pair of sheets; son Robert land; son Daniel land; son James 1 negro; dau. Ursula Lovell land; son Robert 1 negro; grandchildren Ann and Lovell Harrison.

WROE, HENRY, 21 Nov. 1725; 23 Feb. 1725.
Sons Bunch Wroe and Henry Wroe; daus. Sarah, Elizabeth, Mary and Susannah Wroe; Robert Stephens and his wife Elizabeth to pay 500 lbs. tobacco a year for land they live on; wife Mary my personal estate; bro. Bunch Wroe exr.

SPURLING, JEREMIAH, 13 Feb. 1725; 30 March 1726.
Wife Mary 2 beds, cows and calves; eldest son Jeremiah; dau. Sarah; son Thomas and son John Barmuell. Personal property to all my children.

GLASCO, JOHN, 28 Jan. 1725; 30 March 1726.
To John Chalker 4 ells of kersey; to James Courtwell residue of estate; to Garrard Ball my saddle and bridle; to Sarah Ball Jr. 1 rugg and pair of blankets.

STEPHENS, ROBERT, 17 Feb. 1726; 30 March 1726.
To Godson Henry Wroe 1 heifer and 2 piggs; to Godson James Hervey 2 shoats; to Mary Wroe a feather bed; Elizabeth Gough rest of estate and she to be exx.

MUNROE, SPENCE, 15 Jan. 1725; 31 March 1726.
My wife 1 negro and 1 horse; bro. Andrew Munroe my sword and drum; the child my wife goes with and my three children the residue of my estate.

HOWGATE, JAMES, 12 May 1710; 30 March 1726.
Dau. Agnes 3 head of cattle and 1 gold ring; son William 3 head of cattle; if my wife die in widowhood all estate to 2 children; wife and Charles Goddard exrs.

ELLIOTT, WILLIAM, 18 March 1825; 27 April 1726.
Land and personal property to wife Mary for life and at her death to my Godson and nephew William Elliott; son in law Benjamin Weeks a horse, saddle and bridle.

CHANLOR, THOMAS, 11 May 1721; 29 June 1726.
Youngest son Francis land bought of Walter English; son Joseph land and personal property; son John land and personal property at home; grandson Thomas Spurling; exrs. friends Col. Thomas Lee and Capt. Henry Lee.

SANDERS, WILLIAM, 31 March 1726; 29 June 1726.
My sons John, Phillip, William and James to have my land; wife Elizabeth a feather bed and furniture; daus. Mary and Urusla a feather bed and furntiure each; daus. Elizabeth and Sarah Sanders 500 lbs. of tobacco each at 18 years of age.

PURSLEE, PATRICK, 5 April 1726; 29 June 1726.
Wife Ursula; children Anne, John, Thomas and James my estate; bro. Osman Jenkins; bros. John and Gerrard Bricke exrs.

MUSE, ANNE, 14 June 1725; 29 June 1726.
Son Edward the land of my deceased husband; sons William, Hopkins, John, Augustine and George the lands which he leased to Col. William Fitzhugh; my dau. Mary Sanford bed in possession of Thomas Muse Jr.; dau. Anne Muse bed and furniture; dau. Sarah Muse 1 bed, furniture and table; son in law Robert Sanford; friend Benjamin Waddey a ring.

BURN, JAMES, 12 Sept. 1724; 27 July 1726.
Wife Alice; sons William and James; grandson Daniel Burns all of my estate.

BLAGG, MARGARET, 18 May 1724; 27 July 1726.
All my estate to my grandson Abraham Blagg when 18 years of age; James Hore his uncle to advise him.

MINOR, WILLIAM, 30 Jan. 1725; 28 Sept. 1726.
Sons John, William and Nicholas 100 acres of land each; daus. Mary, Jemima and Barbara Minor 10 shillings each; wife Elizabeth exx; bro. Nicholas exr.

CHILTON, JOHN, 7 Aug. 1726; 28 Sept. 1726.
Son John land on Chippawamsic swamp and 8 negroes; son Thomas home plantation; when Richard and John Watts come of age to have negroes in part of their fathers estate.

SORRELL, THOMAS, 12 Jan. 1725; 22 Feb. 1726. (Of Cople).
Son James land; to son John land devised me by my father in law Daniel Occany and land on Nominy where I formerly lived; son James land in James City County bequethed me by my father John Sorrell deceased; nephew Thomas Sorrell land; my bro. John Sorrell of James City County deceased; said nephew and his sisters Elizabeth and Frances a ring each; daus. Anna and Winifred; wife Elizabeth her horse, saddle, bridle, rings, clothing, 3 slaves and use of my plantation for life; friends Capt. George Turbeville and Mr. William Sturman exrs.

BONAM, SAMUEL, St. Stephens Parish Northumberland Co. 6 Dec. 1726; 22 Feb. 1726.
Son Samuel all my land; my bro. Daniel Bonam a ring; to Samuel son of George Haydon 1 cow calf; my sister in law Mary Ball a riding horse; wife Elizabeth and the child she goes with; my children to the care of my uncle George Eskridge until of age.

KING, JOHN, 3 Dec. 1726; 22 Feb. 1726.
Son James; grandson John Spence; my bro's. daughter Mary; son in law John Spence 1 gun; Daniel son of Major George Eskridge 1 gun; wife Margaret rest of estate.

MORRICE, ELIAS, 10 Aug. 1726; 22 Feb. 1726.
To be buried in Nominy Church Yard; wife Bridget 20 head of cattle and household furniture; godchildren Jeremiah and Elizabeth Nash; James son of Jeremiah Nash; my Countrymen David Williams; exrs. my wife and Nathaniel Nash.

WATTS, alias WATKINS, YOUELL, 8 Nov. 1726; 22 Feb. 1726.
Sister in law Hannah Broags my land for life; cousin Patrick Spence land in Virginia and Maryland; to Wharton Ransdell my sermon book; my wife negroes and estate for life; to Youell Hollam and his brother Simon 6 negroes, ½ of personal estate and land.

BROWNING, THOMAS, 31 Jan. 1726; 22 Feb. 1726.
Daughter Jane wife of Andrew Hutchinson land; daughter Ann widow of Morgan Williams 1 slave; daughter Mary wife of Richard Omohundro 1 slave; residue of estate to be equally divided among my children.

BONAM, PHILPOT, 23 Nov. 1726; 22 Feb. 1726.
My wife Rose 3 slaves; brother Daniel Bonam land; brother Samuel; Richard Partridge 1000 lbs. of tobacco; to James Thomas 20 shillings; James Thomas Jr. my wig.

FRANK, ROBERT, 17 Nov. 1725; 22 Feb. 1726.
Granddau. Margaret Spillman my land; grandson Robert Frank; grandson William Plunkett; grandson John Grinning; granddau. Elizabeth Knighton;

grandson Thomas Grinning and grandson Thomas
Frank; exr. John Plunkett.

DUNKIN, JOHN; 20 June 1716; 22 Feb. 1726.
Son Peter land left me by my deceased father Peter
Dunkin; son William; daus. Elizabeth, Anne and Alice
1 shilling each; grandsons John and William Rochester; dau. Phyllis Rochester 1 horse; grandchildren
John and Elizabeth children of James Dunkin; son
James and grandson John son of Peter Dunkin.

AWBREY, JOHN, 19 Dec. 1726; 22 Feb. 1726.
Dau. Hannah Awbrey to my dau. Keziah Attwell until
of age; dau. Kerrenhappuck Awbrey; son Chandler
Awbrey residue of estate.

WALKER, THOMAS, 11 Dec. 1726; 23 Feb. 1726.
Sons James and Thomas land; sons Samuel, William
and Hardidge; dau. Hannah land on Salisbury Plane
in Stafford County; exrs. bro. George Walker; son
James and wife Lydia.

HARDWICH, JOSEPH, 24 Dec. 1726; 29 March 1727.
Wife Anne and all of my children when at age of 16
years to have my estate both real and personal; wife
and nephew James Hardwich exr.

HAMBLETON, JAMES, 17 Nov. 1726; 29 March 1727.
Wife Grace; son James 100 acres of land; son John;
my 3 children.

HAMBLETON, GRACE, 11 Feb. 1727, 29 March 1727.
My deceased husband James; my children James, John
and Anne; said Anne to have my rings and clothes.

CARR, SARAH, widow of William Carr. 21 Nov. 1726; 29
March 1727.
Daughter Elizabeth Bailey my clothes; residue of
estate to daughter Ann Carr.

LAMKIN, GEORGE, 21 April 1718; 29 March 1727.
Daughter Elenor Lamkin; son Peter 100 acres of land; son George land; wife Jean; brother James Lamkin exr.

DISHMAN, SAMUEL, 15 Nov. 1726; 31 May 1727.
Eldest son John land in Westmoreland and Stafford Cos. Daus. Elizabeth Brown and Anne Dishman; son James land in King George; son David; son Peter land in Essex; dau. Mary; wife Cornelia.

RUST, JOHN, 11 April 1727; 31 May 1727.
Sons Samuel and John negroes; Sons John and William land in Stafford and King George; daughter Elizabeth Rust; brother Jeremiah Rust exr.

RUSSELL, ANDREW, 13 April 1727; 31 May 1727.
A debt to be paid which I owe Rev. John Begge of Essex Co. decd; children Francis and Anthony my estate; wife Penelope, John Cockes of Stafford, John Elliott of Westmoreland and Edmund Begge of Essex exrs.

REMY, JACOB, 23 Feb. 1726; 31 May 1727.
Sons John, Jacob, William, Benjamin and Joseph my land; my wife; my decd. father.

LONGWORTH, JOHN, 22 June 1724; 1 June 1727.
Children Anne, Frances, Margaret, Thomas and Elizabeth Longworth my personal property; my son in law John Cockerell and William Sanders exrs.

BRISCO, JAMES, 5 May 1727; 26 July 1727.
Daughter Elizabeth Butler; son John; daughter Ellenor; son James; my wife Margaret and her brother Henry Ward exrs.

FRYER, JOHN, 22 April 1727; 26 July 1727.
Wife Sarah 1 horse and a slave; son William 1 gun;

John 1 gun; rest of estate to be equally divided between wife and sons.

MEACHAM, WILLIAM, 3 Jan. 1726-7; 26 July 1727.
Brothers Richard, Samuel and Benjamin lands in Gloucester Co.; Daniel Jennings, John Morphew and Mary White; Youell Atwell.

NEWTON, (CAPT.) THOMAS, 26 Aug. 1727; 31 Jan. 1727.
Son Willoughby land in Richmond Co. near Totuskey containing 350 acres; daughter Elizabeth Waulhope 3 negroes; daughter Katherine Brent negroes in her possession; grandson Newton Keene; son Rev. Walter Jones and Behethland his wife 3 negroes; wife Elizabeth 5 negroes, 2 horses, 10 cows, 15 sheep, furniture, silver and the use of my plantation for life.

HALLS, JOHN, 29 Jan. 1727; 31 July 1728.
Son George residue of estate after my daughter Mary King has 1 cow and calf, and grandson William Brown 1 mare.

HARTLEY, JOHN, 12 Dec. 1726; 16 April 1728.
Children John, William and Sarah each land; my former wife Elizabeth; my wife Mary my plantation and a third of personal estate for life.

MARTIN, JACOB, 9 Jan. 1727; 30 Oct. 1728.
Daughters Sarah Martin, Anne Lovell and Jane; wife Sarah and son John my land; negroes to each of my daughters.

MOSS, RICHARD, 2 Jan. 1728; 22 Jan. 1728.
Estate to be equally divided between my 3 children Frances, Thomas and Judith; my bro. John Moss to be exr.

BAKER, JOHN, 19 Nov. 1727; 27 March 1728.
To daughter Ann Davice land leased to Thomas English and 2 years after her death to her husband Samuel Davice and at his death to refall to my sons; sons Butler and John the rest of my land and if they die without issue to my daus. Mary and Rebecca; dau. Sarah Munroe 10 shillings; wife residue of estate.

BARNES, THOMAS, 28 Nov. 1728; 29 Jan. 1728.
Wife Ann 5 negroes; my children Abraham, Elizabeth and Frances lands, slaves, etc; brothers Abraham and Richard 2 servants and tobacco.

BRISCOE, MARGARET, 27 Nov. 1728; 29 May 1729.
Daughter Butler a spinning wheel; daughter Ellenor 1 mare; son James 1 horse; exrs. John Butler and John Briscoe.

CHANLOR, WILLIAM, 29 Jan. 1728; 21 July 1729.
To Elizabeth Cooper my former wife's sister; grandson in law Chanlor Awbury; Susannah Appleyard; my present wife.

BERRYMAN, BENJAMIN, 4 Aug. 1729; 27 Aug. 1729.
Sons James, William, Maximilian, Newton, Henry and Benjamin lands in Westmoreland and King George; grandson Gilson Berryman; daus. Elizabeth, Rose, Anne, Sarah, Frankey and Kate; my wife sole exx.

BUTLER, CHRISTOPHER, 2 Oct. 1729; 26 Nov. 1729.
Son Nathaniel; bro. Lawrence; sons William, Lawrence, Joseph, John and Caleb; land to each of my sons; my wife.

COOPER, ELIZA, 9 Jan. 1729; 25 Feb. 1729.
Dau. Marie Taylor 1 feather bed and furniture; son William Walker 1 feather bed and furniture; grandson George Mullins 1 feather bed and furniture; son Spencer Watts exr.

HARRISON, ANDREW, 11 Nov. 1729; 27 Feb. 1729.
Son Joseph land in King George County; my wife Mary and four children residue of my estate.

RUST, MARTHA, 3 Nov. 1726; 25 Feb. 1729.
Dau. Hannah Eskridge; dau. Anne Harrison; son Matthew Rust guardian of my son Peter Rust who is to be my exr.

MELVIN, WILLIAM, 26 April 1726; 25 Feb. 1729.
Son in law John Jennings 1 cow; wife Elizabeth residue of estate.

CARPENTER, ANN, 3 Feb. 1728; 25 Feb. 1729.
Daughter Mary wife of John Halliday and their dau. Mathew my clothing and 1 cow and calf; my son William residue of estate.

ARISS, JOHN, 13 March 1729; 25 March 1730.
Son Spencer Ariss; son John; daughters Elizabeth and Frances slaves, land and personal property. Children under age.

KEATING, PIERCE, 13 Nov. 1729; 23 March 1730.
Son James and daughter Malinda Keating all my estate.

BROWN, DAVID, 8 July 1727; 26 August 1730.
Grandson Original Brown 150 acres of land; daughter Mary Bowling 500 lbs. of tobacco; son Original 100 acres of land; son John and William land whereon I live.

WROE, WILLIAM, 8 Feb. 1725; 30 Sept. 1730.
Wife Hannah; sons Original, William and Richard; daus. Mary, Elizabeth, Sarah and Judith. Wife and

children my negroes and other estate save 20 shillings to Margaret Anderson.

MIDDLETON, BENEDICT, 31 Dec. 1729; 29 March 1730.
Son Robert 100 acres of land & a tract of land where I live with houses etc and 1 negro man; to son Benedict 1 negro boy; carpenter's tools, 1 bed and furniture; to son William a negro man, a negro woman, feather bed and furniture; daughter Mary a negro girl, feather bed, furniture and trunk; daughter Elizabeth a negro boy, feather bed and furniture and trunk; to daughter Jane a negro boy, feather bed, furniture and trunk; one gold ring each (for which I have sent) to Elizabeth and Jane Middleton my daughters; rest of estate to be equally divided between my 3 sons and 3 daughters. Robert Middleton was granted administration with Daniel Bonahm and Samuel Damouvel securities.

SMITH, NICHOLAS, 23 July 1728; 25 Feb. 1730.
Lands between Nicholas, Peter and James the sons of the said Nicholas Smith; son John 1 shilling; ½ of my estate to be equally divided between my three sons and three daus.

BENNETT, JOHN, 21 Jan. 1729; 28 Oct. 1730.
Estate to wife Easter; granddau. Elizabeth Summers 1 shilling.

HARGIS, JOHN, 19 June 1730; 25 Nov. 1730.
Son John; daughters Mary and Milerett Hargis; brothers Roger Hargis and James Woring exrs; all estate to my children.

BINCKS, JOHN, 2 Feb. 1728; 24 Feb. 1730.
Sister Anne Green; wife Elizabeth; brother Thomas Bincks' children Mary and John.

MOTHERSHEAD, JOHN, 13 Nov. 1730; 26 May 1731.
Sons Nathaniel, George, Christopher and John; daus. Elizabeth Quisenberry; dau. Claytor; sons Olvin and George; grandson Brooks Mothershead; wife Elizabeth.

RUST, JEREMIAH, 7 Aug. 1731; 29 Sept. 1731.
Brother Peter land; son Samuel land in Northumberland and Westmoreland; son William the White Marsh Neck; wife Magdalene home plantation for life and then to son Jeremiah; daughters Hannah and Martha Rust 1 negro each; child my wife goes with 2 negroes.

BUTLER, WILLIAM, 20 April 1720; 29 Sept. 1731.
To son Price a negro man and 20 shillings; rest of my negroes to my daus.; cozen Thomas Butler suit of clothes; cozen James Butler a Dueroy coat; dau. Elizabeth 1000 lbs. of tobacco; dau. Mary 20 shillings; residue of estate to my wife and children.

ROBINSON, WILLIAM, 26 June 1731; 27 Oct. 1731.
Children William, Anne and Elizabeth to have my land; my wife; brother Michael Robinson and James Smith exr.

PEYTON, GERRARD, 27 Dec. 1687; 11 Jan. 1687.
To sister Elizabeth Hardidge all estate real and personal; my father in law Mr. William Hardidge of Nominy exr. (will recorded in Book VIII. page 46, which page has been lost).

ASHTON, HENRY, 26 Feb. 1730; 24 Nov. 1731.
My wife; dau. Grace Ashton 2200 acres of land; my granddaus. Elizabeth and Anne Aylett daus. of Capt. William Aylett and Anne his wife who was my dau. deceased, 400 acres of land; granddau. Elizabeth Turbeville 800 acres of land; son Henry my pistols, sword and hostler; son John; dau. Elizabeth Ashton 1000 acres of land in Stafford; cousin Burdett Ash-

ton 1000 acres of land in Stafford; Godson John son of Mr. Charles Ashton decd. land in a back woods on Broad Run Stafford Co. and the other part of same tract to my sons Henry and John which lies near Col. Carter's copper mines; sister Mrs. Sarah Macgill; exrs. in trust Capt. George Turbeville, Capt. Burdett Ashton, Mr. Andrew Munroe, Mr. Richard Watts.

HENRY, ROWLAND, * * *; 26 April 1732.
Dau. Hannah Henry 1 bed and furniture, 2 cows and piggs; wife Mary exx.

SELPH, STEPHEN, 11 Aug. 1731; 31 May 1732.
Son Philip a bed, a bay mare and an iron pott; son Benjamin a mare, bed and iron pott; son Jobe 2 horses, a bed and a pott; son Francis 1 bed, an iron pot and the land where I live adjoining my son Stephen.

McCARTY, ANNE, 7 Nov. 1728; 31 May 1732.
To each of my own brothers and their wives a ring; a ring to Col. John Tayloe; son Henry Fitzhugh all my lands, my first wedding ring and my grandfather Corbin's mourning ring; to Elizabeth dau. of Major John Fitzhugh a gold ring; to dau. Lettice 2 negroes; dau. Sarah Fitzhugh 2 negroes; Billington McCarty my last wedding ring; to Thaddeus McCarty a stone ring; to Sarah Beale my hoop ring. I discharge my bros. Henry Fitzhugh and Thomas and Henry Lee from the bills of exchange to my late husband McCarty. Negroes in the hands of the husband of my daughter Lettice to be hers.

MUSE, THOMAS, 12 March 1729; 28 June 1732.
My wife Elizabeth her horse and saddle; son Christopher £20; son Daniel 1 mare; son James 12 pence Sterling; son Nicholas 12 pence Sterling; sons John and Thomas; daus. Anne Taylor, Mary Muse and Elizabeth Newman the remainder of estate; granddau. Mary George.

STURMAN, WILLIAM, 15 June 1732; 27 Sept. 1732.
Son Foxhall all my lands in Westmoreland and Prince William Counties; dau. Martha Sturman; wife Sarah; my 4 children; William son of Thomas Sturman.

HARDWICK, GEORGE, 30 June 1732; 27 Sept. 1732.
Brother James and his son William; my mother Elizabeth Hardwick to have ½ of my estate and my brother James the other half.

MORTON, RICHARD, 18 Nov. 1731; 27 Sept. 1732.
Wife Massey and my children to have all my estate; father in law Robert Sanford Sr. exr.

BAYLEY, ANN, 13 March 1731; 25 Oct. 1732.
Granddau. Ann Quisenberry; my great grandson Banam Burch; granddau. Elizabeth Cox; great grandson Bayley Washington 2 negroes; Jane wife of Giles Esther; Benjamin Akers 20 shillings; William Brown 20 shillings; granddau. Mary Washington and her husband Henry Washington; granddau. Ann Quisenberry and her son Baman Burch and his sister Ann.

BLUNDALL, THOMAS, 8 Oct. 1731; 25 Oct. 1732.
Dau. Susannah Holladay; sons Thomas, Absolam, William and Garner; daus. Elizabeth McKenne and Jane Blundall; son in law Richard Holladay and son in law William McKenne exrs.

BONUM, DANIEL, 15 Oct. 1732; 28 Nov. 1732.
Son Samuel 196 acres of land; nephews Thomas and Samuel Bonum; wife Sarah 3 negroes; rest of personal estate to my wife and son.

McKENNE, WILLIAM, 3 Nov. 1729; 28 Nov. 1732.
We William and Jane McKenne of Nominy being sick make this our will. Lands to our three sons Gerrard, John and Daniel; son William; grandchild Kenne Williams; 3 daus. Deborah Marmanduke, Jane Williams and Mary Williams 1 shilling each.

BUCKLEY, JOHN, 7 March 1730; 30 Jan. 1732.
Wife Elizabeth and all my children; sons John, Abraham and William lands.

BUTLER, LAWRENCE, (CAPT.) 9 March 1732; 27 March 1733.
Dau. in law Corderoy Sanford; grandson William Bernard 1 negro girl; neice Joyce Butler 1 mare and saddle; son in law Richard Bernard; nephew Lawrence Butler; son Lawrence all my silver spoons and all of my land; to dau. Sarah 1 horse. Friend Capt. Anthony Thornton a mourning ring; Richard Bernard exrs.

MIDDLETON, ELIZABETH, 9 Feb. 1732; 27 March, 1733.
My estate to my 2 daughters Mary and Ellis Middleton except 1 shilling each to my grandson John Middleton, my sons Benjamin, Thomas and Robert Middleton and my son in law John Brown.

WIGGINTON, FRANCES, 24 Dec. 1732; 27 March 1733.
Cousin Elizabeth Cannady; Anne Bannister; Godson Thomas Martin; cousin Barbara Davis; cousin Frances Davis and cousin Gerrard Davis Jr; my dau. Elizabeth Wright; son in law Richard Wright; my husband and childrens' graves to be paled in.

GOLORTHUM, MARTIN, 20 Nov. 1732; 27 March 1733.
Sons John and William; wife Mary and 5 children;
Christopher Pritchett.

FIELD, DANIEL, 2 Feb. 1732; 28 March 1733.
My land to Margaret Gerviss; Mary daughter of
Alice Beckwith land in Prince William; wife Mary
one-third of estate; Daniel Hutson.

RICE, WILLIAM, ***; 17 May 1733.
Wife Mary; sons William, Zerobabel and John; dau.
Rebecca Payne.

PATEN, ANTHONY, 23 Feb. 1731; 29 May 1733.
Son William; dau. Sarah; sons John and Anthony;
dau. Margaret Jett; son in law Frences Jett; son
Samuel and dau. Mary.

WALKER, WILLIAM, ***; 26 June 1733.
Son William 80 acres of land; son Daniel; wife Ann
2 negroes; sons John, Richard and Joseph; my dau.
Martha Walker the chest which was her mothers.

SELF, JOHN, 10 Dec. 1732; 26 June 1733.
Wife Susanna; sons John, Thomas, Moses and William; dau. Mary.

PIERCE, WILLIAM, 1 Aug. 1733; 25 Sept. 1733.
Sons William and Joseph my lands; daus. Sarah,
Mary, Elizabeth and Margaret my lands if bros. die
without issue; personal estate to all my children;
bro. Robert Tomlin and Thomas Dozier exrs.

TANNER, MARTHA, 7 Jan. 1733; 26 Feb. 1733.
To Richard Griffin and his son Lewis all of my estate.
All personal estate and 530 lbs. of tobacco to the
said Lewis.

CREED, JAMES, 16 Oct. 1733; 26 Feb. 1733. (Nuncupative).
Son James 1 horse; wife Elizabeth rest of estate for life and then to my 4 children.

BUTLER, WILLIAM, 18 Jan. 1734; 26 March 1734.
Son Cradock; son Gerrard; my 5 children, Cradock, Gerrard, Elizabeth, Sarah and Hannah Butler; dau. Jane Jeffries; bro. Thomas Butler and Jeremiah Garland exrs.

KIRK, EDWARD, 9 March 1733; 28 May 1734.
Daughter Jemima 1 mare; son Henry 1 horse; residue of my estate to wife Ann and my two children.

LINTON, WILLIAM, 6 Feb. 1733; 26 March 1734.
Sons Anthony, William and John land in Richmond County; dau. Elizabeth Lewis; cousin James Smith and my wife Mary exx.

HARRISON, GEORGE, 7 Feb. 1725; 28 Jan. 1734.
Land whereon I live to son Samuel; sons George and Benjamin land in Richmond Co. purchased of Benjamin Rust; son Jeremiah land purchased of Thomas Harrison; 1 negro child to each son; wife Anne 1 negro woman. Jeremiah and Benjamin to have 2 years schooling at the age of 12 years; rest of estate to wife, sons Samuel, George, Jeremiah and Benjamin.

WILLIAMS, EDWARD, 26 Jan. 1733; 28 May 1734.
Brother William; neice Elizabeth daughter of Joshua Williams; wife Sarah; neice Sarah daughter of William Williams; neice Frances daughter of Richard Haselrig.

HARNESS, WILLIAM, 25 Feb. 1734; 30 July 1734.
Son John; my wife Martha and her son John Jenkins; Thomas Jenkins.

HARDWICK, ELIZABETH, 12 Aug. 1734; 29 Oct. 1734.
Grandchildren Barbara Walker, Rachel Walker and Frences Hardwick; Hannah Asbury and neice Hannah Hardwick; neice Anne Hardwick; son James Hardwick residue of estate.

POPE, HUMPHREY, 10 Jan. 1732; 29 Oct. 1734.
Dau. Ann Conditt ½ of my land in Prince William Co.; dau. Sophia Muse ½ of land in Prince William Co.; sons Humphrey and John; daus. Sarah Pope, Mary Muse and Mary Pope; my wife's dau. Elizabeth Morrison; my wife Mary and 4 youngest children; wife, coz. Daniel McCarty and Peter Jett exrs.

WEEDON, GEORGE, 23 May 1734; 26 Nov. 1734.
To John Pierce my clothes and saddle; my wife the rest of my estate. Nathaniel Gray Jr. and Robert Lovell exrs.

MUSE, THOMAS, 29 Oct. 1734; 26 Nov. 1734.
Bros. Christopher and Daniel Muse; friend Benjamin Waddey 15 shillings; son Thomas Muse residue of estate; my father in law Richard Sanford Jr; brother in law Richard Sanford Jr. and brother John exr.

LOVELL, DANIEL, 9 Aug. 1733; 28 Jan. 1734.
Bro. Robert 5 shillings; bro. James residue of estate after sister Ursula Lovell has 2 negroes.

COOPER, JOHN, 12 Oct. 1734; 25 March 1735.
Wife Hannah; dau. Katherine Chancellor; son in law Thomas Chancellor and grandson John Chancellor.

MUSE, ELIZABETH, 29 March 1735; 27 May 1635.
Sons William, Nicholas and Daniel; daus. Anne Chilton, Elizabeth Barnett, Barbara Minor; granddaus. Mary Minor and Lettice Chilton.

MORE, JOHN, 4 Jan. 1733; 25 Nov. 1735.
Son William my clothes; to Alice Garland a silver tumbler; to Jeremiah Garland my friend the rest of my estate.

MOXLEY, JOSEPH, 18 May 1734; 30 Sept. 1735.
Sons Joseph and Christopher; bro. Daniel; dau. Sarah; wife; bros. John and Samuel.

ESKRIDGE, GEORGE, 27 Oct. 1735; 25 Nov. 1735.
Son Samuel 800 acres of land where I live; son William land on river adjoining his brother; wife use of land given Samuel for her life, slave she brought me in marriage and 10 other slaves for life and at her death to my daughter Elizabeth; land in Machodick to my son Robert; 4 slaves each to the 4 sons of my son George decd.; my daughter Elizabeth land on Pohick, Prince William Co., slaves and stock thereon; son Samuel 500 acres of my Prince William Tract; son in law Willoughby Newton and his wife Sarah; dau. Margaret Kenner wife of Howson Kenner and her dau. a portion of the same tract of land.

VAUGHAN, CORDEROY, 13 July 1735; 25 Nov. 1735.
To Daniel Vaughan 1 shilling; to Anne Merrman 1 shilling; to Peter Vaughan 1 shilling; wife Ellenor my entire estate; her daughter Anne Hays.

COLLINSWORTH, THOMAS, 26 Nov. 1734; 25 Nov. 1735.
Sons Thomas, John and Willoughby; daughters Ann and Sarah Collingsworth.

FINCH, JOHN, 25 Dec. 1735; 27 Jan. 1735.
Sons Thomas, Richard and Blagdon; daughter Mary Finch.

BAILEY, JOHN, 11 June 1729; 30 June 1736.
Sons James and Stephen Bailey; son in law Edward Young.

SMITH, JOHN, 9 Dec. 1735; 27 April 1736.
Sister Margaret Watson; son John; wife Mary and my child unborn.

COLEMAN, JAMES, 28 Dec. 1735; 27 April 1736.
Godson Samuel son of Peter Rust 1000 lbs. of tobacco and 1 horse; bro. Richard Coleman my land and rest of estate.

JEFFRESS, EDMUND, 4 Dec. 1735; 25 May 1736.
Wife Ann; sons Jeremiah, Robert, George and Edmund; the children I have by my wife viz; Elizabeth, Ann, Mary, Catherine, Ellenor, Alice, Jeremiah and Robert; my dau. Elizabeth Garner equal share of mill leased of J. Garner.

BULGER, EDMUND, 29 May 1736; 29 June 1736.
Dau. Mary; sons John and Edmund to share the estate equally.

LEWIS, SURLES, 27 Dec. 1729; 29 June 1736.
Sons Thomas Surles, John and James; dau. Sarah Render; wife Elizabeth; Capt. Anthony Thornton my exr.

SHAW, WILLIAM, 7 June 1736; 29 June 1736.
To Elizabeth Sturman 200 lbs. of tobacco and a chest; to Edward Ransdell Jr. 1 horse; Joseph Stone a gun, saddle and bridle; sisters Sarah and Jane Shaw residue of estate. Edward Ransdell exr.

MUSE, CHRISTOPHER, 18 Jan. 1734; 29 June 1736.
Bro. Nicholas Muse and his son Nicholas my land; my uncle John Muse; land purchased by my father of my uncle John Muse; cousin Thomas son of my decd. bro. Thomas Muse.

STEEL, JOHN, 16 March 1735; 28 July 1736.
  Son John; Sarah Steel; sons Richard and Thomas; daus. Margaret, Mary and Elizabeth; son Charles; wife Margaret. Land on Popes Creek.

BLUNDALL, WILLIAM, 21 July 1736; 30 Aug. 1736.
  To Richard Holladay and wife Susanna all of my estate and said Richard exr.

KENDALL, JOHN, 2 Sept. 1736; 22 Feb. 1736.
  Estate to Mary Brock of King George Co.

TAYLOR, THOMAS, 8 Feb. 1735; Feb. 1736.
  Wife Mary; sons Thomas, William, John and Richard; dau. Elizabeth wife of Amos Bagwell and grandchild Jane Bagwell.

CHILTON, MARY, 3 April 1737; 26 April 1737.
  Granddau. Elizabeth Sanford; Capt. Andrew Munroe and his wife Jane to have care of her estate until she is 18 years of age; son John Watts; son James Bowcock and his children Thomas, James and Jane; son Richard Watts; daus. Jane Munroe, Margaret Strother and Mary Blackburn and the latters husband Mr. Richard Blackburn; Capt. Thomas Chilton and his wife Jemima 1 mourning ring each; Rev. Roderick McCulloch a mourning ring.

MUNROE, WILLIAM, 30 March 1737; 26 April 1737.
  Son Thomas land; grandson Thomas Munroe; grandson Spence and his bro. Andrew Munroe; granddau Jane Munroe; son George; grandson George son of William Munroe; grandson Daniel Payne; Jeane Payne; daus. Sarah Stone and Mary Stone; grandsons William Payne and William Stone; son Andrew Munroe's children Spence Andrew and Jeane; son William exr.

SANFORD, ROBERT, 3 June 1736; * * * 1737.
Sons Robert, John and Joseph land; daus. Margaret Neale, Jemima Minor; grandson Joshua Sanford; daus. Anne and Elizabeth; son Robert and Presley Neale exrs.

JAMES, FRANCIS, 15 Dec. 1736; 31 May 1737.
Daughter Mary Sharpe land; sons Francis and John my home plantation; daus. Margaret and Sarah 1 cow each; Kezia James 1 heifer.

HUDSON, FIELD, died in Sept. last; 28 June 1737. (Nuncupative).
My brother Joshua; my estate to wife Susanna as it is very little.

DICKINSON, THOMAS, mariner, 10 July 1734; 28 June 1737.
To Behethland * * *; sister Mary Dickinson now in Lancaster Co. Great Britain.

WILLIAMS, JOHN, 13 March 1736; 26 July 1737.
Son John; dau. Elizabeth; wife Elizabeth; brother Thomas Williams.

BALL, GERRARD, 13 June 1737; 26 July 1737.
Aunt Mary Courtney 1 negro; brother Benony Ball 800 lbs. of tobacco; bro. Samuel Ball residue of estate when 16 years of age; bro. George Ball exr.

HARDWICK, JAMES, 8 June 1737; 27 Sept. 1737.
Son Aaron the land whereon I live; son George 1 negro; wife Haney Ritta Hardwick 1 negro and ½ of the rest of my estate; son William 3 negroes; my decd. bro. George Hardwick; to William Garland Jr. brother of my wife 50 shillings and 1 mare; daughter Frances Hardwick.

STURMAN, THOMAS, 1 April 1737; 3 Nov. 1737.
Sons Thomas, Richard, William and Valentine land each; to Mary Barker land where she lives and not to entertain any of her brothers and sisters, only her mother this year; dau. Ann Walker 1 negro and at her death to my granddau. Elizabeth Stuart; dau. Dorcas Raffedy 1 feather bed and furniture; dau. Jemima 10,000 lbs. of tobacco.

WELLINGTON, JOHN, 29 Oct. 1737; 30 Nov. 1737.
Sara and Winifred Gibbs to stay with my wife Elizabeth until 18 years of age; to cousin Michael Robinson 1 gold ring; to Elizabeth McCarney 1 gold ring.

CURTIS, THOMAS, 12 Oct. 1737; 30 Nov. 1737.
Wife Honor 128 acres of land; sons John and Robert; dau. Mary Curtis alias Gareing 100 acres in Richmond County.

MOOR, WILLIAM, 28 June 1736; 30 Jan. 1737.
To dau. Jane Creswick 50 acres of land; son William land; dau. Elizabeth; wife Alice and the rest of my children.

LAMKIN, JOHN, 15 Nov. 1737; 31 Jan. 1737.
Dau. Jane Moor; dau. Winifred Howell; to George Duren my tools.

TYLER, JOSEPH, 3 Dec. 1737; 31 Jan. 1737.
My plantation to my bro. Benjamin Tyler; 1 servant to my sister Christian Munroe; 1 negro to cozen Ellenor Munroe; couzens Spence Munroe and Sarah Munroe servants; cousin Andrew Munroe 1 negro; friend James Lovell one feather bed; friend Ann Harrison 1 mare; residue of estate to bro. William Tyler.

REMY, WILLIAM, aged 65; 19 Nov. 1737; 30 May 1738.
Son William; Jacob Remy's heirs; Asbury Remy;

dau. Mary Saunders 1 shilling; to Katherine Wormoth 1 shilling; sons John, James and Daniel; wife Katherine use of plantation for life, and at her death to son Daniel; Elizabeth Sanders 1 feather bed when she marries.

CHAPMAN, JOHN, master of the brigantine "Hopewell"; 15 Sept. 1737; 27 June 1738.
To my bro. Charles all of my personal estate; my friend George Turbeville gent. exr.

CONIER, TARENCE, 10 May 1736; 25 July 1738.
Dau. Sarah 6 head of cattle, bed and furniture; to John Couch 1 mare; residue of estate to my son Tarence and my wife; dau. Sarah stay with my wife until she marry.

SANFORD, ROBERT, 23 March 1737; 29 Aug. 1738.
The plantation whereon I live to son Augustine; son Joshua; sons' mother Mary Sanford now living; son Robert; my 6 daus.; daus. Elizabeth and Mary; exrs. Edward Muse, Presley Neale, wife Mary.

HOWELL, JOHN, * * *; * * * Aug. 1738.
Dau. Martha Atwell; wife Winifred; son John my estate at 21 years of age; exr. Major George Turbeville.

VOLUME IX.

CRABB, DANIEL, 1 Dec. 1738; 30 Jan. 1738.
Bro. Thomas; bro. John; brother Osman and his son Gerrard; sister Lettice McKenney 2 cows and 1 feather bed; my mother Sarah Dumbar 500 lbs. of tobacco a year for life.

PARY, WILLIAM, 11 Feb. 1731; 31 Jan. 1738.
Stricken in years. Wife Anne; grandson Franklin Pary; dau. in law Susanna Pary; my son John to have all my land; granddaus. Anne and Caty, negroes &c.

POPHAM, JOHN, 31 Oct. 1738; 27 March 1739.
Son Job my land and if he dies without issue to my three daus. Sophia, Mary and Anne; son John land purchased of James Kay in King George Co; granddau. Constant Comfort Littleton.

FREEID, WINIFRED, 6 Jan. 1738; 27 March 1738.
To George Durin when 17 years of age; to Jane Moore the use of 1 cow.

COOPER, HANNAH, 26 Dec. 1738; 29 May 1739.
Bushrod Thomas; William Sanford son of my sister Elizabeth decd. of Richmond Co. 2500 lbs. of tobacco; my dau. Elizabeth Meriwether a gold ring; dau. Sarah Berryman a gold ring; son John Bushrod a

ring; dau. Hannah Neale; my late husband Col.
Willoughby Allerton who gave his bond for my dau.
Hannah Neale, by name of Hannah Bushrod; son in
law William Fauntleroy and his wife Apphia; son
Richard Bushrod land purchased of John Jewel and
his wife Elizabeth; I desire my son Richard Bushrod to bury me between his father and Mr. Cooper and
put pedestals to Thomas Bushrod's grave stone; son
Richard exr.

ROWBOTHAN, ELIZABETH, 11 July 1739; 31 July 1739.
I give to Mary Payne all of my estate. [Administration to William Rice who married Mary Payne.]

ALLERTON, ISAAC, 31 March 1739; 27 Nov. 1739.
Wife Anne ½ of all of my estate; my lands to 3 sons Glwen, Willoughby and Isaac; sister Elizabeth Quill's children Sarah and Margaret; coz. Charles Beale and his bros. John, Taverner, Richard and Reuben; exrs. wife Anne, John Bushrod and Daniel Hornby.

DISHMAN, JOHN, 30 Mar. 1738; 27 Nov. 1739.
Land in Prince William to be sold; land and per. estate to wife Frances for life and then to sons John and Samuel; bro. James Dishman and wife Frances exrs.

HIGDON, DANIEL, 26 Oct. 1739; 27 Nov. 1739.
Lands to my daus. Mary and Jane; son in law John Muse; wife Margaret; Humphrey Pope that married my dau. in law Sarah; John McLarran my clothes.

TYNON, WILLIAM, 21 Aug. 1737; 27 Nov. 1737.
Lands in Westmoreland and Northumberland to John Booth; to Ellenor Garner 3 negroes; to James Grase 1 negro; to Mary Anne Garner 1 negro; Re-

becca Eskridge 1 negro; Winifred Benett 2 negroes; Joseph Garner and John Booth exrs.

JETT, MARGARET, 26 Sept. 1739; 27 Nov. 1739.
Granddau. Elizabeth Morris 3 head of cattle; granddau. Margaret Morris rest of estate; Mr. Daniel McCarty exr.

JETT, PETER, of King George Co. 27 Sept. 1728; 27 Nov. 1739.
My wife Margaret my entire estate and she to be exx.

PERRY, JOHN, 27 March 1738; 27 Nov. 1739.
Child's part to my wife Susanna; my son Franklin home plantation; daus. Anne, and Kate and son Roderick Perry; exrs. friends Richard Sanford Jr. and Robert Sanford.

DISHMAN, JOHN, 30 March 1738; 27 Nov. 1739.
Land in Prince William to be sold; land and other estate to my wife Frances for life then to my sons Samuel and John; brother James Dishman and my wife exrs.

FOOTMAN, JOHN, 19 Oct. 1739; 27 Nov. 1739.
My wife Elizabeth; dau. Hannah Footman land in Ragged Point; kinsmen John West of Northumberland Co; Footman Brown and friend Wharton Ransdell exrs.

MONROE, SARAH, 25 July 1739; 27 Nov. 1739.
Son John Elliott; dau. in law Sibella Elliott; grandson John Elliott 1 negro boy; grandson Foxhall Sturman 1 negro girl; grandson Spence Monroe 12 shillings; to Mr. Wharton Ransdell 3 shillings for pair of gloves; dau. Sarah Ransdell; my five grandchildren Elizabeth, Sarah, Martha Sturman, Thomas Ransdell and Sarah Elliott Ransdell; exr. John Elliott.

SPENCE, PATRICK, 10 Dec. 1739; 25 March 1704.
Son Patrick; son Youell Spence the land given me by Youell Watts, decd.; wife Jemima; my four children Elizabeth, Jemima, Mary and Youell Spence; exrs. my wife and son in law Nicholas Minor Jr. until son Patrick comes of age.

HUTT, GERRARD, 15 Nov. 1739; 25 March 1740.
My sons Daniel, Gerrard and Thomas Hutt; wife Anne; my daus. Frances, Elizabeth, Susannah and Anne; grandson John Hutt 1 ring; wife Anne and sons Gerrard and Thomas exrs.

PEARSE, GEORGE, 27 Oct. 1739; 25 March 1740.
To son John land in Stafford, 200 acres; son George 150 acres in Westmoreland; son William; dau. Margaret Pearse.

BEARD, JOHN, 10 Oct. 1739; 25 March 1740.
Sons George and John; wife Anne exx; William Lansdown pay rent 530 pounds tobacco until son John 16 years of age.

BINKS, THOMAS, 1 Feb. 1739; 25 March 1740.
Son John 1 shilling; dau. Mary Binks 1 shilling; sons Thomas and George and daus. Margaret Binks and Mary Binks residue of estate.

ASHTON, JOHN, 6 April 1739; 29 April 1740.
My bro. Burdett Ashton land and slaves; to Richard Rallings his rent now due; bro. Charles Ashton 1 horse; cousin John eldest son of Charles Ashton; exrs. brothers Charles and Burdett Ashton.

BRENAN, OWEN, * * *; 27 May 1740.
Wife Deliverance; sons John and Owen; daus. Hannah and Ann land and slaves.

ASBURY, HENRY, 27 Sept. 1739; 27 May 1740.
Lands to sons Henry, William and Thomas; my wife Hannah personal property and at her death to my children, Sarah, George, Hannah, Isabella and Ann Asbury; exrs. wife and son Henry.

WASHINGTON, LAWRENCE, 5 Feb. 1739; 24 June 1740.
To son John one-half my land; sons James and Thomas the other half between them; to wife Elizabeth all movable estate and she to be exx.

DICKSON, ELIZABETH, 3 Nov. 1740; 25 Nov. 1740.
Son Francis Sharp; son Jeremiah Stephens; grandson James Stephens; son Burdett Stephens to be exr. and he to have rest of estate; granddau. Elizabeth Stephens.

WEEDON, JOHN, Sr., 23 Sept. 1740; 25 Nov. 1740.
100 acres to son John; eldest son Augustine Weedon land; eldest dau. Mary and youngest dau. Sarah; two sons to be exrs.

SMITH, PETER, 10 Jan. 1738; 12 May 1741.
48 acres to my dau. Mary Fleming; son Peter land in Westmoreland; son James the land in Prince William on Bull Run where he now lives which is 325 acres; sons Thomas and William land in Prince William which is 325 acres; dau. Abigail Fleming land in Prince William; granddau. Ann Bailey land in Prince William; heirs of dau. Anne Thomas one shilling; dau. Mary Fleming one shilling; dau. Hannah Ware 1 shilling; dau. Martha McClanahan 1 feather bed; son Peter exr; heirs of son John Smith 1 shilling.

HEADLEY, ROBERT, * * *; 12 June 1741.
Land to son William; son in law David Hacle 1 shill-

ing; granddaus. Mary Smith and Elizabeth Pickrell; wife Mary exx.; Witnesses John Smith, Richard Pickrell.

SANFORD, JOSEPH, 3 April 1741; 26 April 1741.
Wife Mary; dau. Nanny; Son Robert to have estate when 20 years of age; dau. Betty; Presley Neale to have the care of son Robert and dau. Nanny; Thomas Shaw to have the care of dau. Betty; bro. John Sanford; son Robert to be bound to Thomas Sanford Jr., bricklayer, when 14 until he is 21 years of age; estate to be sold and money to children.

MOTHERSHEAD, JOHN * * *; 17 June 1741.
My dau. Ann Quisenberry 1 bed and fur.; dau. Elizabeth Mothershead 1 bed and furniture; son Charles; my wife and three youngest children; sons William and John; daus. Sarah and Mary; wife Ann and son William exrs.

STEELE, CHARLES, 7 April 1741; 30 June 1741.
To brother Thomas Steele 1 mare; sister Sarah Steele 1 horse; my mother Margaret rest of estate and she to be exx.

BUSH, EDWARD, 30 April 1741; 25 Aug. 1741.
To son Edward Francis Bush begot of my now wife Ann land; to Frances Earls 1 cow and calf; wife Ann rest of estate; exrs. Thomas Finch and John Williams.

WRIGHT, RICHARD, 10 March 1740; 27 Oct. 1741.
1 horse, cow, etc. to Godson William Davis; bro. in law Gerrard Davis clothes; sister Ann Davis clothes; bro. John Wright; my wife Elizabeth use of 6 slaves and land for life; son Francis land given me by my bro. John Wright; dau. Elizabeth Wright 4 slaves.

WARD, HENRY, 15 Sept. 1741; 26 Jan. 1741.
> 1 negro to my dau. Jane Ward; dau. Sarah Ward 1 negro; friends John Pownall and his wife Elizabeth to be guardians to my dau. Jane now 11 years of age; my wife Mary residue of estate.

RUST, WILLIAM, 6 Nov. 1741; 26 Jan. 1741.
> To son Samuel land; son William; son Henry land; dau. Mary Rust; my brother Peter Rust and my sister Ann Harrison to see that children comply with will.

CARR, JOSEPH, 12 Sept. 1741; 26 Jan. 1741.
> To son Joseph 126 acres of land; son James land; dau. Mary Carr 2 negroes; to sister Ann Remy's son Joseph Remy land whereon my sister lives.

POPE, THOMAS, 1 May 1741; 23 Feb. 1741.
> 450 acres and negroes to wife and dau. Elizabeth and if she dies without issue to grandchildren of Samuel Hath; £10 to Nominy Church.

TURBEVILLE, GEORGE, of Hickory Hill, 31 Dec. 1741; 30 March 1742.
> Afflicted dau. Elizabeth Turbeville cared for; late wife Frances dau. of Col. Henry Ashton mother of said Elizabeth; my wife Martha dau. of Mrs. Martha Lee, decd. lands of Mrs. Lee's in Suffolk, England; 4 slaves and £600 to dau. Lettice Turbeville; son John plate and books; Col. Henry Lee, Landon Carter and my Godson John Tayloe son of the Honl. John Tayloe of Richmond Co., to be exrs; son John all lands; to John Hobson son and heir of John Hobson; the child my wife now goes with; 1000 acres in Prince William given by Col. H. Ashton; 5000 acres in Prince William called Salisbury Plain on Flatrock.

WESTMORELAND COUNTY WILLS 113

BUNCH, ROE, 10 Feb. 1742; 1 June 1743.
To nephew Bunch Roe 1 negro Dick; to Nephew Henry Roe 1 negro; to W. E. Frank a negro Jemmy; William Taylor and Tho. Whitney some small part estate; to Andrew Monroe.

WILLIAMS, JOHN, 14 Jan. 1741-2; 13 April 1742.
My wife Elizabeth and son Charles estate and if she marry one-half estate to son Charles.

MELDRUM, MICHAEL, 13 Nov. 1741; 27 April 1742.
My wife Mary estate for life and then to all the children of William Jenkins by his wife Mary.

YELLOP, THOMAS, tailor, 18 Jan. 1741; 25 May 1742.
1 negro and a ring to friend Nimrod Hutt of Prince William; friend William Cope mare and clothes; to Winifred and Sarah Gibbs tobacco; John son of John and Mary Murphy; bro. Yellope of County Suffolk in Great Britain and my sisters Mary and Ann.

BRUCE, GEORGE, 27 Jan. 1741-2; 29 June 1742.
To my sons William and George 1 shilling each; dau. Jane wife of Jacobus Jordan 1 shilling; dau. Christian wife of John Young 1 shilling; son Charles 1 gun; wife Margary 100 acres of home plantation for life, then to son Charles; dau. Kezia one pewter dish; dau. Hannah Bruce 1 shilling; brother John Bruce.

BOWCOCK, JAMES, 12 March 1741-2; June 1742.
Son Thomas land; son James 250 acres of land; son John land; son Anthony land and my violin; dau. Jane part of estate; Rev. Roderick McCullock exr.

MOORE, THOMAS, 17 Dec. 1741; 31 Aug. 1742.
To sons William & Thomas ½ of land where I live; dau. Sarah 1 feather bed; dau. Mary Moore ½ per. estate.

SMITH, LAZARUS, 16 July 1742; 31 August 1742.
Bro. James Smith; to Godson Spencer son of Thomas Smith decd. £20 when he is 21 years of age; coz. Richard son of Richard Nutt and his wife Elizabeth horse, saddle etc.; Goddau. Judith dau. of William Smith cattle; bro. John Smith 1 negro boy.

MURPHY, JOHN, 19 July 1742; 26 Oct. 1742.
Son John land; son Samuel £10; dau. Elizabeth personal property; wife Mary.

STONEHOUSE, ELIZABETH, 14 April 1738; 1 Dec. 1742.
My two sons St. John Shropshire and Winfield Shropshire.

BALL, GEORGE, 15 Feb. 1742-3; 29 March 1743.
My brother Emanuel horse, saddle and 2000 lbs. tobacco; bro. Samuel Ball 107 acres where I live and personal property.

CHAMBERS, THOMAS, 7 Jan. 1742; 26 April 1743.
To wife Mary all estate and she to be exx.

GRAY, NATHANIEL, 6 March 1743; 26 April 1743.
To son Nathaniel land in Stafford; son George land in Irish Neck and at his death to grandson Nathaniel Gray son of George, and 7 negroes; dau. Sarah Strother 5000 lbs. tobacco; grandson George Weedon 1 negro; dau. Margaret Gray furniture at new house, 8 cows and calves and £50; son Francis land and 9 negroes; my wife use of plantation and handsome maintenance for life; friend William Strother exr.

BUTLER, CATHERINE, * * * Nov. 1730; 26 April 1743.
Son James 1 negro; son John negro child; coz. Sarah Anderson 1 heifer; coz. Thomas Price 1 sow; exrs. brothers William and James Butler.

THOMAS, JAMES, 1 Dec. 1742; 31 May 1743.
Sons James and George land; dau. Winifred Thomas; dau. Elizabeth Thomas 100 acres in Prince William and 3 negroes; son John rest of estate and 6 negroes; grandson William Thomas son of dau. Katherine 100 acres in Prince William; dau. Hannah Thomas land in Prince William; dau. Sarah Jenkins 1 heifer; wife Sarah to be cared for by son John.

STEEL, JOHN, 3 Oct. 1743; 29 Nov. 1743.
To Mary Steel alias Weeks dau. of Margaret Steel the plantation that Richard Steel now lives on; to Thomas Steel land and clothes; to Sarah Finch land and horse; exr. Benjamin Weeks; my sisters rest of estate.

VOLUME X.

MINOR, NICHOLAS, 11 Oct. 1743; 29 May 1744.
To son William Stewart Minor when 21 years of age and he die without issue to sons John and Nicholas; son John 536 acres of land on Rappahannock River; son Nicholas 496 acres of land in King George; son Stewart land in Richmond County and Westmoreland; dau. Elizabeth Wheret 2000 pounds of tobacco and what she already has; wife Jemima rest of estate for life, still, 10 negroes and 12 silver spoons.

COX, CHARNOCK, JR., 1 March 1743; 26 June 1744.
To sons Presley and Charnock 250 acres of land where I live; sons Vincent and John 2 negroes at death of wife; my wife; rest of estate to four children.

AYLETT, WILLIAM, 29 March 1744; 28 August 1744.
Land and slaves from my decd. father William Aylett of King William Co., and my first wife's father Col. Henry Ashton, decd. to my two daughters Elizabeth and Anne issue of my first marriage, when they are 21 years of age and if they die without issue to my wife Elizabeth; land and mill in Westmoreland and land in Fairfax to Anne and Mary her children; my brother John Aylett decd.; my brother Philip Aylett; brother Benjamin Aylett, decd.; Major Lawrence Washington; son in law Augustine Washington; brother Philip and Daniel McCarty exrs.

FOOTMAN, ELIZABETH, 10 May 1744; 28 Aug. 1744.
Widow of John Footman.

My dau. Frances Youell horse, furniture; granddau. Elizabeth Youell 1 negro; son in law Batteran Youell; William Rice, Sr.; my three children; my two sons Winder and Richard Kenner and dau. Frances Youell rest of estate.

McCARTY, DANIEL, 16 May 1744; 26 June 1744.
Wife Elizabeth all estate, real and personal for life or until son Daniel is 21 years of age, then deliver to him my dwelling plantation, 15 slaves, and if he die without issue to the sons of my brothers Dennis and Billington McCarty; Col. Presley Thornton, Mr. Joseph Morton, Mr. Augustine Washington and Mr. Lawrence Butler Gent exrs.; Witnesses Anthony Thornton, Francis Thornton and James Carter.

DEMOVEL, HANNAH, 8 Sept. 1744; 25 Sept. 1744.
To Peter son of George Lampkin 1 shilling; my granddau. Hannah Demovel 1 feather bed, furniture, cow, 1 wheel and two boxes; grand-dau. Mary Middleton 1 heifer; granddau. Hannah Armistead 1 iron spit and pewter; Sarah dau. of John Armistead and Hannah his wife 1 cow; my grandchildren Jane Moore, Hannah Brown, Magdalen Jackson, Hannah Hartley, James Lamkin, Samuel Lamkin and Magdalen Claughton; my dau. Elizabeth Middleton 1 negro woman; son in law Benjamin Middleton 7 head of cattle and £2; to John Armistead 7 head of cattle, 8 hogs and £2.

JARVIS, JOHN, 7 March 1734-4; 30 Oct. 1744.
My sons John and Field land; daus. Elenor, Catherine and Jane; my wife exx. and rest of estate for life.

MOXLEY, WILLIAM, SENR., 8 May 1744; 30 Oct. 1744.
To my son Daniel and his wife Mary land whereon I live; grandson Richard son of Richard Moxley land; grandson William Peyton horse; son Samuel scales; son William 10 shillings; son Thomas 10 shillings; youngest son Daniel exr; son John Moxley 1 bed and furniture.

ESKRIDGE, ELIZABETH, 20 Oct. 1744; 27 Nov. 1744.
(Widow of George Eskridge.)
To Craddock Butler 1 negro etc.; dau. Elizabeth Aylett; Goddau. Judith Newton 1 negro girl; to Mary Luck 900 lbs. of tobacco; exx. dau. Elizabeth Aylett; widow rest of estate; Mrs. Bray her bed.

FLEMING, JOHN, 15 Nov. 1744; 26 Feb. 1744.
To James Bailey 1 case bottles and he to be exr.; daus. Sarah and Anne 1 feather bed and furniture each; son Peter to care of John Bailey; son Thomas £10 and 10 shillings; son William £10, 10 shillings, etc.

REYNOLDS, ROBERT, 11 Feb. 1744; 26 Feb. 1744.
My wife Nancy exx.; my children; my son 1 horse, saddle, etc.

DODD, JOHN, 16 Sept. 1744; 26 March 1745, of Washington Parish.
My son Joseph land in King George; son Nathaniel home plantation; son Benjamin household goods; dau. Mary McKenny and her husband John a servant maid; dau. Elizabeth; son in law William Goaring 6 shillings; son John Dodd; dau. Elizabeth Weedne.

HAYES, HENRY, 14 June 1744; 26 March 1745.
Son William estate when 21 years of age; wife Jane and all my children residue of estate; William Garland, Jr., of Richmond County, exr.

WALKER, GEORGE, 13 Dec. 1744; 29 Jan. 1744.
Wife Winifred lands in Westmoreland if she does not claim one-third of the Fairfax land, 2 negroes, 2 horses, feather bed and furniture; dau. Barbary 1 still, horse, colt, negro, feather bed and furniture; dau. Winnian 1 negro, 1 colt; dau. Rachel 1 negro, feather bed and furniture; dau. Franky 1 negro girl Grace; four daughters 1504 acres of land in Fairfax Co.; exrs. Danl. Tebbs & John Middleton.

WALKER, PETER, 10 Jan. 1744-5; 26 June 1745.
Wife estate for widowhood, then to all my children divided by persons selected by eldest son John. Widow died before will proved.

SIMMS, ALEXANDER, 26 June 1744; 29 Oct. 1745.
Son Edward ½ of my land with houses; eldest son Henry Simms ½ my land; Franklin Simms, Bethlehen & Margaret Simms.

RUST, MARTHA, 23 Dec. —; 28 May 1745.
My brothers Samuel, Henry and William Rust; uncle Peter Rust exr.; cozen Mary Cox ear bobs and clothes; sister Agness Rust and her son William.

GARNER, HENRY, 4 June 1744; 25 June 1745.
My wife Catherine land; son Thomas land; sons Henry and Bradley Garner; dau. Hannah Allson 1 ewe; dau. Elizabeth Garner 1 shilling, 1 feather bed, 1 cow.

MOTHERSHEAD, CHRISTOPHER, 11 June 1745; 25 June 1745.
My son Christopher land and 4 negroes; wife Elenor and the child she goes with; dau. Sarah wife of John Pope 20 shillings; sister Anne Claytor 250 lbs. tobacco; wife and Alven Claytor exrs.

GRACE, JAMES, 26 Nov. 1744; 30 July 1745.
My wife Johannah and the child she goes with and if no children wife to have estate.

BASHAW, PETER, 9 Oct. 1745; 26 Nov. 1745.
My son Peter land; sons Warrener & James; to Spence Bashaw 1 horse; dau. Elizabeth Bashaw, Mary and Sarah Bashaw; wife Mary residue of estate.

DANELEY, URSULA, 23 April 1745; 28 Jan. 1745-6.
Son Joseph Taylor personal property and he to be

exr; dau. Mary Martin 1 shilling; son Philip Taylor 1 shilling; dau. Ann Rimmer 1 shilling.

FLANAKIN, JOHN, 22 Nov. 1745; 28 Jan. 1745-6.
To Elizabeth Winnix all my pewter, wooden ware and all my estate; Thomas McFarlane and James Clark exrs.

MARADY, PRICE, 20 Dec. 1745; 22 Dec. 1745.
Marady Price heir at law of John Price & Ellenor Brown being sick but of sound mind and memory made verbal will. Said John left John Purtle to his son William Price and to have a negro man and a piece of land called Baccases; to his son Marady Price he gave negroes Moll & Bob and land called Wolf Trap Run; to son William the negroes Tom and Basco and "land whereon I live"; to dau. Martha 1 negro.

TOBEN, MICHAEL, 15 Sept. 1745; 25 March 1746.
Wife Mary use of all estate for life and at her death to my children and my daughter in law Mary Jenkins.

FIELDER, ELIZABETH, 2 Dec. 1745; 25 Feb. 1745-6.
To daughter Jemima all estate; buried at discretion of my children.

McCULLOCK, RODERICK, 11 Nov. 1745; 25 Feb. 1746, clerk, of Washington Parish.
Wife Elizabeth one-third of estate; my son Roderick to be of age at 18 years; dau. Isabel, Elizabeth and son Roderick two-thirds of estate; son Roderick 1 negro Billy; exrs. John Watts and Charles Ashton.

BLACKMORE, GEORGE, 10 Oct. 1745; ?5 Feb. 1746.
To Lovel White the land bought of nis father John White, mare and colt; to William son of my bro. Samuel Blackmore of the Parish of St. Mary Ottry, Co. of Devon in Gt. Britian £100; bro. Samuel Black-

more money, clothes, etc.; coz. Samuel Blackmore son of my bro. Samuel; Gideon Blackmore my cozen, son of Gideon Blackmore; my wife her one-third of negroes.

ROGERS, JOSEPH, 26 Jan. 1736; 25 March 1746.
To wife Mary and Willoughby estate to be equally divided.

MOTHERSHEAD, WILLIAM, 1 May 1746; 27 May 1746.
To Charles Mothershead land; John ½ part; to Sarah wife of Thomas James 1 shilling; John Mothershead and John Quisenberry exrs.

CREED, JOHN, 27 Jan. 1745; 27 May 1746.
To Joseph son of William Weeks horse, saddle, bridle; to Jane dau. of Mary Brown ½ of estate; Robert Vaulx exr.

EARL, SAMUEL, 6 Aug. 1744; 29 July 1746.
My dau. Phillis Mockeridge 1 shilling; dau. Hannah Baley and Elizabeth Hackney 1 shilling each; son Samuel Earl and Peter Rust exrs.; my plantation to grandson Samuel and if die without issue to grandson John Earl; land to continue in Earl name.

RICHARDSON, JONATHAN, 17 Sept. 1746; 28 Oct. 1746.
To wife Elizabeth and all my children estate for life; John Sorrell sole exr.

GREENWOOD, DANIEL, 25 Nov. 1746; 24 Feb. 1746-7.
William Welch to have my son Daniel until he is 21 years of age and he to have 4 years schooling.

GRACE, FRANCES, 4 Oct. 1744; 24 Feb. 1747.
Son Henry Duncan rest of estate, 1 cow and calf after daus. Mary Scott and Elizabeth McBoyd have 1 cow, 2 ewes and clothes.

GARRARD, WILLIAM, 4 Nov. 1746; 25 Feb. 1747.
My son Nathaniel 2 negroes; grandson William Garrard son of Nathaniel; to son Aaron Garrard 1 negro; dau. Jane Garrard 3 negroes; dau. Sarah Garrard 1 negro and £25; wife Mary 3 negroes and she to be exx.

REID, JOHN (son of George Reid in Middle-Heillar, parish of Dallgain, alias, Sorn in the Shire of Ayr.), 17 Jan. 1746; 31 March 1747.
To my father George Reid all my estate; to Capt. John Aitken, commander of the Snow friend-Ship of Ayr, now at Antigua exr.

FORD, GERRARD, 10 Nov. 1746; 26 May 1747.
My son Daniel land and 2 slaves; son Warner home plantation; dau. Elizabeth Ford 1 slave; wife Elizabeth 2 slaves.

LEE, HENRY, Parish of Cople, 28 Aug. 1747; 21 Oct. 1747.
My son John my King Copsico tract and 20 slaves; son Richard land where I live given me by my father Col. Richard Lee decd. and 26 slaves; son Henry land in Prince William given me by my bro. Richard, 3500 acres in Fairfax County and 20 slaves; my grandfather Henry Corbin and his dau. Lettice who was my mother; daughter Lettice; wife Mary; bro. Thomas Lee, Esq., and Col. William Beverley and sons John and Richard exrs. Codicil 15 Oct. 1747. My daughter Lettice wife of William Ball of Lancaster, gent., £40 and household furniture.

LAMBERT, THOMAS, 1 Dec. 1747; 26 Jan. 1747-8.
My daughters Tamer Smith and Elizabeth Stapleton 1 shilling each; my son William 1 shilling; son Thomas clothing; son John clothing; wife Rose rest of estate; to daughter Ann Lambert and son George; wife exx.

SUTTON, RICHARD, 1 Oct. 1747; 23 Feb. 1747-8.
My sons Richard, James and Jacob land; grandson

William son of John and Elizabeth Sutton 1 bed; remainder of estate to all children; dau. Mary Hezelrigg; wife Mary; son John one-third of estate and son William part of remaining estate.

HURLEY, ELIZABETH, 30 Nov. 1747; 24 Feb. 1747-8.
My servant William Baxter; goddaughter Sarah Fisher 1 heifer; to Mrs. Ann Washington servant girl and ½ of my clothes; to friend Augustine Washington residue of my estate.

VOLUME XI.

READ, COLEMAN, 1 March 1747-8; 26 April 1748.
My son Joseph 100 acres of land; to son Richard after the death of my wife Ruth land whereon I live; daus. Mary and Susannah negroes; grandchildren Coleman Brown 1 negro, Coleman Dunkin 1 negro, Ruth Asberry 1 negro, Elizabeth Read 1 negro, and grandson Hutt 1 negro boy.

COX, PETER, 12 Jan. 1747; 26 April 1748.
My wife Mary one-third of estate and use of rest of estate; my five children Mary, Sarah, James, Peter and Hannah estate at age of 21 years or marriage; wife, Daniel Tebbs, George Lamkin and George Cox exrs.

OLIFF, GEORGE, 3 April 1748; 31 May 1748.
Son George tobacco, corn, etc.; son James horse, etc.; dau. Rebecca 1000 lbs. tobacco; grandchild Ann Oliff 1 mare; grandchild Jemima Thrashall one shilling.

WIGGINTON, HENRY, 17 June 1748; 26 July 1748.
To Uncle Roger Wigginton 2 negroes; Roger Wigginton's son Spencer 2 negroes; friend Mistress Mary Lee 1 negro woman; coz. Samuel son of Peter Rust 1 negro; coz. Elizabeth dau. of Richard Wright 1 negro; coz. Elizabeth wife of Dr. Thomas McFarlan residue of estate; exrs. George and Richard Lee.

MINOR, JOHN, 13 Sept. 1748; 25 Oct. 1748.
All my children; wife Mary and my father in law John Barnett and friend John Stowers exrs.; estate to be divided at death of wife among children.

BONUM, SAMUEL, 26 Oct. 1748; 29 Nov. 1748.
Uncle and Aunt Thomas and Elizabeth Bennett 2 negroes and 11 sheep; cousins Mary Thomas 1 negro and Joseph Bennett 2 negroes; to Mrs. Sarah Newton 1 negro; to Mrs. Elizabeth Newton 1 negro; to Miss Judith Newton 1 negro; to John Newton 1 negro and cattle; to Capt. Willoughby Newton residue of estate.

WILLIAMS, CHAMBERS, 12 Jan. 1748-9; 31 Jan. 1748-9.
Edward Guinness and wife Catherine live on my land until son is 18 years of age and pay rent of 800 lbs. of tobacco a year; son Daniel estate at 18 years of age; son Thomas personal estate; John Higdon and his wife Sarah; exr. Humphrey Pope.

BALEY, WILLIAM, 28 Aug. 1748; 31 Jan. 1748-9.
Granddau. Ann Wood her aunt Mary Baley's wearing apparel, 2 feather beds and furniture, pewter, etc.; coz. James Baley clothes; dau. Elizabeth Davis 30 shillings; nephew James Baley and his son William Baley debt for land sold.

DUNKIN, PETER, 13 Sept. 1748; 31 Jan. 1748-9.
Friend James Baley to have charge of my son until said son Charles is 21 years of age; son George my working tools.

SANFORD, WILLIAM, 22 Jan. 1739-40; 28 Feb. 1748-9.
Dau. Martha Rhodes 1 cow and calf; son Joseph 1 steer; dau. Frances Sanford 1 cow, bed and furniture; grandson John Ethel 4 head of cattle; son William land whereon I live.

BELL, THOMAS, 19 Aug. 1742; 25 April 1749.
  To wife Johannah use of my land; sons Thomas and Joseph ½ of land each at death of wife.

BAKER, JOHN, 3 Sept. 1748; 25 April 1749.
  Plantation where he lives and 1 negro to eldest son William; son John land and 1 negro; dau. Anne Baker 1 negro, 1 bed and furniture; dau. Frances 1 negro; dau. Mary Baker 20 shillings; wife Sarah; grandson Presley Baker 1 feather bed.

HALCOM, GEORGE, * * *; 27 June 1749.
  My daus. Susanna, Mary, Milly, Jenny and Hannah Halcom 1 negro child each; wife Isabel 2 negroes; wife and Richard Padgett exrs.

CRITCHER, JOHN, 27 March 1749; 25 July 1749.
  Son John land and 2 slaves; son Richard £30; dau. Anne McClave 1 negro; dau. Mary Critcher 1 negro; son Thomas 3 negroes and land in Fairfax Co.; dau. Jean Critcher 3 slaves; dau. Eleanor Coleman 2 negroes.

GARNER, ARCHIBALD, 15 April 1749; 29 Aug. 1749.
  Children Jemima and Jane Joyce Garner estate at age 18 years; friend Daniel Tebbs exr.; if children die without issue to brother Joseph Garner.

POPE, WORDEN, 14 Jan. 1748; 29 Aug. 1749.
  To children Benjamin, Jean, William and the child my wife goes with all estate; wife Hester one-third of estate; Augusta Washington and Benjamin Weeks exrs.

HARDWICK, JAMES, 12 June 1749; 31 Oct. 1749.
  Land where I live to son Thomas; son John 1 shilling; son in law Elias Davis 1 shilling; dau. Elizabeth Nash 1 shilling; dau. Sarah Summers 1 shilling; dau. Cyonway Lane; wife Elizabeth; son James.

JACKSON, CHRISTOPHER DOMINICK, 1 July 1749; 31 Oct. 1749.
Wife Magdalene and my three sons when they are 21 years of age estate, 3 negroes and stock.

BUTLER, WILLIAM, 15 Jan. 1749; 27 March 1750. (Noncupative.)
All estate to wife Elizabeth; certified to by Jeremiah Kirk and John Whiting; Thomas Butler admr.

BUTLER, ELIZABETH, 19 Jan. 1749; 27 March 1750.
Estate had by my decd. husband William Butler except a gold ring and my riding horse to brother in law Thomas Butler; a gold ring to Catherine Hardidge; horse to my brother Presley Cockrell and also 2 negro girls; to Ellen Clington my side saddle; my aunt Jane Wroe 2 gold rings and residue of estate; exrs. Original Wroe and Thomas Butler.

KILL, CHARLES, 4 Jan. 1749; 30 Jan. 1749.
To Anne, Sarah and Francis Franklin they being the daus. of my sister Elizabeth Franklin decd. £50 each; to Mary Franklin 1 negro; son in law Benjamin Weekes; godson Charles Weekes Steel son of Margaret Weekes; wife Mary residue of land, negroes etc. for life.

DAVIS, ELIAS, 20 Dec. 1748; 30 Jan. 1749.
Feather bed and gun to son Youell; son Elias; dau. Amy Sutton 1 heifer; dau. Ann Packett 1 heifer; son John clothing; wife Elizabeth residue of estate; son Youell and Thomas Templeman exrs.

HARRISON, WILLOUGHBY, 12 Jan. 1749-50; 27 March 1750.
Eldest son Samuel land; son Joshua still; son Daniel land; Dorcas Harrison 1 feather bed and horse; dau. Elizabeth Baley 1 cow; son Willoughby estate already in his possession.

MOTHERSHEAD, JOHN, 28 Nov. 1748; 27 March 1750.
£25 to dau. Mary Mothershead when 21 years of age; my bro. Charles Mothershead use of land for crop when 21 years of age; wife Sarah plantation and rest of estate for life; wife Sarah and brother John Quisenberry exrs.

MOORE, THOMAS, 4 Feb. 1749-50; 24 April 1750.
My son Thomas land in Westmoreland and if he die without issue to son James; wife Winifred use of all estate for life.

RALLINGS, SAMUEL, 17 Aug. 1749; 24 April 1750.
Estate for life to Martha my wife; son Samuel 1 negro and 1 horse; children Benjamin and Martha land; dau. Mary Rallings residue of estate.

DAVIS, SAMUEL, 29 Oct. 1746; 29 May 1750.
Eldest son Joshua land in Prince William, 2 negroes, horse and gun; youngest son Samuel land in Prince William and 1 negro woman; youngest dau. Esther Davis 1 negro child; eldest dau. Ann Davis 1 negro; daus. Mary, Elizabeth, Frances and Catherine Davis 1 negro each; wife Ann land in Westmoreland.

CALLIS, WILLIAM, 5 Nov. 1747; 29 May 1750.
Sons John and Francis land in Prince William; sons Ambrose, Thomas, William, James and Richard; daughter Sarah; wife Sarah; land and negroes to wife and children.

PARTRIDGE, RICHARD, 4 April 1750; 29 May 1750.
Son Mathew 1 bed, horse and 2 cows; wife Jean and her sons Charles and Ashton Lamkin residue of estate for life.

KENDALL, SAMUEL, 22 Jan. 1747; 31 July 1750.
Eldest dau. Sarah 5 shillings; daus. Ann, Martha and Mary 5 shillings each; wife Sarah rest estate for life;

daus. Gladys and Elizabeth; sons Moses and William; coz. John Kendall and John Macormack exrs.

SMITH, JOSEPH, 29 Dec. 1749; 28 Aug. 1750.
Estate in her hands and 1 negro to dau. Jemima Monroe; wife Sarah saddle, bridle, and estate for widowhood; to Augustine Goff 1 heifer; son Joseph 1 negro and land and if he die without issue to son Samuel and if he die without issue to son Gideon; sons Samuel and Gideon 1 negro each.

ELLIOTT, AUGUSTINE, 11 June 1750; 28 Aug. 1750.
Estate for life to Mother Sibella Elliott and she to be exx.; sisters Betty and Mildred Elliott estate at death of mother equally and if they die without issue to sister Martha Elliott.

HOLLAND, SIMON, 7 July 1750; 28 Aug. 1750.
Wife Easter ½ of land; son Youell Holland ½ of land; daus. Hannah and Elizabeth; personal property among all children.

ROCHESTER, WILLIAM, 23 Oct. 1750; 30 Oct. 1750.
4 negroes and 100 acres of land to son John; wife Frances and her son Daniel McKenny 2 negroes for life; son William one-third personal estate.

WHITE, JOHN, aged 63; 18 Feb. 1747; 29 Jan. 1750-1.
Mill and land to son George; dau. Mary household goods; dau. Anne Walker 1 negro and pewter; son William 1 negro; dau. Sarah Russell 20 shillings; grandchildren John and Elizabeth White 5 shillings each; wife Mary 2 negroes and rest of estate.

MARSHALL, JAMES, 2 Feb. 1749; 28 Aug. 1750.
Land (forest) should be sold, other land, negroes, stock etc. to wife Sarah and children.

SMITH, ROBERT, 12 Nov. 1750; 29 Jan. 1750.
Son Samuel land whereon I live and if he die without issue to my grandson Robert son of Stephen Smith; son Samuel 1 feather bed and rest of estate to maintain his mother for life.

GARNER, HENRY, 20 March 1751; 30 April 1751.
To son Vincent all my wearing apparel; to son Henry all my land; wife remainder of estate to raise 2 youngest children and at her death 2 youngest children Henry and Joyce Garner have same; Bradley Garner my brother and wife Jane exr. and exx.

INGLETHORP, THOMAS, 30 Feb. 1750; 30 April 1751.
Friend Mr. Henry Ashton all my estate which is mostly debts due me; Mr. John Storke to pay Dr. James Bankhead.

COX, CHARNOCK, 3 March 1751; 26 March 1751.
Desk and book case to my son Presley; 5 negroes to son George; 2 negroes to son William; dau. Elizabeth Rust 1 negro; grandchildren Peter Rust and Molly Rust 2 negroes each; Elizabeth Rust £25; son in law Samuel Rust exr.

COLLINSWORTH, THOMAS, 11 Dec. 1750; 26 March 1751.
Sons John and Thomas land where I live; daus. Ann and Sarah Collinsworth a looking glass each; wife Ann and 4 children rest of estate; wife Ann and Willoughby Collinsworth exrs.

MUSE, JOHN, 23 Jan. 1750; 26 March 1751.
Dau. Susannah Muse 1 negro; dau. Ann Muse all my land; my three daus.; wife Margaret land for life.

HALL, ANN, 15 Jan. 1750; 26 March 1751.
Ann Crummell; Elizabeth Minor daughter of John

Minor 1 silk and cotton gown; to John Muse's two daughters Ann and Elizabeth clothes; John Muse remainder of estate.

LEWIS, ELIZABETH, 6 Dec. 1750; 26 March 1751.
Land in Prince William and 2 negroes to son John; son in law Lovits Lewis 1 negro; to John son of Catherine Garrott 1 feather bed; to William Roussau 1 negro; his brother James 1 negro; son William Roussau exr. and care of Hillier and James Roussau.

MINOR, WILLIAM STEWART, * * *; 26 Mch. 1751.
Wife Frances household goods and 3 negroes; dau. Frances 5 negroes, 1 doz. large silver spoons and my land when she is of age.

CRAWFORD, ROBERT, 6 Mar. 1750-1; 26 Mar. 1751.
Friend Daniel Tebbs exr.; to Elizabeth Crabb £15; to Thomas Smith my tools.

SANFORD, JOSEPH, 29 Dec. 1750; 30 Apr. 1751.
Wife Barbara 2 negroes, cattle &c, then to son Joseph to whom land in Prince William; dau. Mary Sanford 1 negro, cattle &c; the child unborn to share in estate.

TAYLOR, JAMES, 23 Feb. 1750-1; 30 Apr. 1751.
All of lands to dau. Frances when 15 years of age; wife Sarah; friends George Franklin and Richard Payne exrs.

WHITE, JOHN, 22 Sept. 1750; 30 Apr. 1751.
Eldest son Samuel land, furniture &c; children John, Jenny and Susan White residue of estate; wife Sarah executrix.

ELLIOTT, SABELLAH, 8 Dec. 1750; 29 Jan. 1751.
To dau. Martha 1 feather bed and furniture; dau. Mildred 1 horse; dau. Betty Elliott; dec'd son Augustine Elliott; Richard Barnes of Richmond Co. exr.

LEE, THOMAS, of Stratford, 22 Feb. 1749-50; 30 Apr.
1751.
To be buried by my late dear wife and my honored
mother decd.; to oldest son land in Westmoreland and
Northumberland; my second, third, fourth and my
other younger sons; dau. Alice £1000; nephew George
Lee; dau. Hannah Corbin; executors Richard Corbin,
my eldest son Philip Ludwell Lee, son in law Gawin
Corbin and my second son Thomas Ludwell Lee
guardians to my children.

RUST, MATHEW, 11 July 1751; 30 July 1751.
The sum of £85 to Fleet Cox to pay for 150 acres of
land; son Vincent 20 acres of land; son George; grand
son Daniel Lamkin 1 negro and land in Fairfax Co.
when 21 years of age; dau. Anne Lamkin; daus. Winifred and Sarah Rust; to wife Frances land bought of
Samuel Rust; son Benedict a still and land at death
of wife; daus. Frances and Molly 1 feather bed each;
brother Peter Rust my grist mill.

LAMKIN, SAMUEL, 28 Nov. 1751; 27 Aug. 1751.
To son Daniel estate when 21 years of age and if he die
without issue to my two brothers Ashton and Charles
Lamkin.

LONGWORTH, BURGESS, 7 Nov. 1751; 26 Nov. 1751.
Son John 1 s.; son in law Edward Pridham 1 s.; dau.
Ann Jordan 1 s.; dau. Betty Thornton 1 s.; dau.
Frances Pridham 1 bed; son William land in Richmond
Co.; son Burgess; residue of estate to 2 sons and dau.
Mary.

PRICE, MEREDITH, 1 May 1749; 26 Nov. 1751.
Sister Martha Harrison 1 negro and 3 head of cattle;
cousin John Price 1 table; brother William Price Wolf
Trap Run land and residue of estate.

DOZIER, RICHARD, 5 May 1739; 26 Nov. 1751.
Son in law Thomas Templeman 50 acres land; sons Richard, Thomas and William one third of land each; gr. son Dozier Templeman; dau. Margaret Templeman 1 s.; dau. Elizabeth Wilson 1 s. as she already has her part; to Daniel Muse; to children Sarah Dozier, Hannah Muse, Martha and Mary Dozier residue of estate; wife Elizabeth all estate for life; grand dau. Elizabeth Belfield.

THOMPSON, JOHN, 24 Oct. 1751; 21 Nov. 1751.
Wife Elizabeth one half of land; son William one half of land at age of 20 but if he die without issue to George son of Richard Halliday; friend William Nicholls to bring up son William.

TEMPLEMAN, THOMAS, 25 May 1751; 25 Feb. 1752.
Dau. Mary Templeman house hold goods; son Dodier £5 current money; son William 1 horse and 1/3 of rest of estate; son Richard Hodgson T. 1 horse and 1/3 rest of estate; son John £5 current money; dau. Margaret Brewer 1/3 of rest of estate; dau. Mary Templeman; brother in law Richard Dozier Jr. and son Dozier exrs.

SANFORD, THOMAS, 27 Sept. 1749; 25 Feb. 1752.
Son Thomas 6 ewes; son Robert home plantation; son Richard 1 cow and calf; wife Darius residue of estate for life.

MARSHALL, JOHN, * * *; 1 Apr. 1752.
Dau. Sarah Lovell negro in possession of Robert Lovell; dau. Ann Smith 1 negro in possession of Augustine Smith; dau. Elizabeth 1 negro in possession of John Smith; wife Elizabeth 3 negroes; sons Thomas, John, Abraham and William 2 negroes each; daughters Margaret and Peggy Marshall 2 negroes each.

ARROWSMITH, RICHARD, 5 Feb. 1752; 30 June 1752.
Grandsons William Arrowsmith and William Bittey 1 negro girl; grand daughters Elizabeth Arrowsmith and Mary Bittey 1000 pounds of tobacco each; wife Elizabeth; son Thomas all of land and residue of estate.

POPE, JANE, 3 Apr. 1752; 30 June 1752.
5 negroes to dau. Elizabeth Price; grand ch. Ann and William Price, William and Benjamin Pope 1 negro each; gr. dau. Elizabeth Pope 3 negroes; gr. son John son of my dau. Elizabeth Price; son in law Bourn Price.

BUTLER, JAMES, 27 Jan. 1749; 28 July 1752.
Wife Ann land in Irish Neck and at her death to son Thomas and if he die without issue to my son James; gr. son James Butler; dau. Mary Butler 3 negroes; Elizabeth Sanford; gr. ch. James and Ann Kirk 1 negro; gr. ch. William and Sarah Jackson 1 negro.

GATHAGIN, JAMES, 17 Mar. 1752; 28 July 1752.
Wife Mary; dau. Mary Gathigan.

VOL. XII.

BAYLEY, STEPHEN, Senr., 14 Apr. 1750; 28 Aug. 1753.
Son Stephen land; sons John, William and James; daus. Ann Danielson, Martha Jenkins and Elizabeth * * *; wife Elizabeth; sons and daus. all of estate at death of wife.

WILSON, ALLEN, 12 Aug. 1753; 27 Nov. 1753.
Sister Hannah Borer land whereon I live and residue of estate; exr. Henry Borer.

KENDALL, JOHN, 30 Jan. 1754; 26 Mar. 1754.
Dau. Ann Kendall 1 negro at age of 18 years; Frances dau. of Samuel Kendall; Sarah dau. of Robert Frank; Borrington son of Robert Frank; Stephen son of John Bailey; wife Elizabeth estate for life.

JONES, NATHANIEL, gent., 21 Jan. 1753; 26 Mar. 1754.
Wife Sarah Howson Jones 1 negro, furniture, &c.; son John 50 acres land in Stafford Co. purchased of Thomas Harding; sons John, David, Nathaniel, Charles and Calvert Jones; daus. Mary Peck, Frances Jones, Sarah Franklin, 50 s. each; rest of estate to wife and children.

RALLINS, JAMES, 19 Jan. 1754; 26 Mar. 1754.
Estate to wife Grace who with Augustine Weedon are exrs.

WATTS, JOHN, 4 Nov. 1749; 27 Mar. 1754.
Son John land in Westmoreland and King George; son Richard land in Fairfax and Prince William; to Beheathland Bragg my house keeper the care of my two daus. Frances and Elizabeth Watts estate at age of 21 years; if my children marry a Maryland woman they are to forfeit their part of my estate; sister Margaret Grant a ring; friends Charles Ashton, James Bankhead, James Berryman and George Geay exrs.

BARNET, JOHN, 24 Feb. 1752; 30 Apr. 1754.
Son Richard; gr. son Henry Barnet 1 slave; dau. Elizabeth Finch 1 slave; gr. son John Finch and his sister Mary; dau. Mary Barnet 1 slave, 1 bed and £20; god son Joseph Cockrell 1 heifer; wife Elizabeth use of one half of personal estate and 1 negro.

FLING, WILLIAM, 25 Jan. 1754; 30 April 1754.
Dau. Margaret decd.; James Wilkerson; daus. Elizabeth Fling, Ann Wilkerson and Mary Wilkerson residue of estate; sons in law Thomas and Robert Wilkerson exrs.

RUST, WILLIAM, 26 Mar. 1754; 30 Apr. 1754.
White Marsh Neck to brother Samuel Rust which was left by my father Jeremiah Rust; brother in law Thaddeus Jackson my tools.

HABORN, GEORGE, 10 July 1753; 30 July 1754.
All land to son George; wife Elender; to three children George, Jane and Elender residue of estate; son James clothes; son James, Thomas McFarlane and James Bailey exrs.

MIDDLETON, ROBERT, 20 Aug. 1739; 31 July 1754.
All lands and two negroes to sisters Mary and Alice Middleton and to coz. Thomas Middleton; brother Benjamin Middleton exr.

ARNOLD, WEEDON, 18 Jan. 1754; 27 Aug. 1754.
Two children James and John land; wife Ann 3 negroes for life; I resign Sheriff's Office to friend Lovell Harrison; exrs. Colonel Andrew Monroe, Capt. Robert Vaulx and Mr. Lawrence Butler.

JETT, JOHN, 29 Mar. 1754; 26 Nov. 1754.
Son John land in King George; sons Peter and Francis land and mill in Westmoreland; daus. Mary, Elizabeth and Ann Jett negroes.

RALLINS, BENJAMIN, * * *; 28 Jan. 1755.
Land and negroes to bro. Samuel; sister Mary Whiting 2 negroes; her dau. Ann under 18 years; exr. John Whiting.

SUTTON, MARY, 17 March 1755; 26 Mar. 1755.
Son Jacob; son in law William Hazelrigg a still; grand children Mary Sutton, Elizabeth Thomas, Henrietta Sutton, Kezia Hazelrigg; dau. Mary Hazelrigg Christian and Frances Sutton; Richard Sutton, Jacob and James Sutton.

NEALE, MARGARET, 11 Oct. 1753; 27 May 1755.
To son Shapleigh Neale 1 negro man; dau. Jemima Neale 1 negro girl; son Richard 1 negro; dau. Elizabeth Spence a gold ring; exrs. son Daniel Neale and John Spence Jr.

JONCEL, EDWARD, 21 Apr. 1755; 27 May 1755.
To son John all of estate; Robert Massey, Lionel Massey and his children had by my sister and if they die without issue to my brother's children. Exrs. John Balsher and Thomas Taylor.

McKENNE, WILLIAM, 13 Jan. 1755; 29 July 1755.
All estate to wife Elizabeth for life and at her death to all my children.

PRICE, EVAN, 22 June 1754; 29 June 1755.
Wife Sarah land and other estate during widowhood; dau. Sarah Hutcheson; son John land on which William Hutcheson now lives; son Evan home plantation; daus. Mary and Grace Price and my two sons residue of estate.

RUST, WINIFRED, 8 Aug. 1754; 29 July 1755.
Vincent Rust my part of land divided between us, Sarah, Frances and Mary Rust which belonged to my father; bro. George Rust 1 negro, 1 bed and furniture; sister Sarah Claton all wearing clothes.

EDWARDS, WILLIAM, 18 Jan. 1755; 27 May 1755.
Son George one half of land; son Anthony one half of land; sons Arnold and Joseph 1 s. each; to John Burrus on a/c of my dau. Mary Burrus Settle 1 s.; dau. Grace Edwards; wife Elizabeth rest of estate for life and at her death to son William; dau. Martha Naylor and dau. Grace Edwards my bed and furniture.

QUISENBURY, NICHOLAS, 2 May 1755; 26 August 1755.
Dau. Ann Welch 1 negro; child unborn 1 negro; wife Rose 1 negro, she and my father exrs.

JACKSON, JOSEPH, 16 May 1751; 26 Aug. 1755.
To dau. Lettice Newton £20; father Richard Jackson rest of estate for life and at his death to bro. John Jackson; nieces Ann Jackson and Eleanor Thompson; bros. Richard Jackson and John Thompson.

SPENCE, JEMIMA, 6 May 1755; 30 Sept. 1755.
One trunk marked P. H. 1679 to dau. Elizabeth Sanford; son Patrick 1 silver soup spoon; dau. Jemima Suggett a tea chest; dau. Mary Spence 6 soup spoons and a desk; son Youell Spence a mahogany desk and other furniture; gr. ch. Jemima Suggett and Jemima Sandford.

McFARLANE, THOMAS, 17 Sept. 1755; 25 Nov. 1755.
To Elizabeth Cox 1 mare; to Francis Wright 1 saddle; wife Elizabeth land; my four daughters Mary, Jane, Ann and Hannah McFarlane personal estate when 18 years of age and land to dau. Mary at death of her mother, she to pay ¾ value to other daus.

ASBURY, ANNE, 10 Nov. 1755; 25 Nov. 1755.
Son Thomas; dau. in law Ann Asbury; dau. Elizabeth Muse; Jeremiah Muse; dau. Mary Rochester; grand dau. Anne Wright; Henry Asbury; Coleman Asbury; Ann Asbury; Walker Muse; Penepole Muse; Nicholas and William Rochester.

PRICE, WILLIAM, 13 Oct. 1755; 30 March 1756.
Wife Jane; daus. Betty, Jane, Katy and Patty Price.

VOL. XIII.

MOTHERSHEAD, CHARLES, 12 April 1756; 25 May 1756.
My sister; cousins Elizabeth and Thomas Jeams 3 negroes; sister Mary Wilkerson; cousin Charles Wilkerson; bro. in law Thomas James all estate save the 3 negroes.

ROBERTSON, THOMAS, * * *; 29 June 1756.
All estate to wife Ann; son Richard 1 shilling; grand son John son of Thomas 1 cow at death of wife; grand son Thomas Redmond Robertson 1 feather bed; sons John, William and James land at death of wife.

AWBREY, CHANDLER, 9 Dec. 1755; 25 Sept. 1756.
Son James Sorrell Awbrey at 21 years; daus. A. and — Awbrey; wife Elizabeth one third of land, a horse and saddle; to sister Hannah McAuley, niece Mary McAuley, Mrs. Elizabeth Atwell and to Sarah Atwell a suit of mourning each; children to be educated.

PRICE, EVAN, 3 Nov. 1755; 28 Sept. 1756.
To Valinda Bolthorp a mare and 2 rings; bro. John Price clothes, saddle and bridle; uncle Henry Field; mother Sarah Price and sisters Mary and Grace Price residue of estate.

ROE, BUNCH, 26 July 1756; 28 Sept. 1756.
Nephew William Roe 2 negroes; to Susanna Baker a horse; part of estate to children of William Whiting;

bro. Henry Roe; to Butler Baker a horse and saddle; Amy Pritchett a horse, bed and furniture and her wages for 2 years; William Munroe and John Weedon exrs.

CLAYTOR, THOMAS, 27 Dec. 1750; 28 Sept. 1756.
Eldest son John 5 shillings; sons Thomas and Alvin land; dau. Elizabeth Claytor land; dau. Anne a looking glass; sons William and Samuel land; grand son William son of John land; my seven children.

COURTNEY, MARY, 5 July 1756; 26 Oct. 1756.
A bed and furniture to son Samuel; dau. Rosamond Garner clothes; grand dau. Mary Garner a gold ring; my four sons James, Leonard, Samuel and Jeremiah residue of estate. Sons Leonard and Jeremiah exrs.

ELLIOTT, JOHN, 25 May 1756; 26 Oct. 1756.
To three sons William, Robert and Augustine 2700 acres of land in Prince William Co.; Capt. John Rouzee to care for William and Robert; wife all estate for life.

MIDDLETON, BENJAMIN, 10 Oct. 1756; 30 Nov. 1756.
Wife Jemima; children Mary Brown, Alice Harrison, Benjamin, Jane and Elizabeth. Wife Jemima and William Middleton exrs.

BUTLER, THOMAS, 13 Aug. 1756; 30 Nov. 1756.
Son John land and mill at age of 21 years; dau. Elizabeth Butler, William and Sarah Jackson a bed and furniture; to Ann Butler Jr. schooling and £5; Thomas Butler exr.

BUTLER, THOMAS, 29 May 1756; 26 Apr. 1757.
Son James two tracts of land, 23 and 66 acres, given me by my father; sons William, John and child unborn residue of land; each of my girls 2 years schooling; wife Isabel personal estate for life; George Munroe Jr. exr.

STEPTOE, COL. JAMES, 10 May 1755; 28 June 1757.
Son James land in Fairfax; son George land; son
Thomas land in Fairfax; dau. Ann; dau. Elizabeth to
my sister Carrell; wife Elizabeth one third of estate,
my chariot and six horses.

NAUGHTY, JAMES, 12 Apr. 1755; — July 1757.
Father James Naughty 2 negroes for life and then to
my bro. John; sister Mary Gerrard and her two eldest
children 3 negroes; William Gerrard and John Naughty
exrs.

VAULX, ROBERT, 8 Aug. 1754; 26 Mar. 1755.
Friend John Elliott and his two sons land in Prince
——— County; daus. Milly and Molly Vaulx land in
Brewtons Neck; daus. Katy and Kenner land in
Nominy; daus. Betty and Sally land purchased of John
Elliott; Sally to live with Mrs. Ann Washington; Molly
to live with Mrs. Ransdall; dau. Milly to live with
Sarah Pearce; dau. Elizabeth to stay with my wife
until she is 16 years of age; daus. by a former wife;
children by my present wife; son in law Lawrence
Washington a silver ladle and suit of mourning;
Brererton Kenner clothing; William Bernard law
books; Thomas Shadrack.

DUNKIN, GEORGE, 31 Dec. 1757; 28 Feb. 1758.
Sisters Elizabeth and Sarah Duncan all estate; Samuel
Jackson Sr. exr.

WHITING, THOMAS, 6 Dec. 1757; 28 Mar. 1758.
Daus. Molly, Sally, Nelly and Lizzie all estate; Mary
wife of Samuel Dishman to have care of dau. Molly;
Elizabeth wife of Spence Monroe care of dau. Lizzie;
Henry Roe care of dau. Nelly.

WESTMORELAND COUNTY WILLS 143

RANSDALL, WHARTON, 10 June 1755; 25 Apr. 1758.
Son Edward land; dau. Elizabeth Elliott Pierce land in Stafford and 20 s.; son Wharton a negro and my clothes; son William land on Cobbler Mountain Prince William Co.; wife personal estate.

RICE, ZERUBABEL, 19 May 1758; 30 May 1758.
Eldest son Zerubabel; 2nd son Simon; youngest son John; dau. Mary Rice; wife and all my children; slaves and personal estate to all children.

CALLES, WILLIAM, 20 Jan. 1758; 30 May 1758.
Sons Garland and William Overton Calles negroes and personal estate; wife Mary her horse, saddle and her dower.

BROWN, ORIGINAL, 29 Jan. 1744; 29 Nov. 1757.
All estate to wife Elizabeth and to be exx.

BENNETT, WILLIAM, 18 Sept. 1758; 30 Jan. 1759.
Mother Elizabeth Bennett estate for life, then to my brothers Charles, Daniel and Thos. Bennett.

NEALE, DANIEL, 28 Apr. 1758; 24 Apr. 1759.
Four sons Christopher, Presley, Richard and John land in Fairfax Co.; son Spence land in Fairfax Co.; son Daniel; son Rodham land in Richmond Co.; dau. Penny Spence Neale clothes of her decd. mother and 2 negroes; sons negroes and personal estate; brother Ramsdell Neale, sons Spence, Daniel and Rodham exrs.

ALLERTON, WILLOUGHBY, 30 June 1759; 25 Sept. 1759.
Land, furniture to wife Ann; David Connie's two daus. my sisters in law Jane and Alice; to Capt. Hancock Eustace £700 Sterling; Richard Lee Esq. 100 acres adj. his land.

PIPER, JOHN, 12 Aug. 17—; 25 Sept. 1759.
Land and 5 negroes to dau. Rachel and her husband

William Monroe; son Janathan, his wife Ann and their son John 400 acres of land and 4 negroes; son David 5 negroes; son in law Thomas Muse and my dau. Ann his wife 4 negroes; son William and my dau. Mary Piper land whereon I live and 4 negroes; youngest son Benjamin land in Culpeper.

SANFORD, RICHARD, 25 July 1757; 30 Oct. 1759.
Estate in Westmoreland to wife Susannah; son Richard land in Fairfax where he lives; son Robert; grand dau. Susannah dau. of my son Edward; daus. Frances Harrison, Elizabeth Harrison, Ann Muse; kinsman Aug. Sanford; grand son Franklin Perry est. of his mother Susannah Perry decd.; grand son Richard Muse est. of his mother Mary Muse decd.

BROWN, WILLIAM, 11 Aug. 1759; 30 Oct. 1759.
Son William land; son John land if son William die without issue; dau. Mary Hore 3 negroes; dau. Jane Price 2 negroes; dau. Elizabeth Craighill 2 negroes, bed, furniture and new desk; dau. Margaret Williams 2 negroes, bed and 1 cow; dau. Hannah Butler 2 negroes, bed and furniture, a cow, 10 yds. linen sheeting.

CHANDLER, JOSEPH, 17 Mar. 1758; 29 Jan. 1760.
Sons Thomas and William 5 negroes and 1/3 personal est.; daus. Elizabeth and Mary Chandler 1 negro and personal est. each; dau. Ann 1 negro child; wife Frances maintenance for life.

CORBIN, GAWIN, 29 Oct. 1759; 29 July 1760.
Wife Hannah all est. during widowhood or stay in this country; dau. Martha ½ est. at age of 21 yrs. or marriage and if she die without issue to the 2 youngest sons of my bro. Richard and the other ½ to 2 youngest sons of sister Tucker; god son Thomas son of Rich. Henry Lee £150 towards his education; wife,

Col. Richard Henry Lee, Thos. Ludwell Lee, Francis Lightfoot Lee and Richard Corbin guardians of dau. Martha. exrs.

SPILLMAN, WILLIAM, no date; 29 Apr. 1760.
Daus. Lettice Dulin and Margaret Spillman 1 cow, pewter and bed; land to sons Thomas, William and John Spillman.

POPE, HUMPHREY, 9 Aug. 1759; 27 May 1760.
Land to wife Sarah and at her death to son John; to Humphrey, Benjamin, Mary and Nathaniel Pope my children residue of estate.

LANE, WILLIAM, 19 Aug. 1758; 26 Aug. 1760.
Son James plantation; son William Carr Lane land; sons Joseph and James land; dau. Hannah Middleton 2 negroes and cattle; wife Martha exx.

WILKINSON, TYLER, 6 Apr. 1758; 28 Oct. 1670.
Son Tyler 1 cow; sons William, James, Thomas, Gerrard and Thomas 1 shilling each; to Elizabeth Ribeto 1 shilling; wife Elizabeth est. for life and then to son John.

SANFORD, ROBERT, 23 Aug. 1760; 28 Oct. 1760.
Son James 3 hhs. of tobacco; dau. Winifred Sanford 1 hhd. tobacco; son Robert a Bible and 1 negro; residue of est. to son John, dau. Ann Moxley and Jemima South.

BUSHROD, JOHN, gent., 14 Feb. 1760; 30 Dec. 1760.
Wife Mildred part of est.; dau. Hannah Washington 35 slaves, furniture and land; grand daus. Mary and Jenny Washington 3 slaves each; dau. Elizabeth Bushrod land and 41 slaves; to Lydia Bushrod Pettit dau. of John £10 yearly if her father spend her est.; friends Hon. Richard Corbin and John Washington exrs.

PARTRIDGE, JANE, 18 Sept. 1760; 31 Mar. 1761.
To son Ashton Lamkin 5 shillings; dau. Eleanor Cox 5 shillings; grand dau. Sarah Rust side saddle and clothing; grand son Daniel Lamkin a horse and saddle; son Peter Lamkin 5 shillings; son Mathew Partridge 3 negroes, land on Negro Run Culpeper Co. and residue of estate.

VOL. XIV.

WALKER, JOHN, 25 Sept. 1760; 31 Mar. 1761.
Use of estate to wife Ann; son William land and if he die single to my son James; dau. Elizabeth Walker.

COURTNEY, SAMUEL, 18 July 1759; 31 Mar. 1761.
Godsons Samuel Courtney and Thomas Garner 500 lbs. tobacco each; bros. James, Leonard and Jeremiah Courtney; sister Rosamond Garner; wife Dorcas, no bequest mentioned.

TODD, ROBERT, 18 Jan. 1761; 9 Apr. 1761.
To Richard Cadeen all estate in Va.

CHANCELLOR, THOMAS, 19 Nov. 1760; 31 Mar. 1761.
Wife Katherine; sons John and Thomas; daus. Catherine, Rebecca, Sarah and Grace 1 negro.

JOHNSON, SAMUEL, 22 Dec. 1760; 31 Mar. 1761.
Grand daus. Ann, Margaret and Mary Johnson £20 each; Mary dau. of Thomas Binks decd.; grand son Samuel Johnson 5 negroes and children of 2 others; wife Ann est. for life.

VIVION, THOMAS, 10 Sept. 1760; 28 Apr. 1761.
Son Charles land in King Geo. Co.; son Francis land in Westmoreland; dau. Jane born of late wife before mar. £500, 1 negro, a horse and saddle when of age; dau. Mary £500; dau. Frances Brooking a gold ring; dau. Margaret Pratt a gold ring; Peter Daniel gdn. of sons.

LOWE, JOHN, 6 Mar. 1760; 29 July 1760.
Estate to wife and at her death to children; George Hull and Bradley Garner exrs.

ASHTON, BURDETT, 7 Mar. 1760; 29 July 1760.
Estate to nephew Burdett son of Charles and Sarah Ashton and if he die without issue to bro. Charles Ashton; nephews Lawrence and John Ashton.

REDMAN, WILLIAM, 27 Nov. 1760; 26 May 1761.
Dau. Winifred 1 negro; sons John and William; dau. Lettice 1 negro; wife Frances her saddle, my horse and use of all est. while single.

MULLINS, RACHEL, 2 Feb. 1761; 26 May 1761.
To John Barber 100 lbs. tobacco; son Peter Mullins 1 shilling; dau. Rachel Mullins residue of estate.

SETTLE, WILLIAM, 1 Oct. 1760; 26 May 1761.
All estate to wife Sarah for life and at her death to son Joel.

ROSE, CHARLES, clerk, 7 Mar. 1760; 30 June 1761.
1 negro and £30 to sons Robert and John; son Alexander 1 negro; daus. Catherine and Molly 1 negro; wife Catherine her part of est.; bro. Alexander and nephew John Rose exrs.

WILLIAMS, THOMAS, 20 May 1761; 30 June 1761.
To son Elijah a suit of clothes; son Daniel 1 negro and land; wife Elizabeth and 3 children.

RUST, FRANCES, 23 July 1759; 30 June 1761.
Son Robert Middleton 1 book; dau. Rachel Cox a cow and calf; son Benedict Rust 2 cows, 1 bed and furniture; daus. Frances Sherman and Molly Rust rest of estate.

GARNER, ABRAHAM, 21 Feb. 1761; 30 June 1761.
Dau. Frances dau. of Sarah Garner; daus. Martha, Lettice and Rachel Garner my estate.

ARISS, SPENCER, 23 Nov. 1760; 28 July 1761.
Wife Sarah ½ of estate; dau. Elizabeth Ariss ½ of estate and if she die without issue to my bro. John Ariss; nephew John Ariss Calles; sister Sorrell.

TIDWELL, ROBERT, 27 Sept. 1757; 28 July 1761.
Wife Hannah part of land; son William Carr T. land and 3 negroes; dau. Elizabeth 7 negroes; grand dau. Hannah Tidwell; son John land and 3 negroes; Kath. Jenkins a bed and cow.

MARMANDUKE, CHRISTOPHER, 20 Jan. 1761; 28 July 1761.
To son Christopher and his son Vincent the home plantation; son Daniel £25 and 1 bed; dau. Esther Robinson 1 negro girl; grand daus. Hannah and Elizabeth Holland; dau. Jemima Sandy 1 negro, bed and cow; grand son Thomas Sandy; son John; to Margaret Sandford and grand dau. Elizabeth Marmanduke 1 negro and increase; all my children: Christopher, Jean, John, Daniel, Esther, William and Jemima residue of estate.

BAXTER, EDWARD, 16 June 1761; 28 July 1761.
1 negro girl to George son of William Monroe decd.; to George Monroe's dau. Mary 20 s. to make her a ring; my bros. George and Thomas Baxter residue of estate.

NEWMARCH, JONATHAN, 13 Nov. 1761; 26 Jan. 1762.
Horse, cow and furniture to son Thomas; to son Jonathan same; grand son William Brown a horse; dau. Elizabeth Brown wife of James; to Dorothy Tingle a spinning wheel.

NAUGHTY, JAMES, 22 Aug. 1761; 26 Jan. 1762.
My dau. Mary Gerrard 2 negroes and £5; grand daus. Ann Gerrard and Elizabeth Gerrard to Martha Brown a horse and tobacco; to John Briges a horse and gun; Mary Brown; son John land and 9 negroes; grand son James Gerrard.

SELF, WILLIAM, 10 Mar. 1761; 26 Jan. 1762.
Son William part of land; grand sons William and Peter Self land; dau. Susannah a looking glass; Benjamin Hail's children; daus. Becky and Lettice; Stephen Self to live on plantation and bring up children; son Abraham 1 year's schooling; wife movable estate.

LEE, GEORGE, gent., 13 Sept. 1761; 26 Jan. 1762.
Eldest son George Fairfax Lee; sons Lancelot and William lands in Loudon County; dau. Elizabeth Lee £1000; my late wife Anne; son Lancelot seal with family coat of arms given me by Col. Richard Lee; friends Col. George William Fairfax, Col. Richard Henry Lee, Col. Richard Lee, William Bryant Fairfax and Capt. John Turbeville to be guardians.

RUST, PETER, 9 Nov. 1761; 26 Jan. 1762.
To Daniel Lamkin 712 acres land in Loudon Co.; my sons Richard and Samuel land; sons James, John and Peter; daus. Mary, Martha, Hannah and Elizabeth negroes; wife Elizabeth 100 acres land during widowhood.

DUNBAR, WILLIAM, 11 Nov. 1761; 23 Feb. 1762.
Children Molly, James and William leased land, use of stock and furniture.

WHITE, SARAH, 26 Nov. 1761; 24 Feb. 1762.
To son John, daus. Jenny Smith and Susannah White land, stock, negroes &c; to dau. Margaret Mothershead my clothes.

BAKER, JOHN, 27 Nov. 1761; 30 Mar. 1762.
Wife Elizabeth land for life and then to children William, John and Ann Baker.

NASH, ELIZABETH, no date; 30 Mar. 1762.
Dau. Ann Nash a cow and calf; son John Nash 1 bed; son Thomas Brown 1 shilling; son Nathaniel Nash 1 shilling; dau. Elizabeth Bragg 1 shilling; son William Nash 1 shilling; son Jeremiah Nash residue of estate.

SMITH, STEPHEN, Senr., 22 Nov. 1761; 30 Mar. 1762.
Son Samuel to be bound to his uncle George Banister and have 2 year's schooling; son Robert 1 cow; my wife and children all rest of estate; bro. Samuel Smith exr.

MOORE, ROBERT, 5 Dec. 1761; 30 Mar. 1762.
Wife Elizabeth estate for life and at her death to sons John and Robin; dau. Eleanor Moore 1 chest.

DAVIS, JOHN, 17 Jan. 1754; 30 Mar. 1762.
Son William land; wife Jane and all my children rest of estate.

BRANHAM, MICHAEL, 3 Dec. 1761; 27 Apr. 1762.
To son Barnaby shoemakers tools; wife Rosannah and children Ignatius, Barnaby, Joseph, William, Elizabeth and Rosannah rest of estate.

WASHINGTON, AUGUSTINE, 18 Sept. 1758; 25 May 1762.
Son William Augustine negroes and other per. est. at age of 21 years; decd. bro. Lawrence Washington; daus. Betsey, Nancy and Jane £1000 each; wife Jane to be exx. with Fielding Lewis, Richard Henry Lee, my bros. George and John Washington. Codicil, 16 Feb. 1762. My wife being delivered of a son named George; wife in descent from her grandfather Col. Ashton; my bros. Samuel and Charles; children of my sister Lewis and of my sister in law Mrs. Booth wife of William Booth.

COX, PETER PRESLEY, 6 June 1762; 29 June 1762.
Godson Richard Wright 1 negro; god dau. Molly Cox 1 negro; to Jane Muffitt's daus. Sally and Nancy 1 negro each; bro. William Cox 1 negro; bro. Fleet Cox residue of estate.

BANISTER, GEORGE, 21 May 1762; 29 June 1762.
Sister Ann Smith and her son Robert; sister Elizabeth wife of John Baley clothes and rest of estate.

LAMKIN, PETER, 2 Nov. 1757; 29 June 1762.
Son Mathew land with mill and negroes; son Peter 100 acres land; sons George and James land; wife Ann and all my children rest of estate.

QUISENBERRY, WILLIAM, Sr., 27 May 1762; 27 July 1762.
Dau. Eleanor Bayn 1 shilling; grand sons Nicholas Quisenberry, John Mothershead and William Dodd 1 shilling each; son William land he lives on; daus. Ann and Elizabeth residue of estate.

WHEELER, WILLIAM, 18 Nov. 1761; 28 Sept. 1762.
Wife Elizabeth land; dau. Sarah Horton land and £10; dau. Elizabeth Strother 1 negro; sons Richard and John 5 shillings each; son Thomas land at death of wife.

MOXLEY, ALEXANDER, 5 Aug. 1762; 28 Sept. 1762.
Brother John Moxley's son Rodham 1 negro; cousin Joseph Moxley clothes; wife Frances residue of estate.

DAVIS, ELIZABETH, 20 May 1759; 25 Sept. 1762.
Sister Frances all estate, she and Mary Davis my exxs.

PRITCHETT, THOMAS, 24 May 1762; 30 Nov. 1762.
Died at home of Thos. Robinson. Estate to all of children; bro. James Pritchett exr.

WESTMORELAND COUNTY WILLS 153

BALTHROP, JOHN, 28 Aug. 1762; 30 Nov. 1762.
Sons William and John; daus. Sarah, Elizabeth, Margaret and Nancy Balthrop; sons Sharp and James estate after death of wife Jemima.

BERRYMAN, ELIZABETH, 14 June 1762; 22 Feb. 1763.
Decd. husband Benjamin Berryman; sons Newton, John and Henry all decd. before age of 21 years; son William 16 negroes and land; son James 17 negroes and land; son Maxamilian; daus. Catherine Nowles, Rose Taliaferro, Frances Foot and Sarah Douglass have estate left them by their father.

TEBBS, DANIEL, 25 May 1760; 20 Feb. 1762.
Son William land; son Daniel land and mill; daus. Mary and Elizabeth negroes; wife Elizabeth land.

HORE, JAMES, 12 Apr. 1763; 31 May 1763.
Godson Beckwith Butler 1 negro; cousins Sarah and Elias Hore 1 negro each; to William Berkeley and his wife Peggy 1 negro and at their death to godson John Berkeley; to Mary Nelson Jr., Mary Nelson Sr. and to William Nelson 2 negroes; James son of cousin Elias Hore plantation I live on; residue of estate to Elias Hore and John Triplett.

MIDDLETON, MARY, 6 Mar. 1755; 27 Sept. 1763.
To William and Thomas sons of Thomas Middleton decd. right in land whereon I live, 1 negro man and per. estate; a bed and furniture to Mary Brown dau. of bro. Benjamin Middleton; Leazure widow of bro. Thomas use of estate for life.

JEFFRIES, GEORGE, 30 Aug. 1763; 25 Oct. 1763.
Children William, John, George, Mariah, Elizabeth and Ann to have their parts; wife Elizabeth use of estate during widowhood; wife and Jeremiah Jeffries exrs.

WHITE, JAMES, 21 Oct. 1762; 25 Oct. 1763.
Personal property to Alice Kersey; son Benjamin's daus. Jane, Mildred and Amy 20 shillings each; son John's sons Samuel and John 1 shilling each; son Daniel use of my negro man 4 days each week; daus. Jemima Balthrop and Verlinda Grigsby 1 shilling each; grand dau. Winifred Balthrop 1 trunk; son James 1 shilling.

WEEDON, JAMES, 21 Sept. 1763; 29 Nov. 1763.
Daus. Elizabeth, Jane and Rebecca Weedon 1 negro each; dau. Mary Hilton 1 negro; dau. Sarah £50; 1 bed and furniture to each dau.; sons John, George and Augustine 1 negro each.

DAVIS, FRANCES, 16 Nov. 1763; 29 Nov. 1763.
Sisters Ann and Mary Davis one negro each; sister Katherine Davis residue of estate

DAVIS, ANNE, 12 Oct. 1763; 29 Nov. 1763.
Dau. Anne Davis 1 negro; residue of estate to my five daus.; daus. Anne and Mary exxs.

WILKERSON, JOHN, 21 Feb. 1764; 27 Mar. 1764.
Son Benjamin land and if he die without issue to son John; wife Margaret estate for life and then to all my children.

BAKER, JOHN, 10 Feb. 1764; 29 May 1764.
Daus. Frances and Winny 1 negro man; wife Katherine estate for life, then land and per. estate to be sold, debts paid and residue, save 1 negro man to my son James, and amount divided among children James, Samuel, Rebecca and Richard.

TIDWELL, HANNAH, 27 Jan. 1760; 29 May 1764.
My land to Hannah dau. of son John Tidwell, and grand children Elizabeth and Barbara Tidwell; dau. Elizabeth Tidwell; son William Carr Tidwell.

LEE, MARY, of Lee Hall, 19 Oct. 1762; 29 May 1764.
Personal estate, after legacies are paid, to dau. Lettice Ball; son Richard chariot and horse; £100. to grand dau. Mary Ball; sons John, Richard and Henry Lee; daus. in law Mary and Lucy Lee; grand sons William and Henry Lee Ball; son Richard Lee exr.

BAKER, BUTLER, 21 Jan. 1764; 26 June 1764.
Land to son William; to son Samuel 1 negro girl; negro Peggy to be sold and money divided among daus. Elizabeth Frances and Susannah; son Samuel to be maintained.

HARRISON, SAMUEL, 11 Aug. 1763; 31 July 1764.
Land to son William; father George Harrison decd.; son Jeremiah land; daus. Ann and Hannah Harrison 1 bed each; wife Magdalene 1 bed; Dr. Nicholas Flood to be paid.

DAVIS, ANNE, 9 Jan. 1764; 28 Aug. 1764.
Sister Esther Davis 1 negro girl; sister Katherine Davis 1 negro; sister Mary Davis rest of estate.

OMOHUNDRO, JOHN, 16 Jan. 1765; 26 Feb. 1765.
Sons Thomas, William, John and Richard; daus. Jemima Weaver and Elizabeth Davis 1 negro each; grand son Jesse Davis; son in law Joseph Taylor 1 shilling.

WHITE, MARY, 20 Oct. 1764; 26 Feb. 1765.
Grand dau. Anne Porter; daus. Sarah Russell and Anne Walker; grand daus. Mary dau. of Philip White, and Eliz. Reynolds; son George White.

FINCH, JOHN, 2 Jan. 1765; 26 Feb. 1765.
Bro. Nicholas Muse; sisters Mary Randall and Anne Muse; bro. in law Thomas Randall.

HILTON, JOHN, 24 Sept. 1764; 28 May 1765.
Land to son William; dau. Mary £30; dau. Elizabeth at 21 years; wife ½ estate for life.

MASSEY, LOVELL, 3 June 1764; 28 May 1765.
Use of plantation to wife Martha; sons Lovell, James and Robert; daus. Judith Massey, Mildred and Frances Spillman. Personal estate to children.

GILBERT, MICHAEL, 13 Feb. 1765; 25 June 1765.
Sons William and Thomas; dau. Sarah Morton; wife Mary and all my children.

DELOZIER, THOMAS, 24 Dec. 1764; 30 July 1765.
Wife Susannah 2 negroes; son Richard Davis Delozier 1 negro; son Daniel; dau. Molly Randall Delozier 1 negro.

KIRK, JOHN, 11 Dec. 1764; 27 Aug. 1765.
Wife Sarah estate for life, then to son John and rest of children.

CHILTON, THOMAS, 4 Sept. 1765; 24 Sept. 1765.
Land, 18 negroes, furniture &c to son Thomas; dau. Mary Ransdall 5 negroes; grand son Chilton Ransdell 1 negro; dau. Hannah Sturman 4 negroes; grand dau. Jemima Sturman 1 negro; sons William, John and Charles land in Fauquier; son Stephen land in Prince William; John living in Fauquier Co.; 4 sons residue of estate.

WASHINGTON, ROBERT, 11 Feb. 1763; 24 Sept. 1765.
18 negroes to dau. Sukey; grand children Sarah and Robert Townshend Washington 1 negro each; son John residue of estate; William Bernard guardian to dau. Sukey.

PIPER, JONATHAN, 18 Sept. 1763; 29 July 1766.
Wife Anne; children John, Nancy, Susanna, Jenny, Rachel.

CHRISTIE, GEORGE, — —; 13 Jan. 1766 (Nuncupative).
To George son of Leonard Courteny my silver shoe buckles; to Jeremiah Courtney buttons and residue of estate.

HODGSON, WILLIAM, 31 July 1765; 29 July 1766.
All estate in Virginia to Katherine Baker.

GOFF, WILLIAM O'BRIEN, 19 July 1766; 30 Sept. 1766.
Dau. Frances Johnston 100 acres land in Prince William and £40; wife Jane land and 3 negroes; son William 1 shilling; son Benjamin land, 3 negroes and rest of estate at death of wife.

BENNETT, COSSOM, 14 July 1765; 30 Sept. 1766.
Sons William and Bunbury a horse, saddle and bridle each; wife Catherine and my children rest of estate; Thomas Bunbury and wife exrs.

HURLEY, JOHN, 31 Jan. 1766; 30 Sept. 1766.
Son John my clothes; wife Betheathland residue of estate.

COX, PRESLEY, 18 Feb. 1766; 30 Sept. 1766.
Bible and looking glass to son Fleet Cox; grand sons Richard and Presley Wright £10 each; granddau. Nancy Wright £10; son William Cox; grand ch. Fleet, Presley and Molly Cox; Francis Wright exr.

JEFFRIES, JEREMIAH, 1 May 1766; 28 Oct. 1766.
My still and clothes to bro. Robert; to William Coward his freedom; wife residue of estate.

SANFORD, WINIFRED, 27 Sept. 1766; 28 Oct. 1766.
Son William stock and £5; Ann South clothes; Elizabeth wife of Peter Walker side saddle; sister Ann Moxley part of clothes; John South and Joseph Moxley exrs.

LEE, JOHN, gent., of Essex Co.; 23 Sept. 1765; 24 Feb. 1767.
Wife Mary estate for life; cousin Hancock son of John Lee, Jr., and his wife Susanah land in Essex; bro. Henry Lee land King Copsico in Westmoreland; nephew Henry Lee; bro. Richard Lee; sister Lettice Ball 4 negroes; niece and nephew Mary and Henry Lee Ball; to Mary and Fanny daus. of Baldwin Mathews Smith 1 negro; Lettice, Philip, Mary and Elizabeth children of John Lee Jr. and wife Susannah.

NEWTON, JOHN, 8 Jan. 1767; 24 Feb. 1767.
Estate left me by my father to son Willoughby; the child my wife Elizabeth now goes with land in Westmoreland.

VIGOUR, WILLIAM, —; 31 Mar. 1767.
Wife Sarah Vigour estate for life and at her death to dau. Frances and my six sons.

FLEMING, WILLIAM, 7 Jan. 1767; 28 Apr. 1767.
Estate for life to wife Abigail; sons John and William 1 negro each; dau. Elizabeth wife of Thaddeus Jackson 1 negro; dau. Peggy wife of Rodham Pritchett; dau. Martha Fleming 1 negro and £7.

SEARS, EDWARD, 4 July 1766; 28 Apr. 1767.
Estate to wife Mary for life and then to my son William and my other children.

NEWTON, WILLOUGHBY, 7 Dec. 1766; 26 May 1767.
Son John land in Westmoreland; grand son Richard Jackson furniture; dau. Judith Brent estate I gave her at marriage with Brererton Kenner, land on Rocky Run, Loudon Co.; William Jett and Katherine his wife land I gave them adj. above, and 5 negroes; dau. Katherine Lane; son in law Thomas Lawson negroes and stock; Lettice wife of Thomas Lawson; son in law John Berryman and wife Martha negroes, stock; son

in law Benjamin Berryman and wife Sarah; dau. Elizabeth Newton land whereon I live, stock, chariot with 4 horses, 10 negroes; dau. Mary Newton 21 negroes. Codicil 6 Jan. 1767. Grand son Willoughby son of John who has died since the making of this will; grand daus. Elizabeth Ashton and Ann Jackson; Betty widow of son John.

WEEDON, JANE, 15 Dec. 1763; 28 July 1767.
All estate to sisters Elizabeth, Rebecca and Sarah Weedon.

SPARK, WILLIAM, St. Thomas Par., Co. Surry, Is. of Jamaica, 1 Jan. 1764; 25 Aug. 1767.
Mother Margaret Duthrie of Arbuthink, Kincardine, Scotland; my three sisters Jane, Rebecca and Mary of same place; bro. Alexander Spark of Westmoreland Co. Va. all estate in Jamaica; Eliz. Cooper 2 negroes for care of me in illness.

JACKSON, MAGDALENE, 11 Aug. 1766; 24 Nov. 1767.
Silver box to son Samuel Rust; sons Julius Augustine, Thaddeus and Christopher M. Jackson; decd. husband Christopher D. Jackson. Estate consists of land, slaves, silver, &c.

HUTCHESON, WILLIAM, 14 Apr. 1767; 29 Mar. 1768.
Dau. Mary Hutcheson 1 negro; wife Elizabeth her dower; rest of estate to be sold for credit and interest to estate.

PORTER, WILLIAM, 27 Dec. 1767; 28 Mar. 1768.
Sons Edward and William lands; daus. Ann, Sarah and Betty Porter rest of estate.

CRUTCHER, JOHN, 4 Sept. 1767; 26 Apr. 1768.
Wife Susannah 3 negroes; sons John, Thomas and Joseph negroes; dau. Susannah 2 negroes.

WHITE, JAMES, 3 Jan. 1768; 31 May 1768.
To Elizabeth Weedon 20 shillings; son George residue of estate.

ROWE, WILLIAM, 12 May 1768; 27 Sept. 1768.
Dau. Jane Pope Rowe 11 negroes; grand dau. Elizabeth Fox 1 negro; dau. Angelica Fox land and rest of slaves; son in law Joseph Fox; wife 1 bed and furniture and a room in the house if she desires it.

BEARD, GEORGE, 12 Sept. 1768; 27 Sept. 1768.
Wife Marian, dau. Susannah and son George all personal estate; land to son George; my mother Ann Hilton 50 shillings worth of goods; exrs. William Smith and William Hilton.

VOL. XV.

BUTLER, ANN, 13 Sept. 1763; 27 Nov. 1768.
1 negro to dau. Elizabeth Sanford and at her death to her son William and dau. Frances Sanford; grand dau. Sarah dau. of Mary Sanford 2 negroes; grand dau. Ann Sanford 1 negro; grand sons John and William Butler; grand dau. Ann Kenny 1 negro; friends Hannah and Ann Harrison daus. of Lovell Harrison; grand son James Butler; son in law Willoughby Sanford.

READE, RUTH, 4 Oct. 1768; 29 Nov. 1768.
Dau. Mary Reade 1/3 of estate; grand son Andrew Reade other 2/3 of estate.

NAUGHTY, JOHN, 24 Nov. 1768; 29 Nov. 1768.
To Martha and Mary Brown 2 negroes; John Bridges son of said Martha Brown and his dau. Patty Bridges; James Thomas; Ann dau. of William Gerrard 1 negro; god son Yelverton Quisenberry 1 negro; to John son of William Berkeley 1 negro; god son William Payne; god son John son of William Bridges; god son Richard son of Nathaniel Gerrard.

MIDDLETON, JEREMIAH, 26 Dec. 1768; 30 May 1769.
Son George lands in Richmond and Northumberland Cos.; son John; my four children; wife Sarah Ellen.

GRACE, WILLIAM, 6 Sept. 1769; 28 Nov. 1769.
To wife Ann 3 negroes; son Thomas £2; son John land in North Carolina; son William £65; dau. Ann Bell 1 shilling; son James 5 negroes and residue of estate.

CALLES, FRANCIS, 6 Sept. 1769; 27 Feb. 1770.
To bro. Robert £10; my children; wife Jane rest of estate; exrs. Richard, Ambrose and Thomas Calles.

MIDDLETON, SARAH ELLEN, 23 July 1769; 27 Feb. 1770.
Decd. husband's wishes to be carried out in disposition of will. Exrs. Fleet Cox, Francis Wright and Daniel Bennett.

GARNER, BRADLEY, 13 Oct. 1769; 26 June 1770.
Son George 2 negroes, land my father left me, land bought of Samuel Garner after decease of my wife; sons Vincent and George land in North Carolina whereon William Harden lives; dau. Eleanor Garner 1 negro; daus. Lettice Garner, Hannah Cox and Elizabeth Garner 1 negro each; wife Catherine; son Benjamin 100 acres land; son Jeremiah; Frances dau. of Abraham Garner; grand son Thomas Pertich and his sister Catrin Pritch (Pertich?); to Rodham Pritch a silver watch.

ATTWELL, JOHN, — Apr. 1770; 26 June 1770.
Sons Thomas, John, Richard and Francis; daus. Elizabeth Lafoon, Sarah Coghill, Martha Atwell; sons Youell and William; my wife; bro. Francis Atwell.

JACKSON, DANIEL, 2 May 1767; 31 July 1770.
My children George, Daniel, William, Elizabeth Franklin, Sarah Jackson, land and all estate.

THOMPSON, ANDREW, 5 Sept. 1769; 28 Aug. 1770.
Dau. Mary Burn; daus. Margaret, Sarah, Behathland and Winifred; sons George and Andrew.

HUTT, GERRARD, 4 May 1770; 25 Sept. 1770.
Wife Mary; grand sons William Gerrard Hutt, Joseph son of Andrew Read; dau. Mary Ann Read; son Gerrard and his son Gerrard; grand son John son of William Brown.

SANFORD, THOMAS, 24 May 1767; 27 Nov. 1770.
150 acres of land to grand son Thomas son of Youell and Eliz. Sanford; grand son Thomas Luttrell; son Thomas exr.; wife Margaret residue of estate which at her death goes to my children and grand son Thomas Luttrell.

MUSE, JOHN, 11 Oct. 1770; 27 Nov. 1770.
Wife Eleanor horse, saddle, feather bed and furniture; sons Daniel and James rest of estate; exrs. Richard and Daniel Muse.

MONROE, ANDREW, 1 May 1769; 27 Nov. 1770.
Wife Margaret £5., chair and horse and use of a room for a year; grand son Elliott Monroe land in Loudon Co.; grand son John Monroe land where my son John lived; four grand children John, Jane, Elizabeth and Nancy Monroe; exrs. Dr. James Bankhead, John Ashton and Spence Monroe.

PARTRIDGE, MATHEW, 13 Nov. 1770; 26 Mar. 1771.
Sons Richard and Mathew 5 negroes, daus. Sally, Jenny and Patty 1/5 estate each; wife Jemima my bay mare; exr. Daniel Morgan.

HIGDON, JOHN, 23 Dec. 1770; 26 Mar. 1771.
Children Elizabeth, Original, John and Richard Higdon.

LAWRENCE, CHARLES, 1 May 1770; — Mar. 1771.
Cousin William Lawrence Jr. who lives with me all my estate.

MIDDLETON, BENEDICT, 22 Sept. 1770; 26 Mar. 1771.
Son of Robert Middleton; bro. John all my land, he paying my debts and giving £40 to my bro. William; residue of estate to bro. Robert and cousins Mary and Elizabeth Rust.

BROWN, ELIZABETH, 30 Aug. 1770; 28 May 1771.
Bro. James Dishman land; sister Mary Rutherford a bed and furniture.

CUPINGHEIFER, JOHN, 13 Feb. 1770; 28 May 1771.
Wife Mary estate for life and then to children Mical, Hannah and John; bro. Jacob exr.

BAYNE, MATHEW, Senr., 2 Mar. 1769; 17 Oct. 1771.
Wife Elenor; sons Mathew, Carson, William, Richard and his dau. Mary; sons John, Daniel and George; dau. Sarah Vigor and her husband William V.; dau. Amy Bridges and her son Mathew; dau. Elizabeth Bayne; wife estate for life. (A large estate).

MONROE, GEORGE, Junr., 12 Nov. 1770; 25 June 1771.
Wife Peggy; sons George, John and William; daus. Mary, Sarah and Ann; bro. William Monroe; friend Spense Monroe exr.

WEAVER, ADAM, 30 Nov. 1770; 25 June 1771.
Wife Annamino; sons John, William, Abraham, Benjamin and Zacharias; daus. Elizabeth Bott; Mary Mothershead and Hannah Weaver; sons in law William Walker and William Jyles.

MIDDLETON, ROBERT, 22 Feb. 1771; 24 Sept. 1771.
Estate to be kept together until youngest child 16 yrs; for benefit of wife Elizabeth and children; wife 1/3 of land for life.

MCCLANAHAN, WILLIAM, 15 Sept. 1760; 29 Oct. 1771.
Wife Martha estate for life; son in law Garland Moore land in Richmond Co.; grand children Robert, Garland, Peter and McClanahan and Martha Moore amount from sale of land in Richmond Co. at death of wife; sons Thomas, Peter, William, James and John McClanahan estate at death of wife.

WESTMORELAND COUNTY WILLS 165

STONE, JOSEPH, 10 Dec. 1770; 26 Nov. 1771.
Son Thomas land; wife Ann; son Presley and child unborn; daus. Jemima Neale and Penelope Stone; exrs. wife Ann, Thomas Stone and Rodham Neale.

MOXLEY, JOHN, 14 Aug. 1771; 26 Nov. 1771.
Son Augustine stock and tools where he lives; wife Elizabeth rest of estate.

STOWERS, SAMUEL, 24 Dec. 1762; 31 Oct. 1771.
Wife Ann ½ estate and at her death to cousin Samuel Stowers to whom the other ½.

BULGER, JOHN, 23 Dec. 1771; 31 Dec. 1771.
Daus. Barbara Jenkins and Elizabeth Parsons; children Johnson, Sally and Nancy Bulger 1 negro to each one; lands to be sold.

BROWN, JOHN, 14 May 1770; 31 Dec. 1771.
To son William 1 negro and land that came by William Fryer decd.; son John 2 negroes and land whereon I live; dau. Priscilla Brown 2 negroes, 1 feather bed and furniture; my seven daus. residue of estate.

CAVENDER, HENRY, 24 Dec. 1771; 31 Mar. 1772.
Daus. Ann Davis and Rachel Nash; sons Thomas, John, George and Richard; wife Elizabeth.

READ, MARY, 21 Jan. 1772; 31 Mar. 1772.
4 negroes to sister Ann Asbury; niece Barbara Hutt clothes; bro. Richard Read to be clothed; nephew Andrew Read 5 slaves and rest of estate and at his death to his son Joseph Read.

MONROE, THOMAS, 9 March 1772; 28 Apr. 1772.
Bros. Andrew and James; sisters Martha and Jane residue after bequests to bros.

MIDDLETON, ALICE, 27 Oct. 1766; 28 Apr. 1772.
Thomas son of Thomas Middleton decd.; William son of Thomas Middleton decd. and his bro. Thomas to have estate equally divided among them; exrs. Samuel Walker and William Middleton aforementioned.

SMITH, JOHN, gent., 7 Jan. 1771; 28 Apr. 1772.
Entire estate to sons John, Edward and Mathew Smith and they exrs.

HOLLAND, YOUELL, 7 Dec. 1771; 25 May 1772.
Wife Hannah 1/3 of land; dau. Rockey Holland 2/3 of land.

HALL, LEASURE, 7 Jan. 1770; — 1772.
Dau. Ann Lewis 5 shillings; dau. Mary Bailey 5 shillings; bro. Ashton Hall 1 negro; wife Joanna 1 negro and if she die without issue by me to my daus.; Lewis Hall 1 negro and use of rest of estate for life and then to my daus.

McGUIRE, ALEXANDER, 27 Mar. 1772; 30 June 1772.
Son Travers all stock he to give his bro. Alexander's son Rodham 1 year's schooling; to Charles Scutt's son Thomas 1 year's schooling; dau. Martha McGuire 1 bed and furniture.

BERKELEY, WILLIAM, aged 45 years, 2 Nov. 1769; 28 July, 1772.
Wife Peggy 1/3 of estate and the residue to son John at 21 years.

COLLINSWORTH, JOHN, 9 Oct. 1766; 28 July 1772.
Nephews John and Thomas Collinsworth; son Thomas land and if he die without issue to his brothers John, Jesse and Vincent in succession; daus. Sarah, Peggy and Martha; wife Margaret; bro. Willoughby; personal estate to all children.

HARRISON, JOHN, 4 Apr. 1769; 25 Aug. 1772.
To heirs of son George 1 shilling; son John all land; dau. Abigail; son Robert; grand son Robert Harper; personal estate to all children.

MUSE, JOHN, 5 Jan. 1772; 29 Dec. 1772.
Sons Nicholas, James, Thomas and John; dau. Mary Muse; land and personal estate to all of children.

HUTT, JOHN, 3 Dec. 1772; 29 Dec. 1772.
Sons John and Gerrard Robinson Hutt all lands; son William; dau. Elizabeth R. Hutt; bro. Gerrard Hutt; Gerrard Robinson; residue of estate to all children.

NASH, JOHN, 24 Feb. 1773; 30 Mar. 1773.
Solomon Billings; wife Ann rest of estate.

LAMKIN, GEORGE, 22 Dec. 1772; 30 Mar. 1773.
Wife Agness estate for life and at her death to dau. Lucy and son Youell.

CARPENTER, WILLIAM, 23 Mar. 1773; 31 Mar. 1773.
Debts to be paid and residue of estate to sister Ann Carpenter.

TAYLOR, THOMAS, 25 Sept. 1768; 25 May 1773.
To Jane wife of Thomas Burne 1 cow and calf; to Judith Lilly 1 heifer; to John Stephens 3 negroes and residue of estate.

BERRYMAN, JAMES, 25 Jan. 1772; 27 July 1773.
Son James land in Md.; daus. Katy, Frances and Sarah; sons James, Samuel and Newton; wife Sarah. Estate to wife and children.

VOL. XVI.

MOXLEY, DANIEL, 18 May 1774; no date probate.
Wife Mary estate for life; friends Capt. Thomas and William Chilton; nephew Richard son of Richard Moxley £30.; nephew Joseph son of bro. Joseph 1 negro; Daniel son of nephew a son of bro. Joseph; Daniel son of nephew Richard 1 negro; nephew William son of bro. John rest of estate after death of wife.

McCLANAHAN, PETER, 9 Jan. 1775; no date probate.
Son William land and 1 negro; rest of estate to six children Peter, Thomas, James, Mary, Betty and John.

PINCKARD, THOMAS, 4 Dec. 1776; no date probate.
Wife and sons George Weedon alias Pinckard and Thomas Pinckard estate at death of wife; land in Lancaster to be sold and negroes bought with proceeds.

COLLINS, JOHN, Senr., 30 June 1773; — March 1776.
Dau. Elizabeth Rigg 1 shilling; dau. Jemima Brion 1 shilling; sons Charles and John residue of estate.

SMITH, SPENCE, 18 Aug. 1775; no date probate.
Wife Elizabeth use of estate for life; son Samuel land; son Fleet land in Northumberland; daus. Katy Neale, Jane and Patty Smith; residue of estate to all children.

BAILEY, JOHN, Senr., 11 Jan. 1776; 26 Mar. 1776.
Wife Elizabeth land whereon I live; son Stephen mill, 100 acres land and 2 negroes; dau. Ann and her hus-

band Markham Marshall; sons John and James Bailey
land; grand son Stephen Bailey 50 acres land.

FRANK, ROBERT, 8 Feb. 1776; 24 Sept. 1776.
Wife Mary land and at her death to son Robert and if
he die without issue to son Samuel; son James land;
grand son James Frank.

MONROE, GEORGE, 7 Nov. 1775; 24 Sept. 1776.
Son William a negro man and a negro boy; dau. Sarah
Kitchen 2 negroes and at her death to her dau. Sally;
son Andrew 2 negroes; son John 2 negroes; daus.
Elizabeth, Mary and Molly 2 young negroes each; dau.
in law Elizabeth Monroe 1 negro during widowhood
and at her death or marriage to grand daus. Ann and
Eliz. Monroe.

DEGGES, JAMES, 28 Dec. 1777; 27 Feb. 1778.
8 negroes and land which father purchased of Bunch
Roe to nephew Christopher Edrington; nieces Ann,
Eliz. and Susannah Edrington; nephew James Degge
Dishman land; my sister Harrison's dau. Elizabeth.

JORDAN, ROBERT, 22 Jan. 1776; 24 Sept. 1776.
Son Reuben lands in Richmond and Westmoreland
Cos.; dau. Ann wife of John Rochester 2 negroes and
estate given them at marriage.

DOZER, THOMAS, 23 Feb. 1770; 29 June 1777.
Wife Sarah estate for life and then to son Thomas;
son Joseph 2 cows; residue of estate to all my children;
bro. Richard Dozer.

JORDAN, REUBEN, 7 Dec. 1776; 26 Aug. 1777.
3 year's schooling to god son Longworth son of Burges
Longworth; god son William Rice 2 year's schooling;
nephew William Rochester 1 colt; niece Betsy Rochester 1 colt; bro. in law John Rochester watch and case
of razors; sister Ann Rochester 4 negroes, stock and

land in Richmond Co. and at her death to her son
Robert; nephew John Rochester; wife Ann Jordan may
be with child, she to have 15 negroes, stock, household
furniture and 346 acres land in Westmoreland Co.

EDWARDS, THOMAS, 1 June 1774; 29 Nov. 1774.
Sons William and Thomas 1 gun, horse and negroes;
dau. Mary Sergent Edwards 2 negroes; daus. Franky
and Alice 2 negroes each; wife Alice estate for life and
at her death land to son William; residue of estate to
5 children.

WELCH, THOMAS, 16 Feb. 1777; 29 Mar. 1778. (Nuncupative).
Estate to mother Mary Nugent and at her death to
sister Mary Settles.

SMITH, PETER, Senr., 9 Aug. 1774; no date probate.
Sarah widow of my bro. James Smith care of my daus.
Mary, Nancy, Sallie and Susan for term of 10 years,
she to have use of land, 5.negroes and other per. estate;
if Sarah Smith die my daus. to care of Hannah wife of
Benedict Middleton Sr.; bro. William Smith.

DAVENPORT, JAMES, 30 Apr. 1775; 26 Aug. 1777.
All estate to wife and she to be exx.

CRABB, JOHN, 23 Jan. 1775; 27 Apr. 1779.
Dau. Elizabeth Rogers Middleton 1 negro and 3 head
of cattle; son John 1 negro and my land; dau. Mary
Bennett £5.; son Benedict 4 negroes; dau. Jane Middleton Rust 1 negro; dau. Lettice Crabb 2 negroes; son
William Middleton Crabb 4 negroes and land; John
Middleton gdn. of son William Middleton Crabb.

FEAGINS, WILLIAM, 23 July —; no date probate.
Wife Ann 1/3 estate; children James, George, Thomas
and Betty Feagins; wife Ann, John How and John
Rochester exrs.

WESTMORELAND COUNTY WILLS 171

NASH, JEREMIAH, 10 Nov. 1773! no date probate.
Son Solomon; daus. Mary Ann McKenny, Lydia Nash, Ann Jones stock, cash and house hold furniture.

WASHINGTON, LAWRENCE, 4 Dec. 1773; 29 Mar. 1774.
Wife Susannah 1/3 estate and at her death to daus. Elizabeth Stork and Katy Washington; son Henry land and 3 negroes; bro. in law William Stork Jett; sisters Elizabeth, Ann and Mary Jett and Peggy Skinker; friend John Ashton Sr. my riding horse.

GARNER, JOSEPH, 25 Aug. 1775; 24 Sept. 1776.
All estate to sons Joseph, Benjamin and Nathaniel; daus. Catherine Courtney, Mary Jeffries, Keziah Courtney; grand son Gawin Garner; grand dau. Elizabeth Barecroft; grand son Thomas Garner. Son Joseph and William Barecroft exrs.

BLUNDELL, ABSALOM, 1 Apr. 1774; no date probate.
Son John 1 shilling; son William 1 negro; daus. Sarah Baker Blundell, Suckey Blundell; wife Susannah her dower; sons Thomas and Absalom 1 negro each; dau. Ann Blundell 1 negro; to Molly Randall Delozier 1 negro.

PORTER, ELENDER, 16 Jan. 1778; 31 Aug. 1779.
To heirs of son William 1 shilling; dau. Sarah Headley 1 shilling; dau. Rachel Porter all residue of estate and to be exx.

ROBINSON, HANNAH, 28 July 1778; 29 Sept. 1778.
All estate to sister Apphia Dangerfield and nephew John Pettit; exrs. Beckwith Butler and John Pettit.

BLUNDELL, SUSANNAH, 18 Nov. 1776; 25 Mar. 1777.
1 horse and a gold ring to dau. Molly Randall Delozier; dau. Suckey Blundell silver studs and thimble; son Daniel Delozier 1 horse; children Richard Davis Delozier, Daniel Delozier, Molly Randall Delozier and Sukey Blundell rest of estate.

QUISENBERRY, ANN, 23 Aug. 1773; 29 June 1779.
Sister Elizabeth Quisenberry all of my estate; cousin William Dodd and Nicholas Dodd exrs.

FLOOD, WILLIAM, Dr., 9 Apr. 1775; 27 June 1775.
Land called Kinsail to son William at age of 21 yrs.; son Nicholas; bro. Nicholas; grand son Walter Jones; son William seal with my coat of arms; daus. Elizabeth and Alice Jones; god son Richard Parker Junr.

TEBBS, DANIEL, 25 Feb. 1776; 26 Mar. 1776.
Dau. Martha 6 negroes; son William land in Richmond Co.; dau. Elizabeth 4 negroes; son Fouchee 4 negroes; son Daniel 2 negroes and land in Westmoreland; bro. William Tebbs land given him by my father.

BUTLER, WILLIAM, 5 Sept. 1774; no date probate.
Land in Irish Neck to bro. John Butler; sister Jesse Butler; nephews Thomas and John sons of Benjamin Steward.

BROWN, WILLIAM, 26 Sept. 1774; 24 Sept. 1776.
Son John land in Loudon Co.; dau. Mary Williams 1 shilling; daus. Jane, Hannah, Elizabeth and Sally Brown 1 negro each; son William Brown.

SMITH, SAMUEL, 3 July 1776; 31 Dec. 1776.
Land where I live to wife which adjoins lands of my bros. William and Stephen Smith; son William land; dau. Millia Modiset 1 bed and furniture; grand son Samuel Parsley bed and furniture which I gave my dau. Jane Parsley and now in possession of James Parsley; dau. Alice Smith 1 bed and furniture; sons John, George Bailey and Stephen.

MASSEY, JAMES, 27 Dec. 1777; 25 Aug. 1778.
Wife Sarah all estate and she to be exx.

WESTMORELAND COUNTY WILLS

SMITH, JOHN, 22 Nov. 1777; 24 Nov. 1778.
Wife Elizabeth estate for life; son John; son Augustine land whereon he lives; son Lewis land whereon he lives; my small children; my daus.

RANSDELL, SARAH, 8 Oct. 1778; 27 Mar. 1781.
Dau. Sarah Elliott Pierce my blue cardinal; grand dau. Martha Pierce clothes; grand son Elliott Sturman 40 shillings; son in law Joseph Pierce residue of estate.

WALKER, JAMES, 31 Dec. 1777; 30 June 1778.
Son James now in Great Britain amt. from sale of lands at age of 21 years; bros. Thomas and John Walker now in Gr. Britain; friends William Pierce and John Worden.

QUISENBERRY, HUMPHREY, 30 Jan. 1773; 24 Sept. 1776.
Estate to wife and three children by her, viz: Elizabeth, Peggy and John, dau. Ann Piper 2 negroes; dau. Mary Marshall 1 negro; dau. Bethlune Burshaw 2 negroes; son in law John Pope 5 shillings; exrs. John Carter Senr. and Presley Neale.

BOWCOCK, ANTHONY, 15 Nov. 1777; 25 Nov. 1777.
Cousin John Bowcock land; cousins Richard and Henry Bowcock land; bro. Thomas 1 negro; cousin Mary Ann dau. of James Bowcock decd. residue of estate.

MOORE, JANE, 5 Sept. 1775; no date probate.
Son James Moore 1 mare; dau. Dorcas Moore 1 bed and furniture; Hannah Moore 1 spinning wheel; Jane Lamkin Moore a feather bed and furniture; Sammy Lamkin Moore 1 chest and pewter plates; son Garland Moore exr.

MOXLEY, RICHARD, 5 Jan. 1776; 27 May 1777.
Son Richard 1 negro; dau. Mary Leftwich 1 bed and

furniture; grand ch. Daniel and Katy Moxley land, Mary Moxley £25, Nancy Leftwich 1 negro, and Mary Leftwich 1 negro; son Alvin Moxley rest of estate.

BAYN, WILLIAM, 15 Feb. 1778; 27 Oct. 1778.
Son John land and 1 negro when 21 years of age; use of stock &c for wife Elizabeth and all my children.

BUTLER, LAWRENCE, 18 Nov. 1773; 29 July 1777.
Daus. Joice, Sarah, Elizabeth and Jane 1 negro each; sons Christopher, John, Griffin and Lawrence; wife Eleanor 1 negro. Lands to be sold and money to all children.

CARTER, BENJAMIN, 20 May 1776; 29 June 1779.
Grand father Benjamin Tasker late of Md. decd.; grand mother Ann Tasker decd. each of whom bequeathed me £1000 which I bequeath to my father Robert Carter Esq.

HARRISON, DANIEL, 12 July 1774; 26 Mar. 1782.
Son William Lewis land; son Willoughby; wife Eleanor; children Sally, Daniel and James; bro. Joshua Harrison exr.; estate equally between wife and 5 children.

GILBERT, JANE, 11 Jan. 1778; 31 Mar. 1778.
Dau. Agness Harrison 1 negro; son Youel Rust £30, a table and Dutch oven; grand dau. Nancy 1 bed and furniture.

HILTON, WILLIAM, 17 Dec. 1777; 27 Jan. 1778.
Land, colt and shoe tools to son John; wife Mary her dower; residue of estate to all my children.

HAILEY, RICHARD, 20 Sept. 1774; no date probate.
Furniture and clothes to sons John and Anthony Gerrard; John son of Frances Tupman my gun; to Sarah Hails the clothes of my decd. wife; 1 mare to eldest

son of dau. Mary Rush; grand son Richard Gerrard eldest son of Anthony Gerrard by my dau. tobacco money in hands of Benj. Monroe.

HUNTER, JAMES, 6 Oct. 1777; 30 June 1778.
To wife Winifred if she remain single until son John is of age which will be Sept. 3d 1788; sons William and James £10 each; residue of estate to all my children.

SMITH, SARAH, 21 Jan. 1779; 30 Mar. 1779.
To be buried in Cople Parish Glebe garden at feet of nephew and niece Gregory and Lucy Smith; bro. Edward Smith my negro maid Judy; niece Mary Jacquelin Smith dau. of my sister Mary Smith 3 negroes; niece Ann Smith dau. of same 2 negroes; niece Sarah Smith dau. of same £200; sister Martha Jacquelin Smith £10 for a mourning ring; bros. John and Edward Smith rest of estate.

WROE, ORIGINAL, 21 Apr. 1772; 31 May 1774.
To sons William and Richard lands in Westmoreland and Culpeper Cos.; son Benjamin land; son John 1 shilling; son Thomas land in Culpeper; son Regiland 400 acres land; his sons Taylor and John; dau. Judith Briggs 1 negro until David Briggs come of age; dau. Elizabeth Scott 1 negro, cow and calf; dau. Susannah Edwards 1 negro; dau. Lucretia Wroe 1 negro, bed and furniture, a cow and calf.

MONROE, SPENCE, 16 Feb. 1774; no date probate.
Land to sons James and Spence; son in law William Buckner 1 bed, riding chair; sons Andrew and Joseph Jones rest of estate; bro. in law Joseph Jones and James Bankhead exrs.; dau. Elizabeth Buckner 3 negroes.

PEYTON, JOHN, 13 Mar. 1774; 30 June 1778.
Sons John and William land each; sons Wharton and

Thomas exrs.; wife Margaret use of estate for younger children after which all estate to all of my children.

MUSE, NICHOLAS, 4 May 1778; 30 Mar. 1779.
To wife Elizabeth 100 acres land in Loudon Co.; sons Jeremiah, Walker and Jesse; daus. Penelope Muse, Elizabeth Washington, Mary Randall and Ann Washington 15 shillings each; bro. Daniel Muse.

ROBINSON, HARRY, 22 Sept. 1777; 29 Sept. 1778.
Mother land in King George; William and Alice children of my bro. William 1/3 of estate each at death of my mother.

COURTNEY, LEONARD, Senr., 28 July 1780; 28 Nov. 1780.
Sons James and Leonard land in Fauquier; younger sons William and George; dau. Peggy Courtney a loom and wheels; wife Kezia; grand son Samuel Courtney 1 shilling; daus. Sally Turner and Mary 1 shilling each. Rest of estate to all my children.

CHANDLER, ELIZABETH, ———; 28 Mar. 1780.
To dau. Jane Chandler all estate; John Bailey trustee and exr.

MCKENNY, VINCENT, 9 Oct. 1779; 28 Mar. 1780.
Wife Ann lease of land whereon I live; son Rodham lease with wife; rest of estate to my sons and daughters.

JACKSON, WILLIAM, Senr., 2 June 1780; 25 July 1780.
Sister Elizabeth Franklin 1 negro; to William Franklin 1 mare and colt; to Jane Nash 1 cow and calf.

DRAKE, RICHARD, of King George, 30 Aug. 1760; 25 July 1780.
Son William land; son in law John Green land; wife Frances and children, viz: Elizabeth, Sarah, Eleanor, Thomas, James, Sukey, John, Richard and child unborn; cousin Thomas Drake exr.

KITCHEN, SARAH, 19 Oct. 1789; 31 Oct. 1780.
To dau. Sally my dower in estate of Anthony Kitchen; bro. William Monroe exr.

CARTER, JANE, 15 Feb. 1781; 27 Feb. 1781.
Sons James and John Carpenter; James Nash; dau. Anne Carpenter; dau. Elizabeth Carter; son William Carter; stock and furniture to each.

GRIGGS, WILLIAM, 18 Apr. 1778; 31 July 1781.
Son John; son William under 21 years; wife Mary estate and then to all my children.

COLLINGSWORTH, JOHN, Senr., 17 May 1781; 28 Aug. 1781.
All estate to sons William and Nathaniel; father in law Nathaniel Butler and bro. in law William Smith exrs.

JETT, ANN, 10 Sept. 1781; 25 Sept. 1782.
Grand son Burket 1 cow, bed and furniture; grand dau. Ann Bernard tea chest, spoons and tongs; grand son William Storke Jett large looking glass; son Thomas Jett exr.

RUST, PETER, 6 Mar. 1781; 26 Mar. 1782.
Land to sons Samuel and Peter Cox Rust; youngest son Jeremiah 1 negro and land; daus. Elizabeth, Jane, Charlotte, Mary, Sophia, Harriett; Lucinda and Caroline residue of estate; wife Rebecca her dower; exrs. John Rust, John Crabb, Jeremiah Garland Bailey.

TURNBULL, STEPHEN, 1 Nov. 1783; 30 Mar. 1784.
To be buried by decd. wife; estate equally among children Margaret, Elizabeth, James, George and Reuben.

BERRYMAN, WILLIAM, 21 Aug. 1783; 30 Mar. 1784.
Eldest son Benjamin now decd.; his sons Willoughby Newton and Henry Eskridge Berryman; Mrs. Rose

Grigsby of Stafford slaves; sons Newton, John, Thomas and Gerrard land and negroes; daus. Winifred and Elizabeth 4 negroes each; son Thomas Newton a silver can and silver spoons with crest of Newtons on handle; sons Waters, Gerrard, Thomas, Francis and Josias rest of estate.

SANFORD, WILLIAM, 31 May 1782; 30 Mar. 1784.
Son Charles land; son Richard furniture &c; son William a Bible; son Jeremiah 2 cows and calves; dau. Mary Bulger a safe and table; dau. Sarah Marmanduke a chest; wife Barbara rest of estate and at her death to all children.

HARRISON, SAMUEL, — —; 27 Apr. 1784.
Land to wife and at her death to son Peter; dau. Elsey Harrison 1 year's schooling; to Thomas and Hannah Harrison residue of estate.

WEEKS, BENJAMIN, 2 Dec. 1782; 27 Apr. 1784.
Grand son Benjamin Pope Smith 2 negroes; grand son Benj. Weeks son of Charles Weeks Steel 2 negroes; dau. Sucetty Smith 4 head cattle and 2 negroes; dau. Mary Weeks Steel now living with me land I live on and 1 other tract; dau. Selia Weeks 400 acres land; 2 grand sons land in Richmond Co.

STEPTOE, GEORGE, (Dr.) 22 Jan. 1783; 27 May 1784.
To wife Elizabeth land called Windsor near the court house; child unborn; son Edward residue of estate; bros. James and William Steptoe exrs.

MULLINS, PETER, 23 June 1780; 25 May 1784.
Wife Elizabeth land and at her death to be sold and money used to school 12 poor children who live within 3 miles of Ycomoco Church for 2 years, then 12 more and so on until all money spent save £5. which is for care of graveyard.

DOLMAN, WILLIAM, 31 July 1783; 25 May 1784.
Wife Mary to enjoy estate for life; two sons John Henry and William estate in Gr. Britain; daus. Betsy and Peggy Dolman equal part of estate yearly; children 1 negro each and kept in school.

DRAKE, SARAH, 5 Feb. 1784; 29 June 1784.
Entire estate to son Benjamin.

MEEKS, ANN, 1 Apr. 1784; 27 July 1784.
To Winny Sanford a desk; Ann Y. Kelsick; Henry S. Redman; William Redman Kelsick; sister Sarah Smith a bed and loom; sister Elizabeth Foster my cloth coat; sister Judith Nash my gilt trunk; niece Ann Meeks Packett a gold ring and silver buckles; to Lawrence Waddy Sanford and his son Richard 1 cow; Sally Sanford a bed and furniture left me by Solomon Redman.

MCKENNEY, JOHN, Sen., 12 May 1784; 31 Aug. 1784.
Sons Duke and Joseph land I live on; dau. Barbara Moore; wife Nelly estate I had by marriage with her in lieu of dower; residue of estate to 3 children.

JEFFRIES, ROBERT, 28 Feb. 1784; 30 Nov. 1784.
Estate for life to wife Mary; to John and dau. Catherine Elinore land where they live; son Robert land and if he die without issue to son Jeremiah; son James clothes.

MUSE, JAMES, 20 July 1784; 30 Nov. 1784.
3 negroes, 1 horse to wife Susanna; son Charles clothes; son Lawrence my stock buckle and fiddle; niece Peggy Smith a colt; friends Hudson Muse and Daniel Muse of Northumberland exrs.

WEAVER, JOHN, 28 July 1783; 30 Nov. 1784.
15 acres of land and a bed to bro. Zachariah Weaver; to Eliz. Bayn 1 bed and furniture; to John son of Benj. Weaver 1 Bible, cloth and buttons; bro. Abraham

Weaver 1 saddle and bridle; Robert Moxley and Joseph Moxley Jr.; wife Sarah rest of estate for life, then to Daniel Weaver; Thomas Pritchett the boy I raised.

DEANE, CHARLES, 26 Feb. 1784; 30 Nov. 1784.
Wife Mary 1/3 land, slaves, furniture and stock; sister Lucy Nowel 1 bed and furniture; dau. Anne Deane 1 negro, feather bed and rest of estate.

BUTLER, WILLIAM, 7 Oct. 1784; 30 Nov. 1784.
Estate I got by her and 1 horse to wife Celia; father and mother Nathaniel and Anne Butler residue of estate and at their death to bro. John Butler; sisters Hannah, Betsey, Nelly and Sally Butler estate left to bro. John if he die single.

MCKENNEY, GERRARD, 25 Nov. 1784; 30 Nov. 1784.
Dau. Lettice Porter 1 negro, bed and fur.; son Gerrard 1 negro, bed and fur.; daus. Diana and Katy 1 negro, bed and fur.; dau. Sarah same; son Armstrong same and 1 cow.

FURGESON, MARGARET, 25 Oct. 1784; 25 Jan. 1785.
To William and Isaac sons of my decd. bro. George Stone, the estate I am entitled to at the death of my husband.

SANFORD, MARGARET, 16 Dec. 1784; 22 Feb. 1785.
Sons Reuben and William 27 acres land each; dau. Barbara Sanford a mare and saddle; grand dau. Peggy Sanford 1 horse; residue of estate to all my children.

DEATTERLY, MATHEW, 21 Jan. 1782; 22 Feb. 1785.
Estate to wife Elizabeth for life; sons George, James, John and Thomas estate at death of wife.

POPE, JOHN, 29 Nov. 1784; 29 Mar. 1785.
My wife; sons Elliott, William, Ransdell, John and Thomas all estate; Capt. Benjamin Strother exr.

BUTLER, SARAH, 4 Nov. 1784; 26 Apr. 1785.
Bro. Lawrence Butler 1 negro; niece Elcey Butler 1 negro boy; sister Jane Butler a negro woman for life then to children of bro. Christopher Butler; sister Joice 1 mare.

ATTWELL, RICHARD, 6 Feb. 1782; 28 June 1785.
Son William a horse and gun; my youngest son; wife Mary and my children all estate.

BANKHEAD, JAMES, 8 Jan. 1785; 28 June 1785.
3 negroes and a child's part to my wife; my children; bros. William and John; bros. in law William and Thomas Miller exrs.

VOL. XVII.

THOMSON, WILLIAM, 29 Jan. 1785; 28 June 1785.
Estate for life to wife Ann and at her death to children Richard, Betsey, Lovel, Maria and William; mother in law Margaret Thomson; dau. Margaret land of her grand father Hales.

GREEN, WILLIAM, 3 Sept. 1783; 26 July 1785.
Wife Sarah 1/3 of estate; sons Burkett and Reuben land; son John 2 horses; daus. Letty and Molly 1 feather bed each; daus. Sarah and Margaret 1 colt each.

BENNETT, 12 Mar. 1785; 30 Aug. 1785.
Wife Mary all of estate.

BRAND, NICHOLAS, 17 June 1784; 31 Aug. 1784.
Wife Mary all estate after debts are paid.

BOWCOCK, THOMAS, 6 Aug. 1784; 30 Aug. 1785.
Daus. Sally Bowcock, Susanna Dowling, and Caty Bowcock 1 negro each; dau. Elizabeth Spellman 2 negroes; son Henry 3 negroes.

JETT, THOMAS, 14 Feb. 1785; 25 Oct. 1785.
1/2 of land and stock given by deed to son William Storke Jett; dau. Ann Bernard a gold ring; dau. Mary Storke a gold ring; grand son Thomas Bernard 1 negro girl; Henry son of Lawrence Washington who died in 1776; slaves; nephew Birkett Jett 1 negro; grand son Thomas Storke £200; wife Sukey plantation, 5 negroes

and £5. a year, the mill and at her death to son William Storke Jett; exr. Col. John Skinker.

SANFORD, AUGUSTINE, 30 May 1785; 25 Oct. 1785.
Wife Henrietta estate for life; son Robert land from estate of my uncle John Sanford; sons Richard and Thomas Randall Sanford land; son Augustine 1 negro, horse and £25; dau. Mary Thorn 6 pewter plates and 1 gilt trunk; dau. Elizabeth Gilbert otherwise Rust 6 pewter plates and a leather trunk.

SANFORD, WILLOUGHBY, 5 Dec. 1785; 28 Nov. 1786.
Dau. Ann Templeman 1 shilling only; dau. Elizabeth Barnett 1 shilling only; dau. Mary Butler Harrison Sanford 1 shilling; son John land whereon I live; residue of estate to raise and educate my young children.

MIDDLETON, BENEDICT, 29 May 1782; 27 Sept. 1785.
Wife Hannah use of lands for life, ½ of negroes and personal estate, but if she marry 1/3 of estate; other 2/3 of negroes and personal estate to grand son Benedict Lamkin and my 5 daus. Elizabeth Lewis, Jane Wroe, Hannah, Martha and Ann Middleton; my dau. Elizabeth her share for life and then to children she had by her first husband Mr. Francis Wright decd. and may have by her husband Mr. George Lewis; exx. wife Hannah; exrs. bro. in law Col. Joseph Lane, my nephew Capt. William Middleton and grand son Benedict Lamkin.

BRINNON, JOHN, — —; 30 JUNE 1778.
Wife Hannah estate for life; dau. Ann Crenshaw 1 negro at death of wife; grand daus. Hannah and Ann Rice; dau. Hannah Holland 1 negro at death of wife; dau. Elizabeth Brinnon 1 negro at death of wife; sons John and George land and negroes.

SANFORD, JOHN, 1 Oct. 1776; 27 Oct. 1778.
Grand children Francis Sanford, Jemima Spence, Molly Harrison, Butler and John Sanford; son Wil-

loughby 1 shilling; son in law Thomas Sanford and dau. Jemima Sanford 1 negro, they to be exrs.; wife Sibella use of 1 negro, cow, ewes, bed and fur. for life.

SORRELL, JUDITH, 6 Feb. 1786; 28 Feb. 1786.
Son Thomas 40 shillings; son James rest of estate, lands and negroes.

GORDON, GEORGE, 8 Oct. 1784; 28 Feb. 1786.
Estate in Va. to wife Ursula; son George land in Westmoreland and 8 negroes; son John land in Sheepbridge, Lisduff, etc., in Co. of Down, Ireland; daus. Hannah and Betty Gordon 2 negroes and £200. and arrears in rent due by Mr. Samuel Gordon in Ireland.

RUST, JOHN, 7 Sept. 1785; 28 Feb. 1786.
Land called Essex Lodge in Northumberland to wife Jane, also my negroes and other personal estate and at her death to my children John, Elizabeth, Jane and Molly Rust; bro. Peter Rust.

FITZHUGH, DANIEL, 17 Sept. 1777; 28 Mar. 1786.
To be buried in bro. William's burying yard; son William negroes which I had by his mother Catherine; dau. Jane negroes which I had with her mother Elcey; dau. Sukey negroes I had with her mother Susanna, also sum due from estate of Philip Grymes which was due my wife Susanna; bro. William's children by his wife Hannah; niece Lucy Fitzhugh 1 negro; nieces Ann and Sally daus. of bro. William; nephew McCarty Fitzhugh; friend William Fitzhugh of Chatham.

MONROE, JEMIMA, 2 Dec. 1785; 25 Apr. 1786.
Dau. Elizabeth Monroe ½ estate; son William the other half; exr. Benjamin Monroe.

HIPKINS, RICHARD, 17 Mar. 1786; 25 Apr. 1786.
Son Robert Spottswood Hipkins land; son Thomas negroes; son William Augustus land on Popes Creek; my wife 1/3 estate for life; daus. Mary, Elizabeth and

Charlotte have been provided for by inheritance from their mother and legacies from their grand mother.

HARRISON, MAGDALEN, 16 Dec. 1775; 27 June 1786.
Son Jeremiah 2 feather beds; dau. Hannah Gilbert residue of estate; husband Samuel Harrison.

SANFORD, EDWARD, 25 Dec. 1785; 25 July 1786.
Home plantation and stock to wife Catherine, alias Pope; son Patrick land; son Edward Sanford alias Pope land; heirs of dau. Jemima Stone 1 shilling; heirs of dau. Susanna Sutton 1 shilling; son Robert Sanford alias Pope; son Richard Sanford alias Pope; daus. Elizabeth and Katy Sanford alias Pope 1 negro; grand dau. Eliz. Spence Sutton £10.

BAILEY, DANIEL, 17 Oct. 1785; 30 Nov. 1786.
Bros. John, Samuel and Vincent Smith Bailey.

BRICKEY, PETER, 16 Sept. 1786; 27 Feb. 1787.
Estate for life to wife Winifred; 1 negro each to sons Gerrard, John, Peter and William; gr. son Peter son of Gerrard; gr. son Gerrard son of John; gr. children John and Nancy Kirkham; gr. dau. Winny Lucas Garner; daus. Temperance Morgan, Dorcus Garner, Ann Sanford and Winifred Kirkham; one slave each to daus. and grand children and rest of estate at death of wife.

BEALE, THOMAS, 10 Jan. 1786; 26 June 1787.
Wife Elizabeth estate for life; son William; son Samuel 75 acres land where I live; daus. Alice Rust, Massey, Brand and Elizabeth Olive; daus. to have their parts.

SMITH, WILLIAM, 8 Sept. 1784; 28 Nov. 1786.
Wife Hannah; son Samuel and the rest of my children.

WASHINGTON, JOHN, 3 July 1785; 26 June 1787.
Estate for life to wife Constant and at her death to be sold and money divided among children; child unborn; dau. Sarah Harper 1 ring only as she has her estate; son William Henry seal with family arms on it; son Robert Lund Washington books and saddle; son Robert Townsend W. decd.; my seven ch. Thomas Terrett, William Henry, Thomas Lund, Robert Pitt, George, Louisa Fassaker, Nancy Constantia and child unborn. Exrs. William Fitzhugh of Chatham and my nephew Henry Washington.

LACY, JOSEPH, 13 Feb. 1785; 25 Sept. 1787.
Dau. Margaret Lacy 1 bed and furniture; wife Jane and all my children residue of estate.

MASSEY, LOVELL, 22 Nov. 1777; 30 June 1778.
Daus. Sukey and Patty Massey land given me by my father where my mother lives; wife use of estate during widowhood and she to be exx.

QUISENBERRY, ELIZABETH, 23 May 1784; 22 Feb. 1785.
A horse to Elijah son of William Weaver; to Richard son of same 1 feather bed and furniture; William and Nicholas Dodd 1 horse, bed and fur.; Ann Weaver clothes and saddle and then saddle to her dau. Elizabeth Bayn; a pewter dish and iron spitts to William Quisenberry; John Quisenberry rest of estate.

MORGAN, DANIEL, 20 Sept. 1782; 26 Aug. 1789.
To wife 1/3 of estate; Daniel son of David Morgan my bro. £50; bros. William, Andrew and Benjamin Morgan residue of estate.

CRABB, JANE, 19 Dec. 1773; 30 Oct. 1781.
Son Gerrard 1 shilling; son Vincent 1 bed and cow; son

Osmund estate left dau. Sukey Garner and rest of estate after grand son Abraham Garner has 1 shilling.

FRESHWATER, GEORGE, 14 Dec. 1779; 25 Apr. 1780.
Daus. Mary, Eliz. Ann and Sarah 2 shillings each; son Thomas and wife Elenor each one half of estate.

JETT, CATHERINE, 7 Nov. 1786; 27 Feb. 1787.
Land in King George to be sold and amount paid to daus. Betty and Frances Jett who are also to have 1200 lbs. tobacco; dau. Ann Brown 1 cow, blankets etc; Peter Jett exr.

RANSDELL, EDWARD, 19 June 1773; 30 Nov. 1773.
Land in fee to wife Elizabeth; dau. Elizabeth wife of James Davenport 1 negro woman in trust for her use; Mr. Richard Parker £5 for services rendered; nephew Presley son of bro. Wharton Ransdell 1 ring; nephew Edward son of bro. William a gold ring.

TIDWELL, ANN, 20 Oct. 1784; 28 Mar. 1786.
Daus. Ann and Barbara Tidwell and Betty Muse; son Joseph Sanford; dau. Becky Dozier and her dau. Sarah all personal estate; Thomas Muse and Richard Dozier exrs.

SMITH, PETER, 1 Apr. 1774; — Aug. 1774.
Son Peter 20 shillings; son John land; grand son Peter Smith land; dau. Mary Holloway 20 shillings; dau. Dorcas Neale 1 negro; grand ch. William and Eliz. Turner 20 shillings each.

VOL. XVIII.

WASHINGTON, JOHN AUGUSTINE, 2 June 1784; codicil 19 Nov. 1785; 31 July 1787.
Wife Hannah 1/3 of negroes and ½ other personal estate during widowhood; son Bushrod; son Corbin lands in Loudon and Berkeley Cos.; dau. Jenny Washington £600 with money and negroes advanced her husband; her husband William Augustine Washington; grand dau. Ann Aylette Washington 1 negro girl; dau. Mildred Washington £1000, 1 negro and land conveyed by my mother Mrs. Mary W. and that bought of Robert Washington; my esteemed bro. Gen. George Washington, wife, sons Richard Bushrod and Corbin exrs.

WASHINGTON, WILLIAM, 2 Mar. 1786; 25 Mar. 1788.
Niece Peggy Buckner 6 negro girls; nephew John Hooe Washington 1 negro; nephew Richard Henry Buckner choice of riding horses; bro. John Washington land and rest of estate.

TURNER, THOMAS, 2 June 1787; 30 Oct. 1787.
To wife Jane 1/3 of estate, plate and chariot; dau. Eliz. Cock £500; dau. Jean Turner 1 negro and £1000; eldest son Henry Smith Turner land; sons Thomas, George and Richard lands near Port Conway the latter to have that at Port Royal.

DRAKE, BENJAMIN, 1 Mar. 1788; 29 Apr. 1788.
Cousin Jessy Green all estate and to be exr.

OMOHUNDRO, THOMAS, 14 Apr. 1788; 29 July 1788.
Dau. Ann Moxley 1 negro; her dau. Molly Moxley a cow and calf; son Thomas land, furniture, horse and saddle; son William same; sons Bruce and Richard 1 negro each; dau. Martha Omohundro 1 negro girl; wife Martha.

GILBERT, WILLIAM, 16 Feb. 1785; 29 July 1788.
Wife Hannah estate for life; son William land at her death; residue of estate to children Nancy, Samuel, Uel and child unborn.

CARTER, ANN, 5 Jan. 1789; 31 Mar. 1789.
Sons Robert, Samuel, John, George; daus. Ann Annadale and Sarah Payne 5 shillings each; daus. Mary Neale, Jane and Lucy Carter colt and beds; sons Presley and Richard 1/5 of estate each; son in law Presley Neale and Daniel McCarty exrs.

GILBERT, MARTHA, 7 Aug. 1775; 28 July 1789.
Sister Mary clothes; to Ann Smithy 1 bed; bro. in law William Morton my money.

BENNETT, THOMAS, 15 Oct. 1787; 25 Aug. 1789.
Entire estate to son Richard.

MIDDLETON, JOHN, 3 Jan. 1789; 25 Aug. 1789.
Wife Martha all lands and personal estate save 1 negro woman to son Jeremiah when 21 years of age; said Jeremiah land where Thomas Walker lives, 1/3 of negroes at death of his mother; dau. Sally Middleton £50 and 1/3 of negroes at death of mother; exrs. Richard Bennett and George Middleton.

SMITH, THOMAS, Rector of Cople Parish, 14 Dec. 1788; 27 Oct. 1789.

Lands to sons Thomas Gregory and John Augustine at 21 and £20 each; wife Mary her dower, 2 negroes, chariot and horses; dau. Sarah 1 negro, 1 bed and fur.; 1 negro to Mr. Philip Lee who married my dau. Mary; god son Baldwin Mathews Lee 20 guineas; bro. Col. Gregory Smith.

SMITH, JACOB, 20 May 1789; 27 Oct. 1789.
Son Henry 1 negro and a gun; wife Ann estate for life and then to children Francis, Henry and Jacob.

PAYNE, GEORGE, 6 Apr. 1787; 26 Jan. 1790.
Bro. Richard decd.; sons William, George, John and Richard; daus. Jane Kelly and Mary Morris 2 negroes each; bro. Daniel Payne.

BRISCOE, DANIEL, town of Leeds, 2 Apr. 1789; 27 Apr. 1790.
Wife Elizabeth a suit of mourning and what the law provides; residue of estate to my 5 children John, Elizabeth, Ellen, Martha and Lucy.

SHOATS, GEORGE, 8 Apr. 1790; 25 May 1790.
Dau. Mary Butler 1 negro and 1 horse; dau. Eliz. Shoats 1 negro, 1 horse and furniture.

JETT, JOHN, 2 March 1790; 29 June 1790.
Wife Isabel estate for life and at her death to children Burkett, Newton and Ann Jett who are to be sent to school.

OMOHUNDRO, JAMES, 31 Oct. 1788; 27 July 1790.
Son William land; sons James and Richard 1 shilling each; dau. Ann 1 shilling; wife Elizabeth.

COLLINSWORTH, SARAH, 23 May 1790; 28 Dec. 1790.
To John Collinsworth land left by my father and if he die without issue to William Steel and then to Thomas son of William Franklin.

MIDDLETON, WILLIAM, 26 June 1790; 25 Jan. 1791.
Son Robert lands in Westmoreland and Richmond Cos.; son William manor plantation in Northumberland and purchased of George Eskridge; son John land in Northumberland and 2 negroes; daus. Eliz. and Mary Fleet Middleton land adjoining Mr. Fleet Cox Sr.; dau. Hannah Middleton land adjoining Benjamin Middleton; rest of estate to 5 children.

ATWELL, JOHN, 24 Nov. 1790; 25 Jan. 1791.
Nephew John son of bro. Francis; bro. William Atwell; bro. Youell Atwell's estate; sister Martha Sorrell; to Eliz. Humes and William Redman Jr.

DOZIER, RICHARD, 12 Jan. 1786; 30 May 1791.
James son of Richard Dozier Jr.; nephew Joseph Dozier; nephew Thomas Dozier; niece Betty Walker Dozier.

ATWELL, YOUELL, 1 Jan. 1787; 30 May 1791.
All of estate to Thomas and Daniel sons of Richard Atwell.

SELF, JOHN, 15 Nov. 1790; 26 Apr. 1791.
Wife Anne estate for life; John Cole Self land and to pay his bro. Presley £5; daus. Mary, Margaret and Nelly 1 bed and furniture each; all my children Presley, Elizabeth Wodgerd, John Cole, Mary, Margaret and Elender Self and Ann Moss residue of estate.

DISHMAN, JOHN, 17 Jan. 1790; 26 Apr. 1791.
Wife Anne use of whole estate for life as compensation for her uniform, steady and affectionate deportment to me and also her indefatigable industry, frugality and economy by which it has been acquired. At her death to my children as she sees fit.

DISHMAN, ANN, 20 Mar. 1791; 26 Apr. 1791.
Son William land and 4 negroes; dau. Ann Richardson

2 slaves for life and then to her two children; dau. Elizabeth 2 negroes, a bed and horse; son Samuel plantation in King George; to dau. Frances or rather to Charles Dean what he already has; to Thomas Chancellor who married my dau. Sally 20 shillings; if son William marry one of daus. of Thomas King contrary to wishes of his father and myself to have no part of my estate and it to Samuel, Ann and Elizabeth.

MUSE, GEORGE, 3 May 1791; 2 June 1791.
Daus. Ann Sanford Hall, Peggy and Elizabeth Muse; son George; five small children Burkett, Franky, Rebecca, Eleanor and George; friends Richard Muse and Newton Hall exrs.

COX, FLEET, 7 Jan. 1791; 28 June 1791.
Cherry Point land and 14 negroes to son Peter Presley; sons John, James and Richard land and slaves; dau. Molly Middleton land and brick house where my father lived; dau. Betty Downing a horse and chair; son in law Thomas Downing; son Fleet residue estate

PAYTON, GEORGE C., 12 Nov. 1790; 28 June 1791.
Bro. Anthony Payton land which I sold him; sister Ann Drake corn, cotton and tobacco crop; sister Elizabeth Butler 1 negro in possession of my grand mother.

CLARK, MARGARET, 23 Nov. 1790; 28 June 1791.
Son William Morton Clark 2 negroes and a colt; bro. and sister James and Hannah Morton; father William Morton.

FIELDAN, EDWARD, 8 Aug. 1791; 30 Aug. 1791.
Wife Jane 1/3 land on Greenbrier; son John ½ of land; if son in law William Siddon will go and settle on it he to have ½, 66 2/3 acres on Muddy Creek, Greenbrier.

BAILEY, JEREMIAH GARLAND, 25 Mar. 1791; 25 Oct. 1791.

Estate to be equally divided among all children and
child unborn; if wife choose to have houses built on
her land in Richmond Co.; exrs. son Stephen, John
Sydnor of Richmond Co., Thomas Sanford and Benj.
Middleton.

PAYTON, WILLIAM, 14 Mar. 1791; 25 Oct. 1791.
Wife Mary estate for life then to son James and all
my children; bro. John exr.

JETT, WILLIAM, 21 June 1791; 25 Oct. 1791.
All my land to dau. Peggy Jett Bartlett; Anthony Payton exr.

MUSE, ELIZABETH, 23 May 1791; 29 Nov. 1791.
Sons Jeremiah and Walker Muse; dau. Penelope Muse;
grand dau. Betsey Muse.

MUSE, MARY, 26 Oct. 1790; 28 Feb. 1792.
Niece Susannah Muse; sister in law Eliz. Muse;
nephew Elliott Muse; bros. James, Thomas and
Nicholas Muse.

STURMAN, ELLIOTT, 26 Feb. 1791; 4 Mar. 1792.
Wife Mary; sons William Young and Foxhall the latter
under 21; nephew Elliott Muse.

BUTLER, JANE, 5 Mar. 1791; 27 Mar. 1792.
Cattle to sister Eliz. Briscoe; Eliz. dau. of William
Butler; niece Elcey Butler rest of stock and at her
death to her children Elis. and Wesley Butler; nephew
William Butler exr.

GREOGORY, JAMES, 3 Mar. 1791; 27 Mar. 1792.
Wife Catherine Carr Gregory 40 acres land; son Daniel
Thomas 40 acres; children George Carneby, James G.,
Joseph Carr, John G., Lettice Anthony and Sarah Carr
Howell wife of John Howell.

BUTLER, NATHANIEL, 6 May 1792; 29 May 1792.
Dau. Sarah 2 negroes, bed and furniture; dau. Lee Anna Malser Smith 1 negro during widowhood and then to her son Samuel Smith; grand sons John Butler Pope and William Butler Smith 1 negro each; grand dau. Ann Butler 1 negro child.

HUTCHINGS, JOHN, 24 Oct. 1791; 30 Oct. 1792.
Son William 3 negroes, stock; dau. Betseey 4 negroes, 1 bed and she to live with her aunt Judy Brent.

SUTTON, JOSIAH, 12 Aug. 1792; 27 Nov. 1792.
To Samuel Davis land in Campbell County 200 acres; to Elizabeth Davis part of land in Westmoreland; residue of estate to bro. Jesse Sutton and mother Susa Weston.

TURBEVILLE, GEORGE, 29 June 1790; 29 Jan. 1793.
Of Pecatone, Cople Parish; son Gawin Corbin land which belonged to his grand father Gawin Corbin; son George Richard Lee land which belonged to my father George Turbeville; dau. Hannan Lee Turbeville.

HARRISON, HANNAH, 6 Nov. 1791; 26 Mar. 1793.
Dau. Hannah Harrison 2 negroes and furniture; son Alexander 2 negroes, he to pay my dau. Harriet Peoples £50; my late husband Lovell Harrison; son Joseph; daus. Mary Lovell and Ann Muse.

WRIGHT, FRANCIS, 5 Dec. 1775; 26 Mar. 1793.
Wife Elizabeth house and one third of land; sons Bernard, Johnson and Wright Wright;; exrs. Capt. Benedict Middleton and Fleet Cox.

MIDDLETON, GEORGE, 26 Apr. 1793; 30 July 1793.
God son George M. Wright my silver watch; to Mrs. Eliz. widow of Jeremiah Rust my negro woman and her 3 children; estate bequeathed me by my father to Jeremiah Middleton; George W. Wright and Matilda

Middleton Bennett; all negroes I got by my marriage to Thomas, Mary, Eliz., Sarah and Martha Rust children of Jeremiah Rust.

MORTON, WILLIAM, 11 July 1793; 30 July 1793.
Wife Ann 1/3 estate, 1 bed and furniture; son James 150 acres land; dau. Hannah 1 negro; grand son William Morton Clark £30.

ROSE, FRANCIS, 1 Oct. 1791; 31 Dec. 1793.
Son William 1 shilling; dau. Frances Cecil 1 shilling; wife Mary residue of estate for life and then to my children Bennett, John, Joel and James.

SANFORD, YOUELL, 16 Nov. 1793; 28 Jan. 1794.
Wife Eleanor and then to her son Robert Sanford; sons Daniel and William; daus. Barbara; Caty, Peggy, Jemima, Matilda and Frances; sons Thomas, John and Presley.

TEMPLEMAN, THOMAS, 8 Sept. 1793; 25 Feb. 1794.
Sons Samuel and Thomas; daus. Molly and Fanny; bro. Samuel Templeton and his wife Ann exrs. Land in Hampshire Co. contains 400 acres.

HARVEY, MUNGO, 8 Feb. 1794; 29 Apr. 1794.
To son James land, books; son John land and books; daus. Ann, Sarah and Eliza rest of estate; my wife to have house built for use of her and my family.

VOL. XIX.

BUCKNER, RICHARD, 15 October 1793; 29 April 1794.
A tomb stone to be erected to "Richard and Elizabeth Buckner" nine months after my death. Bro. Francis Buckner's estate. Son Aris Buckner 4 negroes more than he has; gr. son James Richard Miller; gr. dau. Lucy Roy Miller; wife Elizabeth residue of estate and she to be executrix.

RUST, VINCENT, 28 September 1793; 29 April 1794.
Wife Anne estate for life and at her death to grand son George Vincent Cox Hudson, s. of Robert and Anne Hudson, Vincent Rust Payne Wright s. of Bennett and Molly Wright, dau. Winifred Cox Rust, Hannah Rust. Son Mathew Rust disinherited. Richard Lee Esq., Mr. Fleet Cox and Capt. Geo. Garner exrs.

RICHARD HENRY LEE OF CHANTILLY, 4 May 1794; 24 June 1794.
To be buried at the Burnt House on left of late ever dear wife so the present dear Mrs. Lee may be laid on my right. Sons Thomas, Ludwell and Cassius Lee lands in Fauquier Co. and part of West'd estate; son Francis Lightfoot Lee the gold seal wh. was his uncle Arthur's, the 4 silver plates, spoons, knives and pronged fork wh. was Richard Henry Lee's; daus. Mary Washington, Harriet and Sally Lee, Hannah Washington of Walnut Farm, Anne Lee of Alexandria, Henrietta Lee; wife Anne her dower. Sons in law Wm. Augustine Washington, Corbin Washington and Charles Lee of Alexandria.

DAVIS, ELIAS, of Cople Par., 26 January 1794; 24 June 1794.
Wife Sarah est. for life and then to my children William, Youel, Elizabeth, John, Mary and James. Land to s. James.

WASHINGTON, THOMAS, 3 February 1791; 24 June 1794.
Estate to wife Anne for life & at her d. Thomas Muse Washington my s. land whereon I live; dau. Elizabeth Washington; dau. Ann Washington, s. William money due his mother from her father Wm. Walker's estate; dau. Jemima Jenkins.

MAZARETT, JOHN, 5 July 1793; 29 July 1794.
Wife entire estate including claim for services in the American Army.

PRICE, WILLIAM, of Washington Parish, 23 May 1794; 29 July 1794.
Land to friend James Muse for life, then to my nephew John F. Price; friends Mary Ann Muse, Betsy Jett; niece Mary dau. of bro. Meredith Price, & niece Nancy Price.

SELF, MOSES, 23 October 1793; 30 September 1794.
Wife Anne entire estate for life; god dau. Molly Moss; nephew Francis Holliday.

WOOD, SAMUEL, 2 December 1793; 28 October 1794.
Wife Pheba use of land; daus. Nelly, Frances & Hester.

MASSEY, JOHN, of Cople Parish, 7 September 1794; 28 October 1794.
Sister Ellener Maston of Md. 1 negro & £100 specia. Bro. Robert Massey of King Geo. Co.; nephew Thomas

Massey; to Ellender Board of Md.; bro. Thomas Massey's sons Dade, Robert, Segesmund, John and William Massey; Miss Ellener Ann Lee of Md.

COWARD, WILLIAM, of Cople Parish, 7 October 1792; 27 January 1793.
Wife Mary personal estate for life and what is left at her d. to Elizabeth and Letty Thrailkil and Letty Hutt.

MUSE, SAMUEL, 26 August 1794; 28 October 1794.
After debts paid estate to wife Mary and children Nancy, Thomas, Lewis Smith, Susanna and James Muse.

RICHARD LEE, of Lee Hall, Cople Parish, 16 February 1790; 23 March 1795.
Son Richard all estate subject to legacies hereafter named. Wife Sally £50 a year for 4 years beside her dower; dau. born 12 Feb. 1790 and unchristened £1000 to be paid when 21 yrs. of age or marriage and £40 a year for her maintenance; niece Mrs. Mary Graham £100; to each of nephews and nieces a mourning ring; nephew Charles Lee & Richard Bland Lee.

GARNER, ELIZABETH, 22 April 1794; 23 March 1795.
Nephew Wm. Garner. Land in N. C. to be sold and money to my bros. and sisters.

JOHN WASHINGTON of West'd Co. and Cople Parish, 7 April 1794; 22 June 1795.
To Susanna Weston and her dau. Ann 80 acres of land, and at their death to my nephew George Washington; to Joseph Redd personal estate.

McCARTY, DANIEL, 17 January 1793; 28 September 1795.
Son Daniel land in Nominy in trust for support of my

dau. Elizabeth Basset and at her d. to her eldest child; residue of estate to son Daniel.

GREEN, JOHN, 14 August 1795; 28 September 1795.
Sister Caty Green 20 shillings; sister Peggy Green residue of estate.

CAVENDER, THOMAS, 23 November 1786; 28 March 1796.
Wife Sally Sturman Cavender est. during widowhood and then among all my children.

MOORE, WILLIAM, 26 September 1792; 20 April 1796.
Dau. Mary Alverson all of my estate except 5 shilling to s. Vincent Moore.

NELSON, WILLIAM, 3 March 1796; 25 April 1796.
Wife Mary has support from jointure slaves and land; dau. Frances Hore 5 slaves; dau. Susanna Wickliff land; dau. Jane Nelson land wh. came by her mother; s. Wm. land and mill; jointure negroes at d. of wife to three youngest children Betsy, Nancy and John Nelson.

BASHAW, WARNER, 27 November 1795; 26 April 1796.
Son Epaphroditus; dau. Betty Basey, of Frederick Co. 1 negro girl if she keep my dau. Rachel; daus. Caty and Lusetta Bashaw of Fauquier Co.; dau. Franky Bashaw of Culpeper Co.

HAZLERIGG, WILLIAM, 21 May 1795; 22 August 1796.
Wife Mary use of est. for life; grand dau. Mary Porter; Keziah McClanaham my dau. and Edward Porter exrs.

PORTER, NANCY, 7 February 1793; 22 August 1796.
Son Wm. Porter; dau. Eliner Porter; wife Elizabeth; cousin W. Porter.

MATHEW BAYNE, 26 December 1795; 24 April 1797.
Son William; bro. John Bayne; daus. Betsy and Martha; sons John and Richard Bayne; bros. Richard and Caron Bayne.

MORRIS, CHARLES, 8 May 1797; 26 June 1797.
Daus. Molly Butler and Betty Johnston £6 each as proportion for colts given to Sanders Morris, Hannah Moxley and Simon Morris; s. Ewel Morris; daus. Peggy Stone and Susanna Lye; dec'd dau. Hannah Mosley's children.

MOXLEY, AUGUSTINE, 9 June 1797; 28 August 1797.
Wife Caty land whereon I live for life, 1/3 negroes &c. and at her d. to my nephew Robert Sanford; nephew John s. of Wm. Moxley land and mill; Edward s. of Thomas Stone land; niece Fanny Scrimer; niece Betsy Dodd; god dau. Caty Moxley Pope Sanford; nephew Willoughby Sanford; nephew Elijah Sanford; Samuel s. of Jane Moxley; niece Pinney Weaver & her s. Alfred; nephew John s. of Wm. Moxley; sister Elinor Sanford.

OMOHUNDRO, BRUCE, of Cople Par., 2 September 1796; 25 September 1797.
Mother Martha Omohundro 2 negroes for life; bro. Thomas 1 negro; bros. William and Richard residue of estate.

SANFORD, SAMUEL, of City of Baltimore, 2 September 1797; 6 September 1797.
Bros. Edward, Lawrence and Patrick Spence Sanford all estate; negroes to be freed at age of 35 years before which they are to serve my brothers.

ROBINSON, JAMES, of Cople Parish, 20 April 1789; 23 April 1798.

Wife Keziah estate for life or widowhood; dau. Elizabeth Thrift an equal child's part; s. Thomas a child's part; dau. Mary Ann Courtney 5 shillings; daus. Sarah Calaham and Anne Robinson each a child's part; s. William a child's part and 2 negroes.

DRAKE, JOHN, 10 May 1797; 23 July 1798.
My honored parent Rose Drake land, with stock, whereon she lives; wife Anne "Hermits Lodge" whereon I live with furniture, stock &c but if she marry to s. Francis Thomas Drake; sisters Sarah Drake, Leannah Larkin and Rachel Bowin.

PIERCE, JOSEPH, 7 January 1796; 27 August 1798.
Dau. Sebella wife of Samuel Templeman 1 negro and 4 children; daus. Fanny Pierce, Sally Randall, Margaret Pierce; s. Ransdell; dau. Martha Hill; slaves to be gradually freed.

BUTLER, CHRISTOPHER, of Washington Parish, 6 October 1798; 26 November 1798.
Daus. Sarah Butler, Margaret Butler; son Samuel Butler.

TRIPLETT, JAMES, 1 March 1798; 26 November 1798.
My children James, Charles, William, Jane and Catherine Triplett and Elizabeth Monroe.

HARPER, JOHN, 18 April 1798; 28 January 1799.
Land bought of Robt Harrison to wife Hannah Harrison Harper & at her marriage or death to s. William Ramey Harper, he to pay my s. John H. Harper £20 in gold or silver.

RUST, SAMUEL, of Cople Parish, 1 March 1798; 28 January 1799.
Gr. s. Samuel Rust my gun; gr. s. Samuel Crabb my silver watch; gr. s. Thomas Rust land whereon I live;

dau. Elizabeth Crabb 150 acres land; to Hannah Atwell dau. of Mary Beale 25 acres land; Richard s. of William Atwell; Nancy, Molly and Sharlott daus. of Wm. Atwell; sister Hannah Bangus bed and fur. and use of a negro man; Susannah Hume.

CRABB, JOHN, of Cople Parish, 20 November 1798; 25 March 1799.
Wife Elizabeth land at Ragged Point Neck and 1/3 personal estate; s. John 1 negro; dau. Jane Middleton a negro man and woman; residue of estate to children: Samuel, David, Benedict, Molly Rust, Magdalen, Sally Rust, William Middleton Crabb.

BRINNON, GEORGE, 1 January 1798; 25 March 1799.
Son George my land; son Nel; dau. Sally; wife; bro. John.

MUSE, SAMUEL, 2 January 1799.
Estate divided among Sukey, Thomas, Nancy, Lewis S. Muse.

PIERCE, JOSEPH, 6 November 1798.
Inventory returned.

DRAKE, JOHN, 25 March 1799.
Inventory returned.

PUMROY, JACOB, March 1799.
Inventory returned.

VOL. XX.

POOR, CHARLES, 31 October 1798; 24 June 1799.
Dau. Frances wife of Frederick Weaver 20 shillings; dau. Mary Ann wife of David Annadell 1 shilling; son Thomas residue of estate.

COX, FLEET (dates missing).
Son Presley at 21 yrs. land, mill, still, tools &c; s. Fleet land "Brick House" whereon my gr. father Presley Cox lived; s. Downing land on Yeocomoco Neck [rest missing].

OLIFF, SARAH, 23 August 1799; 26 November 1799.
Dau. Ann Oliff feather bed, 2 chests, pewter & house hold goods; s. George 1 bull, feather bed, looking glass & pestle; dau. Lucy Oliff a box and trunk.

STROTHER, MARGARET, 11 February 1799; 26 August 1799.
Grandson John Underwood £100 and feather bed; dau. Elizabeth Muse residue of estate.

ROBINSON, SOLOMON, of Cople Parish, 6 June 1799; 26 August 1799.
Dau. Ann Hutt 1 negro; dau. Keziah Stowers 1 negro girl and a boy; dau. Molly McClanahan 2 negro girls; dau. Hannah Moxley a negro girl; s. Solomon 5 ne-

groes; dau. Fanny Redman negro woman and child; s. James 5 negroes; wife Franky 3 negroes, oxen and cows.

REDMAN, WILLIAM, 7 September 1781; 26 September 1799.
Wife Keziah all estate for life or widowhood and at her death or mar. to all my children.

HUTT, WILLIAM, 18 November 1799; 23 December 1799.
Merchant at Nominy Ferry with Gerrard Hutt; stock in store and ½ of sloop to James s. of Daniel Neale; relation Thomas s. of Gerrard Hutt Senr.; land, mill and her materials; to Corbin and Gerrard sons of Gerrard Hutt Jr. land; to Benjamin s. of Daniel Porter land; Joseph Sutton and wife Rosamond use of land whereon they live.

TURBEVILLE, JOHN, of Hickory Hill, Cople Parish, 21 March 1799; 26 August 1799.
To be buried by wife Martha in the garden; gr. s. John Turbeville whose mother was Elizabeth Tayloe Corbin of Buckingham, 31 negroes; s. George Lee Turbeville dec'd had 30 hd. of sheep, 50 head of cattle of wh. his sd. son John must have 1/3. Dau. Martha Corbin T. land in Loudon, 1000 acres; son Troilus Lewins; gr. s. Philip s. of dau. Lettice Corbin Jones; gr. s. Catesby Jones; gr. s. Roger Jones; gr. daus. Elizabeth Lee Jones, Sally Skelton Jones and Martha Corbin Jones £500 Va. money; dau. Jones and her son Eusebius Jones £500; son all lands; gr. s. John Turbeville lands, one tract lent s. Geo. Lee T.; nep. George Richard Turbeville; wife Anne her dower in estate.

MONROE, ELLIOTT, 19 January 1798; 27 January 1800.
Wife one-fifth of estate for life; son Spence one-fifth of estate; dau. Elizabeth one-fifth; young son unbaptized one-fifth; child unborn one-fifth.

INDEX

A

Abbington, Abigail, 9; Brooks, 24, 61; James, 24; Jane, 9; Joseph, 24; Lawrence, 6, 9, 11, 21, 24, 33, 63; Lydia, 6, 9; Mary, 9, 33.
Alderson, Geo., 54, 59; Jane, 54, 59; Mary, 54; Margaret, 54.
Aitken, John, 122.
Allday, Grace, 11; Henry, 6, 11; Mary, 11.
Allen, Wm., 67.
Allerton, Anne, 107, 143; Eliz., 79; Glwen, 107; Hannah, 79; Isaac, 1, 13, 34, 79, 107; Wm., 39, 61; Willoughby, 34, 79, 107, 143.
Allison, Marg't, 30; Thos., 30.
Allson, Eliz., 119.
Alverson, Mary, 199.
Allworthy, Robt., 66; Ruth, 66.
Anderson, Abr., 69; David, 14.
Angier, John, 9.
Annadale, Ann, 189; Mary A., 202.
Arenton, John, 24; Wansford, 24.
Ariss, Eliz., 149; Fran., 91; John, 91, 149; Sarah, 149; Spencer, 91, 149.
Armistead, Hannah, 117; John, 117; Sarah, 117.
Armsley, Ann, 4; John, 4.
Arnold, Anne, 137; James, 137; Weedon, 137.
Arrington, Dorcas, 56; Eliz., 53, 56; Jane, 56; John, 47, 53; Mildred, 47; Susanna, 47, 50; Thos., 47, 56; Wansford, 56.
Arrowsmith, Richard, 134; Thos., 134; Wm., 134.
Asbury, Ann, 110, 139; Benj., 41; Cath., 41; Coleman, 41; Geo., 110; Hannah, 99, 110; Henry, 41, 110, 139; Isabella, 110; John, 139; Mary, 41; Ruth, 124; Thos., 41, 110; Wm., 110.
Ashton, Burdett, 80, 93, 109, 148; Charles, 80, 94, 109, 120, 148; Eliz., 93, 159; Grace, 93; Henry, 93, 112, 116; Jane, 42, 80; John, 80, 93, 109, 148; Lawrence, 148; Sarah, 42, 148.
Astin, Robt., 3.
Atwell, Daniel, 191; Eliz., 51; Fran., 35, 50, 191; Hannah, 50, 202; John, 16, 35, 50, 51, 191; Keziah, 87; Lydia, 50; Martha, 105; Mary, 11, 181; Molly, 202; Nancy, 202; Richard, 181, 202; Samuel, 50; Sharlott, 202; Thos., 11, 35, 50, 191; Wm., 162, 181, 191, 202; Youell, 50, 162, 191.
Attwell, Fran., 162; John, 162; Richard, 162; Thos., 162.
Atwood, Gilbert, 47, 55.
Auckram, Richard, 17; Wm., 17.
Awbrey, Chandler, 87, 140; Chanlor, 90; Eliz., 140; Hannah, 57, 87; James S., 140; Jemimah, 57; John, 57, 87; K., 87.
Axton, John, 7.
Aylette, Anne, 93, 116; Benj., 116; Eliz., 93, 116, 118; John, 116; Philip, 116; Wm., 93, 116.

B

Bagge, John, 51; Mary, 51.
Bagwell, Amos, 102; Jane, 102.
Bailey, Anne, 16, 21, 110; Basil, 16; Daniel, 185; Eliz., 87, 168; Jere. G., 192; James, 100, 118; John, 21, 100, 168, 185; Mary, 16, 166; Samuel, 185; Stephen, 21, 100, 169, 193; Wm., 21; Vincent S., 185.
Baker, Anne, 54, 126, 151; Butler, 155; Eliz., 23, 54, 151; Fran., 126, 154; James, 154; John, 23, 64, 76, 90, 126, 151, 154; Kath., 154; Mary, 23, 126; Peggy, 155; Presley, 126; Rebecca, 154; Richard, 154; Samuel, 76, 154, 155; Sarah, 64; Susanna, 155; Thos., 78; Wm., 126, 151; Winny, 154.
Baldridge, Charles, 2, 6; Dorothy, 4, 6; Eliz., 2, 7; James, 4, 6, 7; Wm., 2, 6, 7.
Baley, Eliz., 127, 152; Hannah, 121; James, 125; John, 152; Mary, 125; Wm., 125.
Ball, Benoni, 78, 103; Daniel, 78; Emanuel, 78, 114; Geo., 78, 103, 114; Gerrard, 78, 83, 103; Henry L., 155, 158; Lettice, 155, 158; Mary, 85, 155, 158; Robt., 78; Samuel, 103, 114; Sarah, 78, 83; Wm., 122, 155.
Balthrop, Eliz., 153; Jemima, 153; John, 153; Marg't, 153; Nancy, 153; Sarah, 153; Sharp, 153; Wm., 153; Winifred, 154.
Banister, Geo., 151, 152.
Bankhead, James, 130, 136, 181; John, 181; Wm., 181.
Baseley, John, 8; Wm., 8.
Basey, Betty, 199; Caty, 199; Eph., 199; Franky, 199; Rachel, 199; Warner, 199.
Basset, Eliz., 199.
Barber, John, 148.
Barecroft, Eliz., 171; Wm., 171.
Barn, Robt., 75.
Barnes, Abr., 90; Ann, 90; Eliz., 90; Richard, 90; Thos., 90.
Barnett, Eliz., 99, 136, 183; John, 125, 136; Richard, 136.
Bartlett, Peggy J., 193.
Barton, John, 23; Mary, 23.
Batcheldor, Thos., 69.
Bateman, Eliz., 61; John, 61; Mary, 61; Wm., 61.
Bashaw, Eliz., 119; James, 119; Mary, 119; Peter, 119, Sarah, 119; Spence, 119; Warrener, 119.
Batts, Wm., 12.
Bayanham, Anne, 6; Eliz., 6; Mary, 6.
Bayard, James, 73; John, 73.
Baxter, Abr., 59; Anne, 59; Edw., 149; Geo., 149; Mary, 54, 59, 75; Thos., 59, 149; Wm., 59, 123.
Bayley, Anne, 45, 64, 95; Eliz., 135; James, 135; John, 32, 134; Joseph, 45, 53, 58, 64; Michael, 64; Robt., 71; Samuel, 32; Stephen, 135; Thos., 64; Wm., 135.
Bayne, Daniel, 164; Eleanor, 152; Eliz., 174, 186; Geo., 164; John, 174; Wm., 174.
Bayne, Caron, 200; Carson, 164; Elenor, 164; John, 164, 200; Math., 164, 200; Richard, 164, 200; Wm., 164, 200.
Beale, Charles, 107; Eliz., 185; John, 107; Mary, 202; Reuben, 117; Richard, 107; Samuel, 185; Sarah, 94; Tavener, 107; Thomas, 185; Wm., 185.
Beard, Andrew, 41; Anne, 109; Anthony, 41; Eliz., 41; Fran., 41; Geo., 109, 160; John, 8, 24, 41, 46, 109; Mary, 24, 46; Marian, 160; Sarah, 34, 41, 50; Thos., 24, 58; Wm., 41.
Beckwith, Alice, 57, 97; Mary, 97.
Begge, John, 88.

INDEX

Belfield, Eliz., 133.
Bell, Gervace, 3; John, 11, 24; Joseph, 126; Mary, 5, 11; Richard, 5, 73; Thos., 126.
Bennett, Bumbury, 157; Cath., 157; Charles, 143; Corscomb, 34; Cossom, 65, 157; Daniel, 143, 162; Eliz., 125, 143; Esther, 92; John, 1, 92; Joseph, 125; Kath., 65; Lucy, 65; Marg't, 34; Mary, 34, 170, 182; Matilda M., 195; Nicho., 182; Richard, 189; Thos., 125, 143, 189; Wm., 20, 65, 157.
Berkeley, John, 166; Peggy, 153, 166; Wm., 153, 166.
Bernard, Ann, 177, 182; Richard, 96; Robert, 65, 81; Thos., 182; Wm., 96, 156.
Berry, Edward, 28.
Berryman, Anne, 90; Benj., 33, 50, 73, 90, 153, 159, 177; Eliz., 153, 178; Fran., 178; Gerrard, 178; Gilson, 90; Henry, 90, 153; Henry E., 177; James, 90, 153, 167; John, 153, 158; Josias, 178; Kate, 90; Katy, 167; Newton, 90, 153, 167; Rose, 90; Samuel, 167; Sarah, 33, 90, 106, 167; Thos., 178; Waters, 178; Wm., 73, 90, 153, 177; Willo. N., 177.
Beverley, Wm., 122.
Bittey, Wm., 134.
Bincks, Eliz., 92; Geo., 109; John, 92, 109, 138; Mary, 92, 109, 147; Thos., 92, 109, 147.
Biddle, John, 4.
Blackburn, Richard, 102.
Blackmore, Geo., 120; Gideon, 121; Samuel, 120, 121; Wm., 120.
Blagg, Abr., 17, 52, 60, 85; Joane, 5; Marg't, 17, 60, 85; Ralph, 5; Thos., 5.
Blagdon, John, 33; Sarah, 33.
Blanchflower, Benj., 27, 30; Tempe., 27, 30, 48.
Blyton, John, 22.

Blundell, Absalom, 95, 171; Ann, 171; Garner, 95; John, 171; Sarah, 171; Sukey, 171; Thos., 11, 13, 53, 95; Wm., 95, 102, 171.
Bolthrop, Valinda, 140.
Booth, Eliz., 24, 28, 33, 44; Geo., 27; John, 107; Wm., 33, 151.
Bonam, Daniel, 35, 64, 65, 85, 96; Kath., 35, 55; Philpot, 35, 64, 86; Rose, 86; Samuel, 35, 64, 86, 96, 125; Sarah, 96; Thos., 64, 96.
Bond, Richard, 20.
Borer, Hannah, 135; Henry, 35, 82; John, 82.
Bott, Eliz., 164.
Boush, Samuel, 60.
Bowcock, Anthony, 113, 173; Henry, 173, 182; James, 102, 113; Jane, 102, 113; John, 173; Katy, 182; Richard, 173; Sally, 182; Thos., 102, 113, 182.
Bowin, Rachel, 201.
Bowling, Mary, 91.
Boyce, Eleanor, 2; Eliz., 2; Thos., 2.
Bragg, Eliz., 151.
Branham, Barnaby, 151; Eliz., 151; Ignatius, 151; Michael, 151; Owen, 36; Rosanna, 151; Wm., 151.
Breechin, Ann, 77; James, 72, 77; Jane, 77; Sarah, 77; Wm., 77.
Brenan, Ann, 109; Deliv., 109; John, 109; Owen, 109.
Brent, Edmd., 2; Giles, 2; Judith, 158; Judy, 194; Kath., 2, 89; Marg't, 2; Mary, 2; Rebecca, 2.
Brereton, Mrs., 12.
Brewer, Marg't, 133.
Bricke, Gerrard, 84.
Brickey, Gerrard, 185; John, 185; Peter, 185; Wm., 185; Winifred, 185.
Bridges, Amy, 164; Anthony, 8, 9; Eliz., 32; John, 161; Math., 164; Wm., 27, 161.

Briggs, David, 175; Eliz., 175.
Brinnon, Geo., 183, 202; Hannah, 183; John, 183, 202; Sally, 202.
Brion, Jemima, 168.
Briscoe, Daniel, 190; Ellen, 190; Ellenor, 88; Eliz., 190, 193; James, 67, 88, 90; John, 88, 90, 190; Lucy, 190; Marg't, 88, 90.
Broadhurst, Ann, 2; Gerrard, 2; Walter, 1, 2.
Brock, Mary, 102.
Brooks, Dorothy, 6; John, 7; Henry, 6; Joane, 6.
Brooking, Fran., 147.
Brown, Ann, 187; Coleman, 124; David, 38, 82, 91; Eliz., 88, 143, 149, 164; Ellenor, 120; Ellis, 36; Geo., 80; Hannah, 117, 172; Hester, 53; James, 149; Jane, 22, 172; Joane, 11; John, 38, 47, 80, 82, 91, 96, 144, 172; Martha, 150; Mary, 22, 47, 82, 141, 153; Original, 22, 91, 143; Philip, 11; Richard, 82; Rose, 81; Sally, 172; Thos., 80, 151; Wm., 22, 53, 75, 80, 82, 89, 91, 144, 149, 162, 165, 172.
Browning, Thomas, 86.
Bruce, Charles, 113; Geo., 113; Kezia, 113; Margery, 113; Wm., 113.
Bryant, Sarah, 61; Wm., 61.
Buckley, Abr., 30, 31; Eliz., 30, 31, 96; Henrietta, 27; John, 30, 31, 96; Wm., 96.
Buckner, Aris, 196; Eliz., 175, 196; Fran., 196; Peggy, 188; Richard, 196; Richard H., 188; Wm., 175.
Bulger, Edmund, 101; John, 101, 165; Johnson, 165; Mary, 101, 178; Nancy, 165; Sally, 165.
Bunbury, Thos., 157.
Burch, Banam, 95.
Burn, Alice, 85; James, 85; Mary, 85; Wm., 85.
Burshaw, Bethlune, 173.
Burns, Daniel, 85.

Burwell, Herbert, 7; Rebecca, 7.
Bush, Ann, 111; Edw., 111; Wm., 38.
Bushrod, Eliz., 145; Hannah, 70, 79; John, 70, 79, 106, 145; Mary, 80; Mildred, 145; Richard, 70, 107; Sarah, 79; Thos., 70, 107.
Butler, Anne, 134, 161, 180, 194; Beckwith, 153, 171; Betsey, 180; Caleb, 22, 32, 45, 51, 55, 90; Cath., 47, 114; Celia, 180; Chr., 90, 174, 181, 201; Cradock, 98; Elcey, 181, 193; Eleanor, 174; Eliz., 77, 88, 98, 127, 174, 192, 193; Gerrard, 98; Griffin, 74; Hannah, 27, 98, 144, 180; Isobel, 141; James, 27, 47, 54, 73, 93, 114, 134, 141, 161; Jane, 45, 51, 75, 181, 193; Jesse, 172; John, 20, 44, 45, 47, 54, 90, 114, 141, 161, 172, 174, 180; Joice, 174; Jos., 90; Josh., 6; Law., 19, 70, 96, 117, 174, 181; Marg't, 201; Mary, 45, 134, 190, 200; Nath'l, 90, 177, 180, 194; Nelly, 180; Price, 93; Sam'l, 201; Sarah, 96, 174, 181, 194, 201; Thos., 6, 47, 54, 93, 98, 127, 134, 141; Tobias, 16, 27; Wesley, 193; Wm., 47, 54, 90, 93, 98, 114, 127, 161, 172, 180, 193.

C

Cahoe, Alex., 52.
Calaham, Sarah, 201.
Calles, Ambrose, 162; Fran., 162; Garland, 143; Jane, 162; John A., 149; Mary, 143; Robt., 162; Thos., 162; Wm., 143; Wm. O., 143.
Callis, Ambrose, 128; Fran., 128; James, 128; John, 128; Richard, 128; Thos., 128; Wm., 128.
Campain, Geo., 11.
Camose, Philip, 24.

INDEX 209

Campbell, James, 33; Jane, 33.
Canada, John, 34.
Cannady, Eliz., 96.
Carey, Chr., 7; Edw., 7.
Carpenter, Ann, 91, 167, 177; Eliz., 177; James, 177; John, 177; Wm., 91, 167, 177.
Carrier, Eliz., 20; John, 20.
Cardwell, Marg't, 56; Mary, 56; Richard, 56; Winifred, 56.
Carroll, Daniel, 54; Mary, 54.
Carr, Ann, 34, 87; Eliz., 34; Hannah, 34; James, 112; Jane, 34; Joseph, 34, 112; Martha, 34; Mary, 112; Sarah, 34, 87; Wm., 32, 34, 87.
Carter, Ann, 189; Benj., 174; Dorcas, 69; Eliz., 177; Fran., 40; Geo., 189; Giles, 78; Jane, 72, 187, 189; John, 189; Landon, 112; Presley, 189; Richard, 189; Robt., 174, 189; Samuel, 189; Thos., 40; Wm., 177.
Cash, Anish, 43; Eliz., 43; Howard. 43; Joseph, 43; Peter, 43; Thos., 43; Wm., 43.
Cavender, Eliz., 165; Geo., 165; Henry, 165; John, 165; Richard, 165; Sally S., 199; Thos., 165, 199.
Cecil, Fran., 195.
Chalker, John, 83.
Chambers, Mary, 114; Thos., 114.
Chancellor, Grace, 147; John, 99, 147; Kath., 147; Rebecca, 147; Sally, 192; Sarah, 147; Thos., 38, 83, 99, 147, 192.
Chandler, Ann, 144; Eliz., 176; Fran., 144; Jos., 144; Mary, 144; Thos., 144; Wm., 144.
Chanlor, Fran., 84; Joseph, 84; Thos., 84; Wm., 84.
Chapman, Charles, 105; Isaac, 58; John, 105; Richard, 12, 17.
Charles, Thos., 50.

Chilton, Anne, 99; Charles, 62, 156; Jane, 43; John, 43, 60, 85, 156; Lettice, 99; Mary, 102; Sarah, 43; Stephen, 156; Thos., 43, 85, 156; Wm., 156, 168.
Chelton, John, 25.
Christie, Geo., 157.
Christopher, John, 34; Thos., 34.
Chubb, Henry, 30.
Churnell, Joseph, 22.
Clark, Anne, 21; Eliz., 21; Fran., 21; James, 21; Jane, 21; Marg't, 192; Mary, 21, 26; Sarah, 27; Wm., 21, 26, 57; Wm. M., 192, 195.
Claton, Sarah, 138.
Claughton, M., 117.
Clay, Ann, 9; Francis, 9.
Clayton, Thos., 45.
Clayter, Kath., 72; Thos., 72.
Claytor, Anne, 119, 141; Alven, 119, 141; John, 140; Kath., 67; Samuel, 141; Thos., 67, 141; Wm., 67, 141.
Clemens, David, 50; Isabella, 50.
Clements, John, 31, 65; Wm., 13.
Clift, Wm., 22.
Cochren, Christian, 45; Eliz., 45.
Cock, Eliz., 188; John, 88.
Cockerell, John, 33, 88; Mary, 32; Presley, 127.
Coghill, Sarah, 162.
Coggin, Richard, 27.
Cohern, Wm., 31.
Cook, Miles, 3.
Cole, John, 44; Mary, 42, 44; Maryday, 42; Richard, 6, 7; Robt., 42.
Coleman, Eleanor, 126; James, 28, 74, 101; Jane, 74; John, 74; Richard, 8, 74, 101; Wm., 8.
Collin, John, 51; Wm., 51.
Collins, Charles, 168; John, 77, 168; Thos., 11.

Collinsworth, Ann, 130; Jane, 15; Jesse, 166; John, 15, 100, 130, 166, 177, 190; Martha, 166; Nath'l, 177; Peggy, 166; Sarah, 190; Thos., 15, 100, 130, 166; Wm., 177; Willoughby, 100, 130, 166; Vincent, 166.
Colson, Eliz., 56.
Colston, Eliz., 24.
Come, Simon, 19.
Commocke, Susanna, 22.
Conditt, Ann, 99.
Conier, Sarah, 105; Tarence, 105.
Connie, Alice, 143; David, 143.
Conner, David, 68.
Conners, Teague, 5.
Conniers, Daniel, 56.
Cony, Edw., 67.
Cooper, Eliz., 90; Hannah, 99, 106; John, 13, 99.
Cope, Wm., 113.
Corbin, Eliz. T., 204; Gawin, 144, 194; Hannah, 132, 144; Henry, 122; Lettice, 122; Martha, 144; Richard, 132, 144, 145.
Cossum, Henry, 7.
Couch, John, 105.
Court, Wm., 11.
Courtney, Cath., 171; Dorcas, 147; Geo., 157, 176; James, 141, 147, 176; Jere., 141, 147, 157; Kezia, 171, 176; Leonard, 141, 147, 157, 176; Mary, 103, 141; Mary A., 201; Peggy, 176; Samuel, 141, 147, 176; Wm., 176.
Courtwell, James, 67.
Coward, Mary, 198; Wm., 198.
Cox, Anne, 28, 49; Charnock, 28, 116, 130; Downing, 103; Eleanor, 146; Eliz., 28, 95; Fleet, 152, 157, 192, 203; Geo., 124, 130; Hannah, 124; James, 124, 192; Jane, 49; John, 116, 192; Martha, 28; Mary, 119, 124; Molly, 157; Peter, 124; Peter P., 152, 192; Presley, 116, 130, 157, 203; Rachel, 148; Richard, 192; Sarah, 124; Thos.,
28; Vincent, 28, 49, 116, 130; Wm., 130, 152, 157; Winifred, 149.
Crabb, Benedict, 170, 202; Daniel, 60, 69, 106, 202; Eliz., 202; Gerrard, 69, 106, 186; Jane, 186; John, 61, 69, 106, 170, 202; Lettice, 170; Molly R., 202; Osman, 48, 69, 106, 187; Sarah, 69; Samuel, 201; Thos., 106; Vincent, 186; Wm. M., 170, 202.
Craddock, Eliz., 45, 75; Richard, 45, 50, 75.
Cradnuck, Richard, 24.
Craighill, Eliz., 144.
Crawford, Robt., 131.
Creed, Eliz., 98; James, 98; John, 121.
Crenshaw, Ann, 183.
Creswick, Jane, 104.
Critcher, Jean, 126; John, 126; Mary, 126; Richard, 126; Thos., 126.
Cromwell, Gershon, 1.
Cross, Geo., 31, 38.
Crouchman, John, 58; Sarah, 58.
Crumpton, John, 15.
Crutcher, John, 159; Joseph, 159; Susanna, 159; Thos., 159.
Cupingheifer, Hannah, 164; Jacob, 164; John, 164; Mary, 164; Mical, 164.
Cullum, Eliz., 24; Mary, 24.
Curtis, Honor, 104; John, 52, 104; Robt., 104; Thos., 104.

D

Dade, Bethland, 3; Fran., 3, 19.
Damourvell, Samuel, 75.
Daneley, Ursula, 119.
Dangerfield, Apphia, 171.
Daniel, Thos., 5.
Danielson, Anne, 135.
Davenport, Eliz., 187; James, 170, 187; Mary, 37; Randle, 37.
Davice, Anne, 90; Samuel, 90.
Davies, Gerard, 55; Wm., 55.

INDEX 211

Davis, Ann, 28, 48, 111, 128, 154, 155, 165; Barbara, 79, 96; Cath., 128; Elias, 28, 126, 127, 197; Eliz., 78, 125, 152, 155, 197; Esther, 128, 155; Fran., 79, 152, 154; Gerrard, 79, 96, 111; James, 197; Jane, 151; Jesse, 155; John, 15, 28, 151, 197; Joshua, 128; Mary, 154, 155, 197; Samuel, 128; Sarah, 197; Wm., 111, 151, 197; Youell, 127, 197.
Day, George, 1.
Deane, Anne, 180; Charles, 180, 192; Mary, 180.
Deatterly, Eliz., 180; Geo., 180; James, 180; John, 180; Mathew, 180; Thos., 180.
Debria, Lewis, 24; Eliz., 24.
Degges, James, 169.
Delozier, Daniel, 171; Molly R., 156, 171; Richard D., 156, 171; Susannah, 156; Thos., 156.
Demenet, Luke, 32.
Demoval, Hannah, 117.
Dickinson, Thos., 103.
Dickson, Eliz., 110.
Dishman, Anne, 88, 191, 192; Cornelia, 88; David, 88; Fran., 107, 108; James, 107, 108, 163, 169; John, 88, 107, 108, 191; Peter, 88; Samuel, 88, 107, 108, 192; Wm., 191, 192.
Dodd, Benj., 118; Betsey, 200; Eliz., 118; John, 118; Jos., 118; Nath'l, 118; Nicho., 172, 186; Wm., 152, 172, 186.
Dodson, Frances, 10; Thos., 10.
Dolman, Betsy, 179; John H., 179; Mary, 179; Peggy, 179; Wm., 179.
Douglass, Sarah, 153.
Dowling, James, 81; Joanna, 81; Mary, 81; Susanna, 182.
Downing, Betty, 192; Ralph, 60; Thos., 192.
Downton, Grace, 50.
Doyle, Chr., 5.
Dozier, Joseph, 169; Richard, 169; Sarah, 169; Thos., 169.

Dozier, Becky, 187; Betty W., 191; Eliz., 133; James, 191; Joseph, 191; Mary, 133; Richard, 133, 191; Thos., 97, 191.
Drake, Ann, 192, 201; Benj., 179, 188; Eleanor, 176; Fran., 176, 201; James, 176; John, 176, 201, 202; Richard, 76; Rose, 201; Sarah, 176, 179, 201; Thos., 176; Wm., 176.
Draper, John, 1.
Driskall, Darby, 71.
Duckworth, Wm., 8.
Duddlestone, John, 51.
Dudley, Ann, 33; Mary, 77; Richard, 33.
Dunbar, James, 150; Molly, 150; Sarah, 106; Wm., 150.
Duncan, Ann, 63; Blanchflower, 63; Henry, 121; Sarah, 142.
Dunkan, Charles, 46; Fran., 46.
Dunkin, Anne, 87; Charles, 23, 125; Coleman, 124; Eliz., 87, 142; Geo., 125, 142; Henry, 11; James, 87; John, 87; Peter, 23, 87, 125; Wm., 87.
Dunn, Kath., 68; John, 68.
During, Geo., 80, 106.
Dutton, Thos., 6.
Eales, John A., 76.
Earl, John, 121; Samuel, 121.
Earle, Wm., 27.
Earls, Fran., 111.
Eastaff, Judith, 6; Thos., 6.
Eaton, Peter, 68.
Eattle, Benj., 55.
Edrington, Ann, 169; Chr., 169; Eliz., 169; Susanna, 169.
Edwards, Alice, 170; Anne, 47; Anthony, 138; Arnold, 138; Ellenor, 47; Eliz., 138; Franky, 170; Geo., 138; Grace, 138; John, 47; Joseph, 138; Mary S., 170; Merida, 47; Robt., 13; Susannah, 175; Thos., 47, 170; Wm., 47, 138, 170.

Elliott, Aug., 129, 131, 141;
Betty, 129; John, 42, 62,
108, 141; Martha, 22, 131;
Mary, 22, 84; Mildred, 129;
Robt., 141; Sabella, 131;
Sarah, 21, 42, 45, 53; Sibella,
129; Wm., 42, 53, 84, 141.
English, Walter, 11, 31, 84;
Winifred, 16; Youell, 16.
Erwin, John, 57.
Eskridge, Daniel, 86; Eliz., 100,
118; Geo., 18, 32, 39, 64,
85, 100; Hannah, 91; Robt.,
100; Samuel, 100; Wm., 100.
Esther, Giles, 95.
Ethel, Abraham, 25, 60; Kath.,
25; John, 25, 125.
Evans, Eliz., 17; Hester, 17;
Mary, 17, 19; Peter, 17; Rebecca, 17; Richard, 30;
Sarah, 17.
Eversly, Ralph, 6.
Ewell, Anne, 12; Penelope, 12;
Richard, 12; Thos., 12.

F.

Fairfax, Geo. Wm., 150.
Fauntleroy, Apphia, 70, 107;
Wm., 107.
Feagins, Ann, 170; Betty, 170;
Geo., 170, James, 170; Thos.,
170; Wm., 170.
Fendall, Josias, 6.
Field, Abr., 71; Daniel, 71, 97;
Henry, 71; James, 74; Mary,
97.
Fielder, Eliz., 120.
Fieldan, Edward, 192; Jane,
192; John, 192.
Finch, Blagdon, 100; Eliz., 136;
John, 63, 100, 136, 155;
Mary, 63, 100, 136; Richard,
100; Thos., 100.
Finn, Eliz., 56; Thos., 56.
Fitzhugh, Ann, 55, 79, 184;
Cath., 184; Daniel, 184;
Elcy, 184; Henry, 94; Jane,
184; John, 79, 94; Lucy, 184;
McCarty, 184; Wm., 184.
Fleming, Abigail, 110, 158;
Anne, 118; John, 118, 158;
Mary, 110; Peter, 118;
Sarah, 118; Thos., 118; Wm.,
118, 158.

Fletcher, Robt., 50.
Flewelling, John, 21; Thos., 21;
Wm., 21.
Fling, Eliz., 136; Wm., 136.
Flint, Martha, 39; Richard, 4.
Flood, Nicho., 155, 172; Wm.,
172.
Follins, John, 33.
Foot, Frances, 153.
Footman, Eliz., 108, 116; John,
55, 108, 116.
Ford, Daniel, 122; Eliz., 122;
Gerrard, 40, 122; Jarrat, 70;
Warner, 122.
Foster, Anne, 34; Eliz., 179;
Robt., 13, 34; Thos., 12.
Foxcroft, Deborah, 20.
Fox, Eliz., 160; Joseph, 160.
Fowke, Gerrard, 6; Susanna,
6; Thomas, 6.
Foxhall, John, 21, 45.
Frank, James, 169; Martha, 81;
Mary, 169; Neremiah, 81;
Robt., 81, 86, 169; Samuel,
81, 169; Thos., 87.
Franklin, Anne, 127; Eliz., 127,
162, 176; Fran., 17, 127;
Geo. 131; John, 120; Martha,
158; Robt., 135; Sarah, 127,
135; Thos., 190; Wm., 176,
190.
Freeid, Winifred, 106.
Frond, Jane, 76.
Fryer, John, 80, 88; Priscilla,
81; Sarah, 88; Wm., 88.
Furgeson, Marg't, 180.
Furlong, Anne, 60; Mary, 60.

G.

Gamon, John, 73.
Gannack, John, 76.
Garland, Daniel, 17; Geo., 50;
Jere., 18, 35; Nath'l, 18, 35;
Thos., 35; Wm., 50, 103.
Gardner, Wm., 36.
Garrot, Cath., 131.
Gathagin, James, 134; Mary,
134.
Garner, Abr., 48, 49, 149, 162,
187; Arch., 126; Benj., 36,
57, 65, 162, 171; Bradley,
119, 148, 162; Cath., 119,
162; Dorcas, 185; Ellenor,
107; Eliz., 101, 162, 198;

INDEX 213

Gawin, 171; Geo., 162; Henry, 36, 65, 119, 130; Jane J., 126; James, 36, 48, 165; Jemima, 126; Jere, 48; John, 48; Joseph, 48, 65, 126, 171; Joyce, 130; Lettice, 149, 162; Martha, 36, 141; Martha, 149; Nath'l, 171; Parish, 36, 65; Rachel, 149; Rosamond, 141, 147; Sarah, 149; Sukey, 187; Susan, 36; Susanna, 57; Thos., 36, 119, 147; Wm., 48, 49, 198; Winny L., 185; Vincent, 130, 162.
Garrard, Aaron, 122; Ann, 150; Anthony, 174, 175; Eliz., 150; James, 150; Jane, 46, 75, 122; John, 25, 46, 55, 75; Justinian, 13; Mary, 13, 57, 58, 122, 142, 150; Nath'l, 122, 161; Richard, 161, 175; Rose, 13; Sarah, 122; Susanna, 4, 13, 75; Thos., 2, 4, 13, 48; Wm., 58, 122, 142, 161.
George, Mary, 94.
Gerviss, Marg't, 97.
Gibbs, Winifred, 104.
Gilbert, Hannah, 185, 189; Jane, 174; John, 64; Martha, 189; Mary, 156; Michael, 64, 156; Nancy, 189; Samuel, 189; Thos., 156; Wm., 64, 156, 189.
Gilson, Beth'd., 70.
Glasco, John, 83.
Goaring, Wm., 118.
Goddard, Charles, 84.
Golding, Hanlett, 77.
Goff, Ann, 72; Benj., 157; Jane, 157; Wm. O., 157.
Golorthum, John, 97; Martin, 97; Wm., 97.
Good, Francis, 31.
Gordon, Alex., 23; Betty, 184; Eliz., 23; Geo., 184; Hannah, 184; John, 184; Samuel, 184; Urslua, 184.
Gough, Anne, 58; Eliz., 83; Robt., 58.
Gower, Pierce, 31, 55; Stanley, 31.

Guinness, Edw., 125.
Guinning, John, 86.
Gullock, Thos., 28.
Grace, Ann, 161; Fran., 121; James, 119, 161; Johannah, 119; John, 161; Thos., 161; Wm., 161.
Graham, Marg't, 32; Mary, 198; Wm., 31, 60.
Grant, Marg't, 136.
Green, Anne, 92; Burkett, 182; Caty, 199; Erasmus, 30, 39; John, 176, 188, 199; Letty, 182; Molly, 182; Peggy, 199; Reuben, 182; Sarah, 182; Wm., 182.
Greentree, Thos., 15.
Greenwood, Daniel, 121.
Gregory, Cath. C., 193; Daniel L., 193; Geo. C., 193; James, 193; John G., 193; Joseph C., 193; Lettice A., 193.
Grey, Alice, 9; Fran., 9, 114; Geo., 114; John, 54; Marg't, 114; Nath'l, 114.
Griffin, Abr., 59; Lewis, 97; Richard, 97; Wm., 64.
Griffith, Edward, 3.
Griggs, John, 177; Mary, 177; Wm., 177.
Grigsby, Rose, 178; Verlinda, 154.
Grymes, Philip, 184.
Groves, Bryan, 43; Eliz., 43.
Grinning, Thos., 87.
Grimstead, Ann, 44; Thos., 44; Wm. 44.

H.

Haborn, Elender, 136; Geo., 136; James, 136; Jane, 136.
Hackney, Eliz., 121.
Hacle, David, 110.
Hailey, John, 174; Richard, 174.
Haines, Geo., 6; Sibley, 5.
Halcom, Geo., 126; Hannah, 126; Jenny, 126; Mary, 126; Milly, 126; Susanna, 126.
Haley, Eliz., 17.

Hall, Ann, 130; Ann S., 192; Ashton, 166; Joanna, 166; Leasure, 166; Lewis, 166; Newton, 192.
Halls, Geo., 89; John, 89.
Halliday, Geo., 133; John, 91; Mary, 91; Richard, 133.
Hallowes, John, 1; Restitute, 1.
Hallwell, Thos., 24.
Ham, Manuel, 45.
Hambleton, Anne, 87; Grace, 87; James, 87; John, 87.
Hamilton, James, 82.
Hammock, Wm., 40.
Hancock, Richard, 16, 43.
Handley, Jonas, 73.
Hardage, Eliz., 81; Geo., 81; Wm., 81.
Hardicks, Wm., 12.
Hardidge, Eliz., 15, 93; Wm., 3, 15, 93.
Harding, Thos., 135.
Hardwick, Aaron, 103; Anne, 21, 87; Eliz., 68, 95, 99, 126; Fran., 103; Geo., 39, 48, 68, 95, 103; Haney R., 103; James, 21, 27, 68, 87, 95, 99, 103, 126; John, 126; Joseph, 20, 21, 27, 87; Lydia, 21; Robt., 39; Thos., 21, 27, 126; Wm., 13, 21, 68, 103.
Harper, Daniel, 11; Hannah, 201; John, 201; Robt., 167; Sarah, 186; Thos., 45; Wm., 45; Wm. R., 145.
Harpin, Henry, 11.
Hartley, Hannah, 117; John, 89; Mary, 89; Sarah, 89; Wm., 89.
Haselrig, Fran., 98; James, 51; Richard, 51, 98.
Hardy, John, 55.
Harford, Thos., 12.
Hargis, John, 92; Mary, 92; Milerett, 92; Roger, 92.
Harness, John, 98, Martha, 98; Wm., 98.
Harris, Ann, 23; Arthur, 23; Ellenor, 23; James, 28; Valentine, 23; Wm., 23.
Harrison, Abigail, 167; Alice, 141; Agness, 174; Andrew, 91; Alex., 194; Anne, 65, 83, 91, 98, 112, 155; Benj.,
98; Daniel, 127, 174; Eleanor, 174; Elsey, 178; Eliz., 75, 144, 178; Fran., 144; Geo., 51, 98, 155, 167; Hannah, 155, 178, 194; James, 51, 174; Jere., 98, 155, 185; John, 51, 167; Joseph, 91, 194; Joshua, 127, 174; Lovell, 83, 137, 194; Magdalen, 185; Martha, 132; Mary, 83, 91; Molly, 183; Peter, 51, 178; Robt., 12, 167; Samuel, 98, 127, 155, 178, 185; Thos., 98, 178; Wm., 51, 155, 174; Willo., 51, 127, 154.
Harvey, Ann, 195; Eliza, 195; James, 83, 195; John, 195; Mary, 82; Mungo, 195; Sarah, 195.
Hath, Samuel, 112.
Haven, Arthur, 61; Stephen, 61.
Hawkins, John, 32.
Hawley, Edw., 33; Eliz., 33, 62; John, 33; Sarah, 33.
Hayden, Mary, 11; Penelope, 11.
Haydon, Geo., 85; Samuel, 85.
Hayes, Henry, 118; Jane, 118; Wm., 118.
Hazelrigg, Mary, 137, 199; Wm., 137, 199.
Heabedred, John, 5.
Headley, Ann, 52; Eliz., 52; Fran., 62; Henry, 52; John, 52, 62; Robt., 52, 110; Sarah, 171; Wm., 52, 110.
Hearn, Alice, 24; Philip, 24.
Hemmings, Eliz., 66; Joseph, 66.
Hemmons, John, 50.
Hennings, Joseph, 40.
Henman, 36.
Henry, Rowland, 94.
Herra, Marg't, 61.
Hewes, Thomas, 25.
Hicking, Eliz., 58.
Hicks, John, 16.
Hid, Anne, 26; Eliz., 26; Thos., 26.
Higdon, Daniel, 33, 67, 72, 107; Eliz., 163; Jane, 7; John, 33, 67, 72, 82, 125, 163; Marg't, 107; Original, 33, 163; Richard, 7, 163.

INDEX 215

Higgins, Aug., 46, 72; Ann, 72; John, 46; Penelope, 15.
Hill, Martha, 201.
Hiller, John, 2.
Hillier, John 2.
Hilton, Ann, 160; Eliz., 156; John, 156, 174; Mary, 156, 174; Wm., 156, 174.
Hindmer, John, 49; Sarah, 49.
Hines, Jane, 19; John, 55; Zach., 19.
Hipkins, Richard, 184; Robt. S., 184; Wm. A., 154.
Hobson, John, 57, 112.
Hoburd, Edw., 75.
Hodgson, Wm., 157.
Hogg, Roger, 27, 42; Wm., 27.
Holloday, Richard, 95, 102; Susanna, 95.
Hollam, Youell, 86.
Holland, Eliz., 129, 149; Esther, 129; Hannah, 129, 149, 166, 183; Rocky, 166; Simon, 129; Youell, 129, 166.
Holliday, Fran., 197.
Holloway, Mary, 187.
Hopkins, Blanche, 39; Rice, 39.
Hopwood, Mary, 82; Moses, 82; Richard, 82.
Hord, Geo., 23; Thos., 23.
Horde, James, 82.
Hore, Elias, 46, 153; Fran., 199; James, 46, 85, 153; John, 146; Mary, 144; Robt., 48; Sarah, 48, 153.
Hornbuckle, Ellener, 41; Henry, 23, 41; Richard, 41; Thos., 23, 41.
Horrell, Eliz., 36; Paul, 36.
Horton, Sarah, 152; Wm., 19, 27, 28.
House, Wm., 24.
Howard, John, 57; Susanna, 57, 63.
Howell, John, 60, 105, 193; Paul, 34; Ruth, 60; Sarah C., 193; Winifred, 104.
Howgate, Agnes, 84; James, 84; Wm., 84.
Hubard, Jane, 17.
Hudson, Anne, 196; Caleb, 38; Field, 103; Geo. V. C., 196; John, 43; Joseph, 17; Joshua, 17, 27, 38, 43, 103; Joyce, 71; Marg't, 43; Mary, 43; Robt., 196; Rush, 38; Ruth, 17; Susanna, 103.
Hull, Ann, 11, 12; Edw., 38; Geo. 148; Penelope, 12; Winifrut, 12.
Hume, Susannah, 202.
Humphreys, Wm., 62.
Hunter, James, 175; Wm., 175; Winifred, 175.
Hurley, Betheathland, 157; Eliz., 123; John, 157; Morris, 42, 56.
Hurst, Rebecca, 19.
Hutcheson, Eliz., 159; Mary, 159; Sarah, 138; Wm., 138, 159.
Hutchings, Betsey, 194; Wm., 194.
Hutchinson, Andrew, 86; Jane, 86.
Hutson, Daniel, 97.
Hutt, Anne, 109, 203; Corbin, 204; Daniel, 2, 109; Eliz., 109; Fran., 109; Gerrard, 48, 109, 162, 167, 204; John, 167; Letty, 198; Nimrod, 113; Susanna, 109; Thos., 109, 204; Wm., 204; Wm. G., 204.

I.

Igdon, John, 31.
Inglethorp, Thos., 130.
Inman, Abr., 6.
Ireland, Eliz., 8.
Isham, Grace, 4.

J.

Jackson, Ann, 138; Chr. D., 127; Chr. M., 159; Daniel, 81, 162; Eliz., 158; Geo. 81, 162; John, 138; Joseph, 138; Julius A., 159; Magdalene, 117, 159; Richard, 138, 158; Sarah, 134, 162; Thaddeus, 136, 158, 159; Wm., 134, 162, 176.
Jadwin, Bartho., 10, 20; Jere., 10, 20; John, 10, 20.

James, Fran., 103; John, 103; Sarah, 103.
Jarvis, Eliz., 51; Field, 117; James, 51; John, 51, 117; Richard, 39.
Jeams, Eliz., 140; Thos., 140.
Jeffress, Ann, 101; Cath., 101; Edmund, 101; Eliz., 101; Ellenor, 101; Geo., 101; Jere., 101; Robt., 101.
Jeffries, Ann, 153; Cath., 179; Eliz., 153; Geo., 153; James, 179; Jane, 98; Jere., 153, 157, 179; John, 153; Mariah, 153; Mary, 171, 179; Wm., 153.
Jenkins, Amy, 13; Barbara, 165; Eliz., 76; Jemima, 197; Jere., 76; John, 63, 98; Martha, 135; Nicho., 13; Osman, 84; Sarah, 115; Thos., 76.
Jennings, Eleanor, 50; John, 91; Wm., 69.
Jett, Ann, 137, 177, 190; Betty, 187; Birkett, 182; Burkett, 190; Isabel, 190; Kath., 158, 187; Eliz., 137; Fran., 97, 137, 187; John, 137, 190; Marg't, 97, 108; Mary, 137, 171; Newton, 190; Peter, 108, 137, 187; Sukey, 182; Thos., 177, 182; Wm., 158, 193; Wm. S., 171, 177, 182.
Jewell, John, 78.
Johnson, Ann, 25, 46, 55, 147; Barbara, 25; Eliz., 25, 46, 55; Fran., 25, 46, 57; James, 25, 46, 55; Joanna, 9; Mary, 33, 147; Robt., 33; Samuel, 147; Thos., 9.
Johnston, Betty, 200.
Joncel, Edw., 137; John, 137.
Jones, Alice, 172; Ann, 49, 171; Ashton, 16; Charles, 49, 135; Catesby, 204; David, 135; Eliz., 16, 49, 172; Eliz. L., 204; Eusebius, 204; Fran., 135; Hugh, 1; Humph., 5; John, 16, 50, 66, 135; Joseph, 175; Judith, 6; Lettice C., 204; Manwaring, 16; Marg't, 6; Martha, 204; Mary, 16; Nath'l, 5, 49, 135; Philip, 204; Robt., 63; Roger, 204; Sally S., 204; Sarah, 6, 49, 135; Stephen, 34; Susan, 32; Thos., 27; Walter, 172.
Jordan, Ann, 132, 170; Dorcas, 44; Jane, 113; Jacobus, 113; John, 17; Reuben, 169; Robert, 159.
Journey, Sisley, 10.
Jyles, Wm., 164.

K.

Keating, James, 91; Malinda, 91; Pierce, 91.
Keene, Newton, 89.
Keesee, John, 76.
Kelly, Edm'd, 5; Jane, 190.
Kelley, Ann, 70; John, 80; Wm., 70.
Kendall, Ann, 128, 135: Fran., 135; Gladys, 128; John, 102, 129, 135; Martha, 128; Moses, 129; Samuel, 128, 135· Sarah, 128; Wm., 129.
Kenner, Brererton, 142, 158; Eliz., 68; Howson, 100; Marg't, 100; Richard, 68, 117; Rodham, 68; Winder, 68, 117.
Kersey, Alice, 154; John, 48.
Kill, Charles, 127; Mary, 127.
Kimball, Lydia, 24.
King, Arthur, 65; James, 86; John, 19, 86; Marg't, 86; Mary, 42, 89; Smith, 42.
Kirk, Ann, 98, 134; Edw., 98; Henry, 12, 98; James, 134; John, 156; Sarah, 156.
Kirkham, John, 185; Nancy, 185.
Kitchen, Anthony, 177; Sarah, 169, 177.
Kitching, Eliz., 74; Wm., 74.

L.

Lacy, Jane, 186; Joseph, 186.
Lafoon, Sarah, 162.
Lambee, Wm., 32.
Lambert, Geo., 122; John, 122; Rose, 122; Thos., 122; Wm., 122.

INDEX 217

Lamkin, Agness, 167; Anne, 132, 152; Ashton, 128, 146; Benedict, 183; Benj., 172; Charles, 128, 132; Connegan, 9; Daniel, 132, 146, 150; Elenor, 88; Geo., 9, 88, 117, 152, 167; James, 88, 117, 152; Jane, 76; Jean, 88: John, 9, 104; Lucy, 167; Mathew, 152; Peter, 88, 117, 146, 152; Samuel, 117, 132; Thos., 9; Winifred, 76; Youell, 167.
Landman, John, 16; Wm., 16.
Lane, Cyonway, 126; James, 69, 145; Joseph, 145, 183; Martha, 145, 183; Wm., 145.
Lankford, Thos., 56.
Lansdowne, Mary, 8; Nicho., 8.
Larkin, Leannah, 201.
L tham, Mary, 32; Stephen, 81.
Launcelott, Ann, 9, 12; Jane, 47; Joane, 12; John, 9, 12, 15· Mary, 15, 47; Wm., 12, 40.
Lawrence, Charles, 163; Wm., 163.
Lawson, Lettice, 158; Thos., 158.
Lee, Alice, 132; Anne, 150, 196; Arthur, 196; Baldwin M., 190; Cassius, 196; Charles, 196, 198; Ellener A., 198; Eliz., 150, 158; Fran., 55, 80; Fran. L., 145, 196; Geo., 124, 132, 150; Hancock, 158; Harriet, 196; Henrietta, 196; Henry, 55, 61, 80, 84, 94, 112, 122, 155, 158; John, 122, 155, 158; Lancelot, 150; Lettice, 34, 122; Ludwell, 196; Martha, 112; Mary, 122, 124, 158, 190; Philip, 55, 80, 158, 190; Philip L., 132; Richard, 20, 34, 48, 55, 122, 143, 150, 155, 158, 198; Richard B., 198; Richard H., 144, 145, 150, 196; Sally, 196, 198; Sarah, 34; Susanna, 158; Thos., 55, 56, 80, 84, 90, 122, 132; Thos. L., 132, 145, 196; Wm., 150.

Leftwich, Eliz., 39; Mary, 173, 174; Nancy, 174.
Legg, Eliz., 37; James, 37; Mary, 37; Robt., 37.
Lenham, John, 29; Joshan, 29.
Lewis, Ann, 166; Eliz., 98, 131, 183; Fielding, 151; Fran., 12; Geo., 183; John, 101, 131; Lovits, 131; Surles, 101; Vincent, 65; Wm., 69.
Lett, Peter, 9.
Lindsey, Edmund, 2.
Linton, Anthy., 98; John, 98; Mary, 98; Wm., 98.
Lisson, Frances B., 25.
London, Wm., 1.
Longford, Thos., 27.
Longworth, Anne, 88; Burgess, 132; John, 73, 88, 132; Marg't, 88; Millicent, 80; Thos., 88; Wm., 80, 132.
Lord, John, 8.
Lovell, Anne, 89; Daniel, 83, 99; James, 58, 83, 99; John, 54; Mary, 37, 58, 194; Robt., 24, 58, 83, 99, 133; Ursula, 83, 99.
Lowe, John, 148.
Lucas, Anne, 17; Charles, 35, 57; John, 57; Jacob, 35; Temperence, 42, 57; Samuel, 17.
Luck, Mary, 118.
Luke, Nicholas, 54.
Lund, Chr., 5; Robt., 5; Thos., 5; Wm., 5.
Luttrell, Eliz., 76; John, 76; Simon, 76; Thos., 163.
Lye, Susanna, 200.

M

Macclanacon, Wm., 64.
Macormack, John, 129.
Maddox, Rice, 4.
Madison, Edward, 4; John, 4.
Macgill, Sarah, 94.
Maiders, Ann, 24.
Manner, John, 42.
Manning, Eliz., 81.
Maphe, Eliz., 5; Mary, 5, 6; Rob't, 5, 6.

Marcey, Edw., 81; John, 81; Martha, 81; Robt., 34; Thos., 81.
Markham, Eliz., 50; Lewis, &' 50.
Marloe, John, 65.
Marmanduke, Chr., 16, 149; Daniel, 149; Jane, 16; John, 149; Miles, 16; Sarah, 178; Vincent, 149.
Marrean, Daniel, 56; Eliz., 56; John, 56; Wm., 56.
Marshall, Abr., 133; James, 29; John, 133; Marg't, 133; Martha, 38; Markham, 168; Mary, 173; Peggy, 133; Sarah, 129; Thos., 38; Wm., 38, 133.
Marson, Thos., 17, 32, 49.
Martin, Elias, 82; Hester, 82; Jacob, 89; John, 71, 89; Mary, 11, 120; Mathew, 82; Sarah, 89; Stephen, 82; Thos., 11; Wm., 71.
Martyn, Jacob, 38.
Mason, John, 82; Wm., 69.
Massey, Dade, 65, 198; David, 70; James, 156, 172; John, 197, 198; Judith, 156; Lionel, 137; Lovell, 58, 156, 186; Mildred, 156; Patty, 186; Robt., 137, 156, 197, 198; Sarah, 172; Segesmund, 198; Sukey, 186; Thos., 198; Wm., 198.
Maston, Ellener, 197.
Maunder, Sarah, 9; Wilkes, 9.
Mazarett, John, 197.
Mazingo, Edw., 44; John, 44; Thos., 44.
Meachum, Benj., 89; Samuel, 89; Richard, 89; Wm., 89.
Medford, Henry, 64; Jarrett, 64; John, 64.
Meeks, Ann, 179.
Meldrum, Michael, 113.
Melvin, Eliz., 91; Wm., 91.
Merchant, Thos., 48.
Meriwether, Eliz., 70, 106.
Merrman, Ann, 100.
Middleton, Alice, 40, 136, 166; Anne, 183; Benedict, 17, 40, 92, 163, 170, 183; Benj., 40, 96, 117, 136, 141, 153, 191; Eliz., 18, 40, 92, 96, 117, 164, 170, 191; Ellis, 96; Geo. 161, 189, 194; Hannah, 146, 170, 187, 191; Jane, 92, 141, 202; Jemima, 141; Jere., 161, 189, 191; John, 16, 17, 18, 96, 119, 161, 163, 170, 189, 191; Leazure, 153; Martha, 183, 189; Mary, 35, 40, 92, 96, 117, 136, 153, 191; Robt., 17, 18, 35, 92, 96, 136, 148, 163, 164, 191; Sarah, 161, 162; Sally, 189; Thos., 18, 40, 96, 136, 153, 166; Wm., 92, 141, 163, 166, 183, 191.
Miller, James R., 196; John, 24; Lucy R., 196; Thos., 181; Wm., 181.
Mills, Daniel, 40.
Minor, Barbara, 85, 99; Ellenor, 29; Eliz., 29, 130; Fran., 28, 131; Jemima, 85, 103, 116; John, 28, 85, 116, 125, 130; Mary, 85, 99, 125; Nicho., 28, 74, 109, 116; Sarah, 73; Wm., 85; Wm. S., 116, 131.
Minty, Edward, 16.
Mockeridge, Phillis, 121.
Modiset, Millea, 172.
Monroe, Andrew, 17, 31, 38, 53, 83, 102, 104, 163, 165, 169, 175; Ann, 169; Benj., 184; Christian, 104; Elenor, 17; Elliott, 163, 204; Eliz., 17, 169, 184, 201, 204; Geo., 102, 149, 164, 169; James, 165, 175; Jane, 102, 163, 165; Jemima, 129, 184; John, 163, 164; Joseph J., 175; Marg't, 163; Martha, 165; Nancy, 163; Peggy, 164; Sarah, 90, 108, 164; Spence, 53, 84, 102, 104, 108, 142, 163, 164, 175, 204; Susanna, 53; Thos., 102, 165; Wm., 53, 102, 144, 164, 169, 177, 184.
Moon, John, 12, 62.

Moore, Alice, 104; Ann, 49; Barbara, 179; Dorcas, 173; Eleanor, 151; Eliz., 151; Garland, 164, 173; Hannah, 173; James, 49, 128, 173; Jane, 117, 173; Jane L., 173; John, 100, 151; Marg't, 49; Martha, 164; Mary, 113; McC., 164; Peter, 164; Robert, 20, 151, 164; Robin, 151; Sammy L., 173; Thos., 49, 113, 128; Vincent, 199; Wm., 49, 104, 113, 199; Winifred, 128.
More, Wm., 100.
Morgan, Andrew, 186; Anthony, 37; Benj., 186; Daniel, 163, 186; David, 186; John, 9; Robt., 37; Temperence, 185; Wm., 186.
Morrice, Bridget, 86; Elias, 86.
Morris, Abr., 82; Charles, 51, 200; Eliz., 108; Edw., 51; Ewell, 200; John, 51, 71; Marg't, 82; Mary, 90; Robt., 51; Samuel, 51; Sanders, 200; Simon, 200; Wm., 51.
Morrison, Eliz., 99.
Morton, Ann, 69, 195; Hannah, 195; James, 192, 195; John, 69; Joseph, 117; Massey, 195; Richard, 95; Sarah, 156; Wm., 189, 192, 195.
Mosley, Hannah, 200.
Moss, Ann, 191; Eliz., 42; Fran., 89; John, 89; Judith, 89; Richard, 89; Roger, 42; Thos., 89.
Mothershead, Ann, 111; Brooks, 67, 93; Charles, 111, 121, 128, 140; Chr., 93, 119; Elenor, 119; Eliz., 119; Geo., 93; John, 93, 111, 121, 128, 152; Mary, 128, 164; Nath'l, 93; Olvin, 93; Sarah, 128; Wm., 111, 121.
Moulton, John, 13.
Mourning, John, 27.
Moxley, Alex., 152; Alvin, 174; Ann, 145, 157, 188; Aug., 165, 200; Caty, 200; Chr., 100; Daniel, 100, 168, 174; Eliz., 165; Fran., 152; Hannah, 200, 203; John, 117, 152, 165, 168, 200; Joseph, 100, 152, 157, 168; Katy, 174; Mary, 117, 174; Molly, 189; Richard, 117, 168, 173; Rodham, 152; Samuel, 100, 117, 200; Sarah, 100; Thos., 117; Wm., 117, 200.
Muckleroy, Eliz., 66.
Mullins, Eliz., 178; Geo., 90; Peter, 148, 178; Rachel, 148.
Munn, Eliz., 3; Thos., 3.
Murphy, Bryant, 55; Eliz., 76; John, 114; Mary, 114; Samuel, 114.
Muse, Anne, 84, 130, 131, 144, 155, 194; Aug., 84; Burkett, 192; Betsey, 193; Betty, 187; Charles, 179; Chr., 94, 99, 101; Daniel, 94, 99, 133, 163, 176; Edw., 84; Eleanor, 163; Eliz., 94, 99, 139, 176, 192, 193, 203; Elliott, 193; Fran., 192; Geo., 84, 192; Hannah, 133; Hopkins, 84; Hudson, 179; James, 163, 167, 179, 193, 197, 198; Jere., 139, 176, 193; John, 74, 76, 84, 101, 107, 130, 131, 163, 167; Law., 179; Lewis S., 198, 202; Marg't, 130; Mary, 167, 193, 198; Nancy, 198, 202; Nicholas, 99, 101, 155, 167, 176, 193; Peggy, 192; Penelope, 139, 176, 193; Rebecca, 192; Richard, 144, 163, 192; Samuel, 198, 202; Sarah, 84; Sophia, 99; Sukey, 202; Susanna, 130, 179, 193; Thos., 76, 84, 94, 99, 101, 144, 167, 187, 193, 198, 202; Walker, 139, 176, 193; Wm., 84, 99.
Mustin, Thos., 53.

Mc

McAuley, Hannah, 140; Mary, 140.
McBoyd, Eliz., 121; Mary, 68; Patrick, 68; Thos., 68.

McCarty, Anna, 80; Anne, 94; Billington, 79, 94, 117; Daniel, 34, 71, 79, 99, 117, 198, 199; Dennis, 79, 117; Eliz., 117; Kath., 71; Thaddeus, 79, 94; Winifred, 79.
M c C l a n a h a n, Betty, 168; James, 164, 168; John, 168; Keziah, 199; Martha, 110, 164; Mary, 168; Molly, 203; Peter, 164, 168; Thos., 164, 168; Wm., 164, 168.
McClave, Anne, 126.
McCullock, Eliz., 120; Isabel, 120; Roderick, 120.
McFarlane, Ann, 139; Eliz., 139; Hannah, 139; Mary, 139; Thos., 124, 139.
McGuire, Alex., 166; Martha, 166; Rodham, 166; Travers, 166.
McKenne, Daniel, 96; Eliz., 95, 137; Gerrard, 96; Jane, 96; John, 96, 118; Lettice, 106; Mary, 118; Wm., 95, 96, 137.
McKenny, Ann, 176; Armstrong, 180; Diana, 180; Duke, 179; Gerrard, 180; John, 179; Joseph, 179; Katy, 180; Mary A., 171; Nelly, 179; Rodham, 176; Sarah, 180; Vincent, 176.

N

Nash, Anne, 167; Eliz., 126, 151; James, 86, 177; Jere., 13, 86, 151, 171; John, 151, 167; Lydia, 171; Nath'l, 86, 151; Rachel, 165; Solomon, 171.
Naughty, James, 150; John, 142, 150, 161.
Naylor, Martha, 138.
Neale, Chr., 52, 143; Daniel, 52, 137, 143, 204; Dorcas, 187; Fran., 52; Hannah, 52, 107; James, 204; Jemima, 137; John, 143; Katy, 168; Marg't, 103, 137; Penny S., 143; Presley, 52, 103, 111, 143, 189; Richard, 137, 143; Rodham, 52, 143; Spence, 143; Ursula, 52.

Nelson, Betsy, 199; John, 199; Joshua, 79; Mary, 153, 199; Nancy, 199; Wm., 153, 199.
Newberry, Wm., 9.
Newell, John, 28; Wm., 28.
Newjent, Elias, 63.
Newman, Eliz., 94.
Newmarch, Jona, 149; Thos., 149.
Newmarch, Thos., 149.
Newstubbs, Sarah, 36.
Newton, Barbara, 46; Benj., 18, 77; Betty, 159; Eliz., 18, 77, 89, 125, 158, 159; Fran., 77; Gerrard, 18; John, 18, 55, 77, 125, 158, 159; Joseph, 18; Judith, 118, 125; Lettice, 138; Mary, 159; Rose, 18, 48; Sarah, 77, 100, 125; Thos., 48, 89; Wm., 77; Willoughby, 89, 100, 125, 158, 159.
Netherton, Henry, 62.
Nevitt, James, 40.
Nicholas, Lewis, 19, 22, 25; Vasula, 22.
Nicholls, Mary, 63.
Nicholson, Eliz., 83.
Nobell, Robt., 38.
Nowles, Cath., 153.
Nowel, Lucy, 180.
Notts, John, 26.
Norrie, Bridget, 13; David, 13; John, 13.
Nutt, Eliz., 114; Richard, 114.

O

Ocanny, Daniel, 61.
Offlie, Wm., 47.
Olathman, Teague, 11.
Oliff, Ann, 124, 203; Geo., 124, 203; James, 124; Lucy, 203; Rebecca, 124; Sarah, 203.
Omohundro, Anne, 23; Bruce, 189, 200; Eliz., 23, 190; James, 190; John, 23, 155; Martha, 189, 200; Mary, 86; Richard, 23, 86, 155, 189, 190, 200; Thos., 23, 155, 189, 200; Wm., 23, 155, 189, 190, 200.

INDEX 221

Oneal, Garrett, 77; John, 77.
Orchard, James, 36; Rebecca, 36.
Organ, Richard, 48.
Osborne, Robt., 34.
Overall, John, 49; Mary, 49; Wm., 49.
Owen, Edmd., 68; Henry, 11; Sarah, 63.

P

Packett, Anne, 127; Ann M., 179.
Paite, Henry, 5.
Palmer, Sarah, 66.
Parker, Eliz., 16; Richard, 172, 187; Ruth, 16; Wm., 16.
Parsley, James, 172; Jane, 172; Samuel, 172.
Parsons, Dorothy, 63; Eliz., 165; John, 63; Joseph, 63.
Partington, Thos., 4.
Partridge, Jane, 146; Jean, 128; Jemima, 163; Mathew, 128, 146, 163; Richard, 86, 128, 163.
Pary, Anne, 106; Franklin, 106; John, 106; Wm., 106.
Paten, Anthony, 97; John, 97; Samuel, 97; Wm., 97.
Paine, Anne, 20; Betty, 20; Edw., 32; Mary, 20; Wm., 20.
Payne, Daniel, 102, 190; Eliz., 10, 20, 26; Geo., 190; James, 10; Jeane, 102; John, 10, 20, 26, 190; Mary, 107; Millicent, 10; Rebecca, 97; Richard, 190; Sarah, 189; Wm., 79, 102, 190.
Payton, Anthony, 192; Geo. C., 192; James, 193; John, 193; Mary, 193; Wm., 193.
Peach, Geo., 82; Mary, 82; Thos., 82.
Peachey, Samuel, 79.
Peale, Malachi, 13.
Pearce, Geo., 109; John, 109; Sarah, 142; Wm., 109.
Pears, Geo., 22; John, 22; Mary, 22.
Pease, Mary, 54.
Peck, Mary, 135.

Pennell, Thos., 23, 25.
Peoples, Harriet, 194.
Peper, David, 28; John, 26, 28; Marg't, 26.
Perry, Franklin, 108; Franklyn, 144; John, 108; Roderick, 108; Susanna, 108, 144.
Petit, John, 145.
Pettit, John, 171; Lydia B., 145.
Peyton, Ellen, 3; Frances, 8; Gerrard, 13, 93; Henry, 3; John, 175; Marg't, 176; Thos., 176; Valentine, 3, 8; Wharton, 175; Wm., 117, 175.
Picknell, Henry, 22; Jane, 22; John, 22; Mary, 22; Wm., 22.
Pickerell, Eliz., 35, 111; Henry, 35.
Piecroft, Deborah, 15; Marg't, 15; Nath'l, 15; Phila., 15.
Pearce, John, 26, 32.
Pierce, Eliz. E., 143; Fanny, 201; Geo., 81; John, 81, 99; Joseph, 97, 173, 201, 202; Marg't, 201; Martha, 173; Mary, 26; Ransdell, 201; Sarah, 32; Sarah E., 173; Sibella, 56; Wm., 21, 31, 56, 97.
Pinckard, Geo., 168; Thos., 168.
Piper, Anne, 156; Ann, 173; Benj., 144; Jenny, 156; John, 13, 42, 81, 143, 144, 156; Jona., 144, 156; Mary, 81; Rachel, 156; Rebecca, 13.
Phelps, Ann, 14; Thos., 14.
Phillips, Michael, 6 Robt., 36.
Plunkett, John, 81, 87; Wm., 86.
Poindexter, Thos., 77.
Poor, Charles, 203; Thos., 202.
Pope, Benj., 126, 134, 145; Elliott, 180; Eliz., 66, 112, 134; Humph., 64, 68, 74, 79, 99, 107, 125, 145; Hester, 126; Jane, 22, 66, 134; Jean. 126; Jemima, 66, 74; John, 66, 73, 74, 99, 119, 145, 173, 180; John B., 194; Law., 44,

66, 74; Lewis, 25; Lucy, 3, 4; Mary, 33, 74, 145; Nath'l, 2, 3, 4, 25, 33, 39, 53, 59, 70, 145; Penelope, 74; Ransdell, 180; Sarah, 107, 119, 145; Thos., 3, 4, 11, 14, 74, 112, 180; Wm., 33, 126, 134, 180; Worden, 59, 126.
Popham, Job, 106; John, 106; Sophia, 106.
Porten, Cradock, 60; Daniel, 51, 60; Eliz., 50, 51, 60.
Porter, Anne, 155; Ann, 159; Benj., 204; Betty, 159; Daniel, 204; Edw., 159, 199; Elender, 171; Elinor, 199; Eliz., 199; Lettice, 180; Mary, 199; Nancy, 199; Rachel, 171; Wm., 159, 171, 199.
Potter, Fran., 67; Wm., 67.
Powell, Thos., 53; Wm., 43.
Power, Hannah, 71; Robt., 71.
Pratt, Margaret, 54, 147; John, 54, 61.
Prescott, Edw., 6.
Price, Ann, 134; Betty, 139; Bourn, 134; Eliz., 134; Evan, 71, 138, 140; Grace, 44, 138, 140; Jane, 139, 144; John, 44, 120, 132, 134, 138, 140; John F., 197; Kath., 44; Katy, 139; Marg't, 63; Mary, 65, 138, 197; Meraday, 120; Meridice, 63; Meredith, 132, 197; Nancy, 197; Patty, 139; Sarah, 138, 140; Susanna, 63; Thos., 63, 114; Wm., 63, 120, 132, 134, 139, 197.
Pridham, Edw., 132; Fran., 132.
Pritch, Rodham, 162.
Pertich, Thos., 162.
Pritchett, Ann, 76; James, 152; Peggy, 158; Rodham, 158; Thos., 152, 180.
Pumroy, Jacob, 202.
Purkins, John, 30.
Purslee, James, 84; John, 84; Patrick, 84; Thos., 84; Ursula, 84.
Pye, Ann, 35; John, 35.

Q

Quill, Eliz., 107; Marg't, 107; Sarah, 107.
Quisenberry, Ann, 64, 95, 152, 172; Eliz., 93, 152, 172, 173, 186; Fran., 64; Humph., 64, 173; John, 27, 64, 121, 128, 173, 186; Mary, 76; Nicho., 138, 152; Peggy, 173; Rose, 138; Wm., 64, 152, 186.
Quoanes, Eliz., 8.

R

Raffedy, Dorcas, 104.
Rallings, Benj., 128; Martha, 128; Mary, 128; Samuel, 128.
Rallins, Benj., 137; Grace, 135; James, 137; Samuel, 137.
Ramey, Jacob, 75; Mary, 75; Wm., 75.
Randolph, Francis, 38; Henrietta, 38.
Ransdall, Chilton, 156; Mary, 156.
Ransdell, Amy, 80; Edw., 56, 80, 101, 143, 187; Eliz., 187; Presley, 187; Sarah, 108, 173; Sarah E., 108; Thos., 108; Wm., 143, 187; Wharton, 80, 86, 108, 143, 187.
Randall, Sally, 201; Thos., 155.
Ratte, Solomon, 14.
Rawlings, Anthony, 60; Martha, 60; Richard, 60; Samuel, 60.
Read, Andrew, 19, 162, 165; Coleman, 19, 124; Eliz., 124; Jos., 124, 162, 165; Mary, 124, 165; Mary A., 162; Richard, 124, 165; Robert, 30; Ruth, 124; Susanna, 124.
Reade, Andrew, 161; Mary, 161; Ruth, 161.
Readman, Anne, 12; Fran., 24; John, 12; Mary, 12, 24; Robt., 15.
Redd, Joseph, 198.

Redman, Fran., 37, 58, 148; Fanny, 204; John, 148; Keziah, 204; Lettice, 148; Solomon, 69, 179; Robt., 24, 37; Thos., 24; Wm., 148, 204; Winifred, 148.
Reed, Claytor, 78; Eliz., 28; Jane, 78; John, 28, 78; Thos., 78; Wm., 60, 78.
Reid, Geo., 122; John, 122.
Remy, Ann, 112; Asbury, 104; Benj., 88; Daniel, 105; Jacob, 16, 88, 104; James, 105; John, 88, 105; Joseph, 112; Wm., 88, 104.
Reynes, John, 7.
Reynolds, Eliz., 155; Nancy, 118; Robert, 118.
Rhodes, Martha, 125.
Ribeto, Eliz., 145.
Rice, Ann, 183; Eleanor, 17; Eliz., 41; Hannah, 183; John, 17, 41, 79, 97, 143; Marg't, 28; Mary, 28; Mary, 97, 143; Ralph, 17; Simon, 143; Wm., 17, 107, 117, 197; Zero, 17, 97, 143.
Richardson, Ann, 191; Eliz., 121; Jona., 121.
Rigg, Eliz., 168.
Riley, Edw., 81.
Rimmer, Ann, 120.
Roberts, Maurice, 31.
Robins, Simon, 36; Thos., 16.
Robertson, Ann, 140; James, 140; Mary, 62; Priscilla, 62; Richard, 140; Thos., 140; Wm., 140.
Robinson, Alice, 176; Ann, 40, 72, 83, 93; Anne, 201; Esther, 149; Eliz., Franky, 204; Gerrard, 167; Hannah, 171; Harry, 176; James, 200, 204; John, 83; Keziah, 201; Mary, 83; Michael, 40, 93; Solomon, 203; Thos., 72, 152, 201; Wm., 40, 93, 176, 201.
Robottom, Wm., 62.
Rochester, Ann, 169: Betsy, 169; Fran., 129; John, 87, 129, 169, 170; Mary, 139; Nicho., 139; Phyllis, 87; Robt., 170; Wm., 87, 129, 139, 169.
Roe, Bunch, 44, 113, 140; Henry, 113, 141, 142; Judith, 22; Original, 33; Sutton, 58; Wm., 140.
Rodgers, Mary, 24.
Rogers, Joseph, 121; Mary, 121; Willoughby, 121.
Rollins, Mary, 65; Phillip, 65; Thos., 65; Wm., 65.
Rose, Alex., 148; Bennett, 195; Cath., 148; Charles, 148; Fran., 195; James, 195; Joel, 195; John, 148, 195; Mary, 195; Robt., 148; Wm., 195.
Rosier, Bridges, 15, 27, 37; Wmson., 27.
Rosse, Henry, 20.
Rouzee, John, 141.
Rousseau, Hillier, 131; James, 131; Wm., 131.
Rowe, Jane, 160; Wm., 160.
Rowbothan, Eliz., 107.
Rowland, David, 75.
Rowsey, Mary, 31.
Rozier, Eliz., 2, 3, 37; John, 2, 3, 5, 33, 37, 39; Mary, 39.
Ruch, Wm., 44.
Rush, Eliz., 46; Wm., 46.
Russell, Andrew, 88; Anthony, 88; Fran., 88; Penelope, 88; Sarah, 129, 155.
Rust, Agness, 119; Anne, 9, 18, 185, 196; Benedict, 132, 148; Benj., 65, 98; Caroline, 177; Charlotte, 177; Eliz., 130, 177, 184, 194; Fran., 132, 138, 148; Geo., 65, 132, 138, 177; Henry, 112, 119, James, 150; Jane, 177, 184; Jane M., 170; Jere., 65, 88, 93, 136, 177, 194, 195; John, 65, 88, 150, 177, 184; Lucinda, 177; Magdalen, 75; Marg't, 18; Martha, 65, 91, 93, 119, 195; Mary, 112, 138, 163, 175; Math., 91, 65, 132, 196; Molly, 130, 132, 184; Peter, 65, 91, 93, 112, 119, 124, 130, 132, 150, 177, 184; Rebecca, 177; Richard,

150; Samuel, 64, 88, 93, 112, 119, 130, 132, 136, 150, 159, 177, 201; Sarah, 138, 146, 195; Sophia, 177; Thos., 194, 195, 201; Vincent, 132, 138, 196; Wm., 9, 18, 29, 88, 93, 112, 119, 136; Winifred, 132, 138, 196; Youel, 174.
Rutherford, Mary, 164.

S

Salter, Wm., 8.
Sammons, Geo., 22.
Sanders, Eliz., 74, 84; James, 84; John, 74, 84; Mary, 84; Philip, 74, 84; Ursula, 84; Wm., 74, 84.
Sandy, Jemima, 149.
Saunders, Mary, 105.
Sanford, Anne, 103, 144, 161, 185; Aug., 106, 183; Barbara, 131, 178, 180; Butler, 183; Cath., 185; Caty M. P., 200; Charles, 178; Cordery, 96; Daniel, 195; Darius, 133; Dorcas, 44, 78; Edw., 144, 185, 200; Eleanor, 195; Elinor, 200; Elijah, 200; Eliz., 102, 138, 161, 163; Fran., 125, 161, 183; Henrietta, 182; James, 145; Jemima, 138, 195; Jere., 178; John, 103, 111, 145, 183, 195; Joseph, 111, 125, 131, 182, 187; Joshua, 103, 105; Law., 200; Law. W., 179; Matilda, 195; Marg't, 180; Mary, 84, 105, 131; Mary B. H., 183; Nanny, 111; Patrick, 185; Patrick S., 200; Peggy, 180; Presley, 195; Reuben, 180; Richard, 99, 133, 144, 178, 179, 182; Robert, 84, 95, 103, 105, 111, 133, 144, 145, 182, 195, 200; Sally, 179; Samuel, 200; Sibella, 184; Thomas, 133, 163, 184, 195; Thomas R., 183; Wm., 27, 106, 125, 157, 161, 178, 180, 183, 184, 195; Willoughby, 161, 200; Winifred, 145, 157; Winny, 179; Youell, 163, 195.
Saxton, Alice, 10; Ann, 10; Eliz., 10; Henry, 6, 10; Nicho., 7; Wm., 10, 43.
Scott, Eliz., 175; Gustavus, 31; James, 31; Jane, 31, 37; John, 31, 32, 37; Mary, 121; Sarah, 31.
Scrimer, Fanny, 200.
Sears, Edw., 158; Mary, 158; Wm., 158.
Sebastian, Sarah, 65.
Scott, Eliz., 175; Gustavus, 31; James, 31; Jane, 31, 37; John, 37, 31, 32; Mary, 121; Sarah, 31.
Self, Abraham, 150; Anne, 191, 197; Jane, 62; Jane J., 48; John, 62, 97, 196; Lettice, 150; Mary, 97, 191; Moses, 97, 197; Nelly, 191; Peter, 150; Presley, 191; Robert, 62; Stephen, 62, 150; Susanna, 97; Thomas, 97; Walter, 62; Wm., 97, 150.
Selph, Benj., 94; Fran., 94; Philip, 94; Stephen, 94.
Settle, Joel, 148; Mary, 170; Mary B., 138; Sarah, 148; Wm., 148.
Sharp, John, 14, 43; Mary, 43; Robert, 1; Thomas, 14.
Sharpe, Mary, 103.
Shaw, Jane, 62, 101; Jenny, 45; Thomas, 33, 45, 62, 63, 111; Wm., 101.
Sheadrick, John, 60; Thomas, 60.
Shephard, Ann, 49; Geo., 35; Hindmer, 49; Isaac, 72.
Sherman, Eliz., 80; Fran., 148.
Shoares, Wm., 16.
Shoats, Eliz., 190; Geo., 190.
Shore, Arthur, 7; Patience, 7; Susan, 7.
Short, Wm., 16.
Shortridge, Wm., 64.
Shropshire, St. John, 114; Winifred, 114.
Siddon, Wm., 192.

Simmons, Jacob, 25; Jane, 47; Law., 25; Marg't, 25; Wm., 25.
Simms, Alex., 119; Bethlehn, 119; Edw., 119; Franklin, 119; Henry, 119.
Sisson, Daniel, 4.
Skinker, John, 183; Peggy, 171.
Slye, Robert, 2, 4, 8.
Smith, Alice, 172; Ann, 18, 52, 53, 152, 175, 190; Anne, 57, 58, 133; Aug., 133, 173; Baldwin M., 158; Benj. P., 178; Caleb, 16, 19, 81; Charles, 53; Edw., 166, 175; Eliz., 12, 52, 71, 81, 133, 168, 173; Fanny, 158; Fleet, 168; Fran., 53, 190; Geo. B., 172; Gideon, 129; Gregory, 175, 190; Hannah, 185; Henry, 190; Herbert, 6; Humph., 19; Isaac, 27; Jacob, 190; James, 52, 92, 98, 110, 114, 170; Jane, 52, 168; Jenny, 150; John, 16, 81, 82, 101, 110, 114, 166, 172, 173, 175, 187; John Aug., 190; Joseph, 66, 129; Joyce, 66; Judith, 114; Lazarus, 114; Lee A. M., 194; Lewis, 173; Lucy, 175; Martha J., 175; Mary, 12, 53, 57, 66, 82, 101, 111, 158, 170, 190; Mary J., 175; Mathew, 166; Nancy, 170; Nath'l, 66; Nicho., 92; Patty, 168; Peggy, 179; Peter, 92, 110, 170, 187; Rebecca, 6; Robt., 33, 130, 151, 152; Sally, 170; Samuel, 129, 130, 151, 168, 172, 185, 194; Sarah, 129, 175, 179; Scuetty, 178; Spence, 168; Stephen, 130, 151, 172; Tamer, 122; Thos., 19, 82, 110, 189; Thos. G., 190; Wm., 12, 13, 19, 42, 53, 110, 170, 172, 177, 185; Wm. B., 194.
Smoot, Ellenor, 42; Mary, 41; Sarah, 41; Thos., 42; Wm., 23, 41, 42; Winnifrut, 42.
Solley, Eliz., 3; Thomas, 3.

Sorrell, Anna, 53; Fran., 57; Eliz., 53, 57, 85; James, 85, 184; John, 57, 85, 184; Judith, 184; Martha, 191; Thos., 53, 57, 61, 69, 85.
South, Ann, 57, 72; Geo., 57, 72; Jemima, 145; John, 57, 72.
Spark, Alex., 159; Wm., 159.
Sparrow, Robt., 22, 64.
Speake, Ann, 1; Thos., 1.
Speke, Fran., 4; John, 4; Thos., 4, 8.
Speed, Ralph, 59.
Spence, Alex., 15, 17, 20, 38, 44; Dorcas, 17, 20, 39; Eliz., 38, 109; Jane, 44; Jemima, 74, 109, 138, 183; John, 86, 137; Joseph, 103; Mary, 38, 109, 138; Patrick, 15, 17, 38, 44, 56, 109, 138; Thos., 16, 17, 56; Wm., 1; Youell, 109, 138.
Spencer, Anne, 17; Fran., 43, 72; John, 43, 72; Mary, 43; Nicholas, 10, 12, 43; Richard, 17.
Spellman, Eliz., 182.
Spiller, Dorothy, 73; John, 73.
Spillman, Fran., 24, 156; John, 145; Lettice D., 145; Marg't, 86, 145; Richard, 145; Thos., 24, 67, 145; Wm., 145.
Spurling, Jere., 83; Mary, 83; Thos., 83, 84.
Stapleton, Eliz., 122.
Stands, John, 6.
Starr, Eliz., 34.
Steel, Charles, 102, 111; Charles W., 127; Eliz., 102; John, 76, 102, 115; Mary, 102; Mary W., 178; Richard, 102, 115; Sarah, 102, 111; Weeks, 115.
Steele, Marg't, 111; Thos., 111.
Stephens, Burdette, 110; Edw., 44; Eliz., 83; James, 110; Jere., 110; John, 167; Robt., 83.
Steptoe, Edw., 178; Geo., 142, 178; Eliz., 142, 178; James, 142, 178; Thos., 142; Wm., 178.

Stewart, Benj., 172; John, 172; Kath., 39; Mary, 39; Susanna, 39; Thos., 172; Wm., 39.
Stuart, Eliz., 104.
Stoddard, Wm., 13.
Stone, Ann, 165; Edw., 200; Geo., 180; Isaac, 180; Jemima, 78, 185; Joseph, 101, 165; Mary, 102; Peggy, 200; Penelope, 165; Presley, 165; Sarah, 102; Thos., 65, 68, 165, 200; Wm., 102, 180.
Stonehouse, Eliz., 114.
Stopper, Chr., 15.
Stork, Eliz., 171.
Storke, Mary, 182; Thos., 182; Wm., 3, 70.
Stowers, Ann, 165; Keziah, 203; Samuel, 165.
Strother, Eliz., 152; Marg't, 102, 203; Sarah, 114; Wm., 114.
Sturman, Ann, 44; Anna, 78; Elliott, 173, 193; Eliz., 17, 44; Dorcas, 17; Foxhall, 95, 108, 193; Hannah, 156; John, 15, 17, 44, 78; Jemima, 156; Marg't, 10; Martha, 108; Mary, 193; Rebecca, 10; Richard, 10, 15, 104; Sarah, 95, 108; Thos., 95, 104; Val., 10, 104; Wm., 62, 78, 95, 104; Wm. Y., 193.
Suggett, Jemima, 138.
Sullivant, Darby, 16, 28; Eliz., 28.
Sumett, Alex., 5.
Summers, Eliz., 92, 126.
Summerville, John, 62; Mary, 62.
Sutherland, John, 72; Kath., 72.
Sutton, Amy, 127; Eliz. S., 185; Henrietta, 137; Jacob, 123, 137; James, 122, 137; John, 123; Joseph, 204; Josiah, 194; Mary, 123, 137; Rosamond, 204; Richard, 27, 122, 137; Wm., 123.
Sydnor, John, 193.

T

Talbot, James, 26; Eliz., 80.
Taliaferro, Rose, 153.
Tancell, John, 52.
Tankersley, Chas., 38.
Tanner, Fran., 35, 44; Hannah, 35, 44; John, 15; Martha, 97; Mary, 35: Thos., 35, 44.
Tasker, Ann, 174; Benj., 174; John, 1.
Tayler, James, 23, 33, 45.
Tayloe, John, 79, 94, 112.
Taylor, Anne, 94; Fran., 131; James, 131: John, 102; Joseph, 73, 80, 119, 155; Marie, 90; Mary, 102; Philip, 120; Richard, 102; Sarah, 131; Thos., 102, 167; Urslee, 74; Wm., 33, 102.
Tebbs, Daniel, 124, 153, 172; Eliz., 153; Fouchee, 172; Martha, 172; Wm., 153, 172.
Templeman, Ann, 183, 195; Dozier, 133; Fanny, 195; Molly, 195; Richard, 133; Samuel, 195, 201; Sebella, 201; Thos., 127, 133, 195.
Tew, Grace, 1; John, 1.
Thomas, Ann, 66, 69, 110; Bushrod, 106; Daniel, 66; Eliz., 115; Geo., 114; Hannah, 115; Hugh, 66; John, 25, 66; James, 115; Kath., 115; Marg't, 25; Mary, 125; Sarah, 115; Winifred, 115.
Thompson, Alice, 56; Andrew, 162; Anna, 56; Eliz., 133; Geo., 162; John, 133, 138; Samuel, 19; Susanna, 62; Thos., 30, 56; Wm., 19, 29, 62, 133.
Thomson, Ann, 182; Betsey, 182; Lovel, 182; Maria, 182; Richard, 182; Wm., 182.
Thorn, Mary, 183.
Thorne, Fran., 22, 27, 39; Geo., 22, 40.
Thornbury, Mary, 58; Samuel, 58.
Thornton, Anthony, 96; Betty, 132; Presley, 117.
Thrailkil, Letty, 198.
Threshall, Jemima, 124.

INDEX 227

Thrift, Eliz., 200.
Tidwell, Ann, 187; Barbara, 154, 187; Eliz., 154; Hannah. 149, 154; John, 149, 154; Robt., 149; Wm. C., 149, 154.
Tilson, Hannah, 32; Rebecca, 32; Robt., 32; Roger, 32.
Toben, Mary, 120; Michael, 120.
Todd, Robt., 147.
Tomlin, Robt., 97.
Travers, Eliz., 34; Rebecca, 34; Winifred, 34.
Triplet, Cath., 201; Charles, 201; James, 201; Jane, 201; John, 153; Mary, 33; Wm., 201.
Trussell, Daniel, 9; Eliz., 9; John, 9.
Tucker, Benj., 73; Eliz., 73; Gerrard, 13; Henry, 73; John, 14, 73; Joseph, 73; Rebecca, 73; Rose, 14; Sarah, 14.
Tupman, John, 174.
Turbeville, Anne, 204; Eliz., 93; Fran., 112; Gawin C., 194; Geo., 77, 94, 112, 194; Geo. L., 204; Geo. R., 204; Geo. R. L., 194; Hannah L., 194; Martha, 204; John, 112, 204; Lettice, 112; Martha, 112; Trolius L., 204.
Turnbridge, Geo., 22, 26.
Turnbull, Eliz., 177; Geo., 177; James, 177; Reuben, 177; Stephen, 177.
Turner, Eliz., 187; Geo., 188; Henry S., 188; Jane, 188; Richard, 188; Robt., 76; Sally, 176; Sarah, 66; Thos., 188; Wm., 187.
Tyler, Benj., 104; Charles, 25, 53; Joseph, 104; Wm., 104.
Tynon, Wm., 107.

U

Underwood, John, 203; Mary, 42.

V

Vanlendgen, Richard, 52.
Vaughan, Cordery, 100; Daniel, 100; Ellener, 100; Eliz., 6; John, 5, 7; Peter, 100; Samuel, 7; Wm., 7.
Vaulx, Betty, 142; Eliz., 75, 142; James, 22, 44, 45, 46, 74, 75; Katy, 142; Kenner, 142; Mary, 51; Milly, 142; Molly, 142; Robt., 21, 45, 51, 75, 142; Sally, 142.
Veal, John, 68; Morris, 68.
Veale, Amey, 16; Dorothy, 16; Elenor, 16; John, 16; Mary, 16; Morris, 16; Wm., 16.
Vigour, Fran., 158; Sarah, 158; Wm., 158.
Vigor, Sarah, 164; Wm., 164.
Vincent, Eliz., 8; Henry, 8; John, 8; Joseph, 30.
Vivion, Charles, 141; Fran., 147; Mary, 147; Thos., 147.

W

Waddy, Benj., 84.
Walker, Ann, 57, 97, 104, 147; Anne, 129, 155; Barbara, 99; Barbary, 118; Benj., 57, 65; Charles, 58; Daniel, 97; Edmund, 56; Eliz., 32, 58; Franky, 118; Geo., 56, 87, 118; Hardidge, 87; Jas., 5, 87, 147, 173; Jane, 32; John, 9, 56, 97, 119, 147, 173; Joseph, 97; Lydia, 87; Margery, 57; Martha, 97; Mary, 8, 13, 21, 57; Peter, 119, 157; Rachel, 99, 118; Richard, 8, 13, 97; Samuel, 57, 87, 166; Thos., 8, 13, 53, 56, 87, 173; Wm., 21, 87, 90, 97, 147, 164, 197; Winifred, 118.
Wall, Richard, 17.
Walls, Richard, 61.
Ware, Eliz., 37; John, 37, 39; Hannah, 110.
Ward, Henry, 67, 88, 112; Jane, 67, 112; John, 8, 67; Mary, 112; Sarah, 112.
Warner, John, 80.

Washington, Anne, 14, 19, 29, 123, 142, 176, 197; Ann A., 188; Aug., 19, 72, 82, 116, 117, 123, 151; Bayley, 95; Betsey, 151; Bushrod, 188; Corbin, 188, 196; Charles, 151; Constant, 186; Eliz., 110, 176; Geo., 151, 186, 188, 198; Hannah, 145, 188, 196; Henry, 19, 95, 171, 182, 186; James, 110; Jane, 151; Jenny, 145, 188; John, 3, 10, 14, 19, 38, 51, 110, 145, 151, 186, 188, 198; John H., 188; John Aug., 188; Katy, 171; Law., 3, 14, 19, 25, 48, 110, 116, 142, 151, 171, 182; Louisa F., 186; Mary, 95, 145, 188, 196; Mildred, 19, 188; Nancy, 151; Nancy C., 186; Nath'l, 19, 51; Robert, 156, 188; Robt. L., 186; Robt. T., 156, 186; Richard B., 188; Samuel, 151; Sarah, 156; Susanna, 171; Thos., 110, 197; Thos. M., 197; Thos. T., 186; Wm., 188, 197; Wm. Aug., 151, 188, 196; Wm. H., 186.
Waters, Dorothy, 63; John, 58, 64.
Wattey, Geo., 52.
Watts, Ann, 1, 16; Eliz., 7, 136; Geo., 1; James, 29; John, 7, 29, 59, 62, 85, 102, 120, 136; Mary, 59; Richard, 37, 59, 63, 60, 85, 102, 136; Spencer, 29, 90; Wm., 50; Youell, 16, 86, 109.
Watson, Marg't, 101; Thos., 76.
Waugh, John, 13.
Waulhope, Eliz., 89.
Weaver, Abr., 164, 180; Adam, 164; Alfred, 200; Annamino, 164; Benj., 164, 179; Daniel, 180; Elijah, 186; Frederick, 202; Fran., 202; Jemima, 155; John, 164, 179; Pinney, 200; Sarah, 180; Wm., 164; Zach., 164, 179.
Webb, Barbary, 52; Hannah, 24; Joane, 11; Michael, 26; Rebecca, 26; Thos., 7, 11; Wm., 11, 12, 24.
Webster, Alex., 33, 35; Ann, 33, 35.
Weedon, Aug., 110, 154; Benj., 38, 47; Eliz., 154, 159; Geo., 7, 17, 37, 38, 99, 114, 154, 168; James, 154; Jane, 154, 159; John, 110, 154; Jordan, 17, 37, 44; Mary, 38, 44, 110; Rebecca, 154, 159; Sarah, 110, 159; Susanna, 38, 47; Thos., 38.
Weeks, Benj., 84, 115, 127, 178; Charles, 178; Joseph, 60, 121; Mary, 60; Sarah, 60; Selia, 178; Wm., 61.
Welch, Ann, 138; Garratt, 61; Thos., 170; Wm., 121.
Wellington, John, 40; Eliz., 104; John, 104; Michael, 40.
West, John, 108; Richard, 23.
Westcomb, James, 39, 56.
Weston, Ann, 198.
Wharton, Eliz., 4^ Henry, 40.
Wheeler, Eliz., 152; John, 71, 152; Richard, 152; Samuel, 58; Thos., 23, 58, 152; Wm., 58, 152.
Wheret, Eliz., 116.
Whetstone, Edw., 15.
White, Alice, 26; Amy, 153; Ann, 14; Benj., 154; Daniel, 6, 154; Dennis, 14; Geo., 129, 155, 160; James, 154, 160; Jane, 154; Jenny, 131; John, 120, 129, 131, 150, 154; Lovel, 120; Mary, 129, 155; Mildred, 153; Philip, 26, 155; Samuel, 131, 154; Sarah, 150; Thos., 31.
Whiting, John, 137; Mary, 137; Molly, 142; Nelly, 142; Sally, 142; Thos., 142; Ursula, 71; Wm., 71.
Whitstone, John, 8.
Whistens, John, 7.
Whiston, Ann, 11; John, 11; Restitute, 11.
Wickers, Benj., 38; Thos., 38.
Wickleff, David, 21; Henry, 29; Marg't, 21; Robt., 21, 26.
Wickliff, Susanna, 199.

Wiggington, Ann, 66; Eliz., 55; Fran., 77, 96; Henry, 66, 77, 124; James J., 77; Roger, 66, 124; Spencer, 124; Wm., 66, 77.
Wilkerson, Anne, 136; Benj., 154; James, 136; John, 154; Marg't, 154; Mary, 136; Robt., 136; Thos., 136.
Wilkinson, Ann, 22; Gerrard, 145; James, 145; John, 22, 145; Mary, 140; Thos., 145; Tyler, 145; Wm., 145.
Williams, Ann, 86; Chambers, 125; Charles, 113; Daniel, 125, 148; David, 86; Elijah, 148; Edw., 98; Eliz., 103, 113, 148; Jane, 32, 96; John, 32, 103, 113; Joshua, 98; Kenne, 96; Marg't, 144; Mary, 96; Morgan, 16; Sarah, 63, 98; Thos., 103, 125, 148; Wm., 52, 98.
Williamson, David, 71.
Willis, Wm., 52.
Willson, Allen, 69; John, 69; Wm., 68.
Wilsford, Andrew, 10; Jas., 10; Thos., 2, 10, 37.
Wilson, Allen, 135; Ann, 52, 76; Eliz., 133; Henry, 52; John, 11.
Winder, Eliz., 68.
Windzor, Anthony, 25; Anne, 25; Eliz., 25; Marg't, 25; Mary, 25; Sarah, 25.
Winnix, Eliz., 120.
Withrington, Constance, 13; Edward, 13.
Wood, Ann, 125; Edward, 50; Fran., 197; Hester, 197; John, 1; Nelly, 197; Pheba, 197; Samuel, 197.
Woodier, Thos., 70.
Woodlock, Thos., 36.
Woodward, Mary, 73.
Wophendall, Adam, 11.
Worden, John, 59.
Woring, James, 92.
Wright, Anne, 19, 53, 139; Bennett, 196; Bernard, 194; Eliz., 96, 111, 124, 194; Fran., 19, 51, 111, 139, 157, 162, 183, 194; Geo. M., 194; John, 53, 111; Johnson, 194; Martha, 51; Molly, 196; Nancy, 157; Presley, 157; Richard, 96, 111, 124, 152, 157; Thos., 57; Vincent R. P., 196; Wright, 194.
Wroe, Benj., 175; Bunch, 83; Eliz., 83; Hannah, 82, 91; Henry, 83; Jane, 127, 183; John, 175; Judith, 91; Lucretia, 175; Mary, 91; Original, 82, 91, 127, 175; Regiland, 175; Richard, 82, 175; Sarah, 83, 91; Susanna, 83; Taylor, 175; Thos., 175; Wm., 91, 175.
Wyatt, Math., 71; Vincent, 51, 71; Wm., 51, 71.

Y

Yellop, Thos., 113.
Young, Christian, 113; Edw., 100.
Youel, Dinah, 66; Harman, 67; Thos., 67.
Youell, Eliz., 117; Fran., 117; Thos., 16, 29.

www.ingramcontent.com/pod-product-compliance
Lightning Source LLC
Chambersburg PA
CBHW050441240426
43661CB00055B/2468